Hackers & Painters

Big Ideas from the Computer Age

Hackers & Painters
Big Ideas from the Computer Age

Paul Graham

O'REILLY®

Beijing · Cambridge · Farnham · Köln · Sebastopol · Tokyo

Hackers & Painters: Big Ideas from the Computer Age
by Paul Graham

Published by O'Reilly Media, Inc., 1005 Gravenstein Highway North, Sebastopol, CA 95472.

O'Reilly books may be purchased for educational, business, or sales promotional use. Online editions are also available for most titles (*http://my.safaribooksonline.com*). For more information, contact our corporate/institutional sales department: (800) 998-9938 or *corporate@oreilly.com*.

Editor: Allen Noren
Production Editor: Matt Hutchinson

Printing History:

May 2010:   First Edition.

ISBN: 978-1-449-38955-0
[LSI]   [2011-01-20]

FOR MOM

Note to readers

The chapters are all independent of one another, so you don't have to read them in order, and you can skip any that bore you. If you come across a technical term you don't know, take a look in the Glossary, or in Chapter 10, which explains a lot of the concepts underlying software.

We regret to inform readers that, after reading Chapter 5, Microsoft's PR firm were unable to grant us permission to reproduce any of their photographs of Bill Gates. We thank the Albuquerque Police Department for the substitute reproduced on page 86.

www.paulgraham.com

Contents

Preface

THIS BOOK IS AN ATTEMPT TO EXPLAIN TO THE WORLD AT LARGE what goes on in the world of computers. So it's not just for programmers. For example, Chapter 6 is about how to get rich. I believe this is a topic of general interest.

You may have noticed that a lot of the people getting rich in the last thirty years have been programmers. Bill Gates, Steve Jobs, Larry Ellison. Why? Why programmers, rather than civil engineers or photographers or actuaries? "How to Make Wealth" explains why.

The money in software is one instance of a more general trend, and that trend is the theme of this book. This is the Computer Age. It was supposed to be the Space Age, or the Atomic Age. But those were just names invented by PR people. Computers have had far more effect on the form of our lives than space travel or nuclear technology.

Everything around us is turning into computers. Your typewriter is gone, replaced by a computer. Your phone has turned into one. So has your camera. Soon your TV will. Your car has more processing power in it than a room-sized mainframe had in 1970. Letters, encyclopedias, newspapers, and even your local store are being replaced by the Internet. So if you want to understand where we are, and where we're going, it will help if you understand what's going on inside the heads of hackers.

Hackers? Aren't those the people who break into computers? Among outsiders, that's what the word means. But within the computer world, expert programmers refer to themselves as hackers. And since the purpose of this book is to explain how things really are in our world, I decided it was worth the risk to use the words we use.

The earlier chapters answer questions we have probably all thought about. What makes a startup succeed? Will technology create a gap between those who understand it and those who don't? What do programmers do? Why do kids who can't master high school end up as some of the most powerful people in the world? Will Microsoft take over the Internet? What to do about spam?

Several later chapters are about something most people outside the computer world haven't thought about: programming languages. Why should you care about programming languages? Because if you want to understand hacking, this is the thread to follow—just as, if you wanted to understand the technology of 1880, steam engines were the thread to follow.

Computer programs are all just text. And the language you choose determines what you can say. Programming languages are what programmers think in.

Naturally, this has a big effect on the kind of thoughts they have. And you can see it in the software they write. Orbitz, the travel web site, managed to break into a market dominated by two very formidable competitors: Sabre, who owned electronic reservations for decades, and Microsoft. How on earth did Orbitz pull this off? Largely by using a better programming language.

Programmers tend to be divided into tribes by the languages they use. More even than by the kinds of programs they write. And so it's considered bad manners to say that one language is better than another. But no language designer can afford to believe this polite fiction. What I have to say about programming languages may upset a lot of people, but I think there is no better way to understand hacking.

Some might wonder about "What You Can't Say" (Chapter 3). What does that have to do with computers? The fact is, hackers are obsessed with free speech. Slashdot, the *New York Times* of hacking, has a whole section about it. I think most Slashdot readers take this for granted. But *Plane & Pilot* doesn't have a section about free speech.

Why do hackers care so much about free speech? Partly, I think, because innovation is so important in software, and innovation and heresy are practically the same thing. Good hackers develop a habit of questioning everything. You have to when you work on machines made of words that are as complex as a mechanical watch and a thousand times the size.

But I think that misfits and iconoclasts are also more likely to *become* hackers. The computer world is like an intellectual Wild West, where you can think anything you want, if you're willing to risk the consequences.

And this book, if I've done what I intended, is an intellectual Western. I wouldn't want you to read it in a spirit of duty, thinking, "Well, these nerds do seem to be taking over the world. I suppose I'd better understand what they're doing, so I'm not blindsided by whatever they cook up next." If you like ideas, this book ought to be *fun*. Though hackers generally look dull on the outside, the insides of their heads are surprisingly interesting places.

Cambridge, Massachusetts
April 2004

Chapter 1

Why Nerds Are Unpopular

WHEN WE WERE IN JUNIOR HIGH SCHOOL, MY FRIEND RICH AND I made a map of the school lunch tables according to popularity. This was easy to do, because kids only ate lunch with others of about the same popularity. We graded them from A to E. A tables were full of football players and cheerleaders and so on. E tables contained the kids with mild cases of Down's Syndrome, what in the language of the time we called "retards."

We sat at a D table, as low as you could get without looking physically different. We were not being especially candid to grade ourselves as D. It would have taken a deliberate lie to say otherwise. Everyone in the school knew exactly how popular everyone else was, including us.

I know a lot of people who were nerds in school, and they all tell the same story: there is a strong correlation between being smart and being a nerd, and an even stronger inverse correlation between being a nerd and being popular. Being smart seems to *make* you unpopular.

Why? To someone in school now, that may seem an odd question to ask. The mere fact is so overwhelming that it may seem strange to imagine that it could be any other way. But it could. Being smart doesn't make you an outcast in elementary school. Nor does it harm you in the real world. Nor, as far as I can tell, is the problem so bad in most other countries. But in a typical American secondary school, being smart is likely to make your life difficult. Why?

The key to this mystery is to rephrase the question slightly. Why don't smart kids make themselves popular? If they're so smart, why don't they figure out how popularity works and beat the system, just as they do for standardized tests?

One argument says that this would be impossible, that the smart kids are unpopular because the other kids envy them for being smart, and nothing they could do could make them popular. I wish. If the other kids in junior high school envied me, they did a great job of concealing it. And in any case, if being smart were really an enviable quality, the girls would have broken ranks. The guys that guys envy, girls like.

In the schools I went to, being smart just didn't matter much. Kids didn't admire it or despise it. All other things being equal, they would have preferred to be on the smart side of average rather than the dumb side, but intelligence counted far less than, say, physical appearance, charisma, or athletic ability.

So if intelligence in itself is not a factor in popularity, why are smart kids so consistently unpopular? The answer, I think, is that they don't really want to be popular.

If someone had told me that at the time, I would have laughed at him. Being unpopular in school makes kids miserable, some of them so miserable that they commit suicide. Telling me that I didn't want to be popular would have seemed like telling someone dying of thirst in a desert that he didn't want a glass of water. Of course I wanted to be popular.

But in fact I didn't, not enough. There was something else I wanted more: to be smart. Not simply to do well in school, though that counted for something, but to design beautiful rockets, or to write well, or to understand how to program computers. In general, to make great things.

At the time I never tried to separate my wants and weigh them against one another. If I had, I would have seen that being smart was more important. If someone had offered me the chance to be the most popular kid in school, but only at the price of being of average intelligence (humor me here), I wouldn't have taken it.

Much as they suffer from their unpopularity, I don't think many nerds would. To them the thought of average intelligence is unbearable. But most kids would take that deal. For half of them, it would be a step up. Even for someone in the eightieth percentile (assuming, as everyone seemed to then, that intelligence is a scalar), who wouldn't drop thirty points in exchange for being loved and admired by everyone?

And that, I think, is the root of the problem. Nerds serve two masters. They want to be popular, certainly, but they want even more to be smart. And popularity is not something you can do in your spare time, not in the fiercely competitive environment of an American secondary school.

Alberti, arguably the archetype of the Renaissance Man, writes that "no art, however minor, demands less than total dedication if you want to excel in it."¹ I wonder if anyone in the world works harder at anything than American school kids work at popularity. Navy SEALS and neurosurgery residents seem slackers by comparison. They occasionally take vacations; some even have hobbies. An American teenager may work at being popular every waking hour, 365 days a year.

I don't mean to suggest they do this consciously. Some of them truly are little Machiavellis, but what I really mean here is that teenagers are always on duty as conformists.

For example, teenage kids pay a great deal of attention to clothes. They don't consciously dress to be popular. They dress to look good. But to who? To the other kids. Other kids' opinions become their definition of right, not just for clothes, but for almost everything they do, right down to the way they walk. And so every effort they make to do things "right" is also, consciously or not, an effort to be more popular.

Nerds don't realize this. They don't realize that it takes work to be popular. In general, people outside some very demanding field don't realize the extent to which success depends on constant (though often unconscious) effort. For example, most people seem to consider the ability to draw as some kind of innate quality, like being tall. In fact, most people who "can draw" like drawing, and have spent many hours doing it; that's why they're good at it.

Gateway High School chess club, 1981. That's me, upper left.

Likewise, popular isn't just something you are or you aren't, but something you make yourself.

The main reason nerds are unpopular is that they have other things to think about. Their attention is drawn to books or the natural world, not fashions and parties. They're like someone trying to play soccer while balancing a glass of water on his head. Other players who can focus their whole attention on the game beat them effortlessly, and wonder why they seem so incapable.

Even if nerds cared as much as other kids about popularity, being popular would be more work for them. The popular kids learned to be popular, and to want to be popular, the same way the nerds learned to be smart, and to want to be smart: from their parents. While the nerds were being trained to get the right answers, the popular kids were being trained to please.

So far I've been finessing the relationship between smart and nerd, using them as if they were interchangeable. In fact it's only the context that makes them so. A nerd is someone who isn't socially

4

adept enough. But "enough" depends on where you are. In a typical American school, standards for coolness are so high (or at least, so specific) that you don't have to be especially awkward to look awkward by comparison.

Few smart kids can spare the attention that popularity requires. Unless they also happen to be good-looking, natural athletes, or siblings of popular kids, they'll tend to become nerds. And that's why smart people's lives are worst between, say, the ages of eleven and seventeen. Life at that age revolves far more around popularity than before or after.

Before that, kids' lives are dominated by their parents, not by other kids. Kids do care what their peers think in elementary school, but this isn't their whole life, as it later becomes.

Around the age of eleven, though, kids seem to start treating their family as a day job. They create a new world among themselves, and standing in this world is what matters, not standing in their family. Indeed, being in trouble in their family can win them points in the world they care about.

The problem is, the world these kids create for themselves is at first a very crude one. If you leave a bunch of eleven-year-olds to their own devices, what you get is *Lord of the Flies*. Like a lot of American kids, I read this book in school. Presumably it was not a coincidence. Presumably someone wanted to point out to us that we were savages, and that we had made ourselves a cruel and stupid world. This was too subtle for me. While the book seemed entirely believable, I didn't get the additional message. I wish they had just told us outright that we were savages and our world was stupid.

Nerds would find their unpopularity more bearable if it merely caused them to be ignored. Unfortunately, to be unpopular in school is to be actively persecuted.

Why? Once again, anyone currently in school might think this a strange question to ask. How could things be any other way?

But they could be. Adults don't normally persecute nerds. Why do teenage kids do it?

Partly because teenagers are still half children, and many children are just intrinsically cruel. Some torture nerds for the same reason they pull the legs off spiders. Before you develop a conscience, torture is amusing.

Another reason kids persecute nerds is to make themselves feel better. When you tread water, you lift yourself up by pushing water down. Likewise, in any social hierarchy, people unsure of their own position will try to emphasize it by maltreating those they think rank below. I've read that this is why poor whites in the United States are the group most hostile to blacks.

But I think the main reason other kids persecute nerds is that it's part of the mechanism of popularity. Popularity is only partially about individual attractiveness. It's much more about alliances. To become more popular, you need to be constantly doing things that bring you close to other popular people, and nothing brings people closer than a common enemy.

Like a politician who wants to distract voters from bad times at home, you can create an enemy if there isn't a real one. By singling out and persecuting a nerd, a group of kids from higher in the hierarchy create bonds between themselves. Attacking an outsider makes them all insiders. This is why the worst cases of bullying happen with groups. Ask any nerd: you get much worse treatment from a group of kids than from any individual bully, however sadistic.

If it's any consolation to the nerds, it's nothing personal. The group of kids who band together to pick on you are doing the same thing, and for the same reason, as a bunch of guys who get together to go hunting. They don't actually hate you. They just need something to chase.

Because they're at the bottom of the scale, nerds are a safe target for the entire school. If I remember correctly, the most popular kids don't persecute nerds; they don't need to stoop to such things. Most of the persecution comes from kids lower down, the nervous middle classes.

The trouble is, there are a lot of them. The distribution of popularity is not a pyramid, but tapers at the bottom like a pear. The least popular group is quite small. (I believe we were the only D table in our cafeteria map.) So there are more people who want to pick on nerds than there are nerds.

As well as gaining points by distancing oneself from unpopular kids, one loses points by being close to them. A woman I know says that in high school she liked nerds, but was afraid to be seen talking to them because the other girls would make fun of her. Unpopularity is a communicable disease; kids too nice to pick on nerds will still ostracize them in self-defense.

It's no wonder, then, that smart kids tend to be unhappy in middle school and high school. Their other interests leave them little attention to spare for popularity, and since popularity resembles a zero-sum game, this in turn makes them targets for the whole school. And the strange thing is, this nightmare scenario happens without any conscious malice, merely because of the shape of the situation.

For me the worst stretch was junior high, when kid culture was new and harsh, and the specialization that would later gradually separate the smarter kids had barely begun. Nearly everyone I've talked to agrees: the nadir is somewhere between eleven and fourteen.

In our school it was eighth grade, which was ages twelve and thirteen for me. There was a brief sensation that year when one of our teachers overheard a group of girls waiting for the school bus, and was so shocked that the next day she devoted the whole class to an eloquent plea not to be so cruel to one another.

It didn't have any noticeable effect. What struck me at the time was that she was surprised. You mean she doesn't know the kind of things they say to one another? You mean this isn't normal?

It's important to realize that, no, the adults don't know what the kids are doing to one another. They know, in the abstract, that kids are monstrously cruel to one another, just as we know in the abstract that people get tortured in poorer countries. But, like us, they don't like to dwell on this depressing fact, and they don't see evidence of specific abuses unless they go looking for it.

Public school teachers are in much the same position as prison wardens. Wardens' main concern is to keep the prisoners on the premises. They also need to keep them fed, and as far as possible prevent them from killing one another. Beyond that, they want to have as little to do with the prisoners as possible, so they leave them to create whatever social organization they want. From what I've read, the society that the prisoners create is warped, savage, and pervasive, and it is no fun to be at the bottom of it.

In outline, it was the same at the schools I went to. The most important thing was to stay on the premises. While there, the authorities fed you, prevented overt violence, and made some effort to teach you something. But beyond that they didn't want to have too much to do with the kids. Like prison wardens, the teachers mostly left us to ourselves. And, like prisoners, the culture we created was barbaric.

Why is the real world more hospitable to nerds? It might seem that the answer is simply that it's populated by adults, who are too mature to pick on one another. But I don't think this is true. Adults in prison certainly pick on one another. And so, apparently, do society wives; in some parts of Manhattan, life for women sounds like a continuation of high school, with all the same petty intrigues.

I think the important thing about the real world is not that it's populated by adults, but that it's very large, and the things you do have real effects. That's what school, prison, and ladies-who-lunch all lack. The inhabitants of all those worlds are trapped in little bubbles where nothing they do can have more than a local effect. Naturally these societies degenerate into savagery. They have no function for their form to follow.

When the things you do have real effects, it's no longer enough just to be pleasing. It starts to be important to get the right answers, and that's where nerds show to advantage. Bill Gates will of course come to mind. Though notoriously lacking in social skills, he gets the right answers, at least as measured in revenue.

The other thing that's different about the real world is that it's much larger. In a large enough pool, even the smallest minorities can achieve a critical mass if they clump together. Out in the real world, nerds collect in certain places and form their own societies where intelligence is the most important thing. Sometimes the current even starts to flow in the other direction: sometimes, particularly in university math and science departments, nerds deliberately exaggerate their awkwardness in order to seem smarter. John Nash so admired Norbert Wiener that he adopted his habit of touching the wall as he walked down a corridor.

As a thirteen-year-old kid, I didn't have much more experience of the world than what I saw immediately around me. The warped little world we lived in was, I thought, *the world*. The world seemed cruel and boring, and I'm not sure which was worse.

Because I didn't fit into this world, I thought that something must be wrong with me. I didn't realize that the reason we nerds didn't fit in was that in some ways we were a step ahead. We were already thinking about the kind of things that matter in the real world, instead of spending all our time playing an exacting but mostly pointless game like the others.

We were a bit like an adult would be if he were thrust back into middle school. He wouldn't know the right clothes to wear, the right music to like, the right slang to use. He'd seem to the kids a complete alien. The thing is, he'd know enough not to care what they thought. We had no such confidence.

A lot of people seem to think it's good for smart kids to be thrown together with "normal" kids at this stage of their lives. Perhaps. But in at least some cases the reason the nerds don't fit in really is that everyone else is crazy. I remember sitting in the audience at a "pep rally" at my high school, watching as the cheerleaders threw an effigy of an opposing player into the audience to be torn to pieces. I felt like an explorer witnessing some bizarre tribal ritual.

If I could go back and give my thirteen year old self some advice, the main thing I'd tell him would be to stick his head up and look around. I didn't really grasp it at the time, but the whole world we lived in was as fake as a Twinkie. Not just school, but the entire town. Why do people move to suburbia? To have kids! So no wonder it seemed boring and sterile. The whole place was a giant nursery, an artificial town created explicitly for the purpose of breeding children.

Where I grew up, it felt as if there was nowhere to go, and nothing to do. This was no accident. Suburbs are deliberately designed to exclude the outside world, because it contains things that could endanger children.

And as for the schools, they were just holding pens within this fake world. Officially the purpose of schools is to teach kids. In fact their primary purpose is to keep kids locked up in one place for a big chunk of the day so adults can get things done. And I have no problem with this: in a specialized industrial society, it would be a disaster to have kids running around loose.

What bothers me is not that the kids are kept in prisons, but that (a) they aren't told about it, and (b) the prisons are run mostly by the inmates. Kids are sent off to spend six years memorizing meaningless facts in a world ruled by a caste of giants who run after an oblong brown ball, as if this were the most natural thing in the world. And if they balk at this surreal cocktail, they're called misfits.

Life in this twisted world is stressful for the kids. And not just for the nerds. Like any war, it's damaging even to the winners.

Adults can't avoid seeing that teenage kids are tormented. So why don't they do something about it? Because they blame it on puberty. The reason kids are so unhappy, adults tell them-

selves, is that monstrous new chemicals, *hormones*, are now cours-
ing through their bloodstream and messing up everything. There's
nothing wrong with the system; it's just inevitable that kids will
be miserable at that age.

This idea is so pervasive that even the kids believe it, which
probably doesn't help. Someone who thinks his feet naturally hurt
is not going to stop to consider the possibility that he is wearing
the wrong size shoes.

I'm suspicious of this theory that thirteen-year-old kids are
intrinsically messed up. If it's physiological, it should be universal.
Are Mongol nomads all nihilists at thirteen? I've read a lot of
history, and I have not seen a single reference to this supposedly
universal fact before the twentieth century. Teenage apprentices
in the Renaissance seem to have been cheerful and eager. They got
in fights and played tricks on one another of course (Michelangelo
had his nose broken by a bully), but they weren't crazy.

As far as I can tell, the concept of the hormone-crazed teenager
is coeval with suburbia. I don't think this is a coincidence. I think
teenagers are driven crazy by the life they're made to lead. Teenage
apprentices in the Renaissance were working dogs. Teenagers now
are neurotic lapdogs. Their craziness is the craziness of the idle
everywhere.

When I was in school, suicide was a constant topic among the
smarter kids. No one I knew did it, but several planned to, and
some may have tried. Mostly this was just a pose. Like other
teenagers, we loved the dramatic, and suicide seemed very dramatic. But partly it was because our lives were at times genuinely
miserable.

Bullying was only part of the problem. Another problem, and
possibly an even worse one, was that we never had anything real
to work on. Humans like to work; in most of the world, your
work is your identity. And all the work we did was pointless, or
seemed so at the time.

At best it was practice for real work we might do far in the future, so far that we didn't even know at the time what we were practicing for. More often it was just an arbitrary series of hoops to jump through, words without content designed mainly for testability. (The three main causes of the Civil War were.... Test: List the three main causes of the Civil War.)

And there was no way to opt out. The adults had agreed among themselves that this was to be the route to college. The only way to escape this empty life was to submit to it.

Teenage kids used to have a more active role in society. In pre-industrial times, they were all apprentices of one sort or another, whether in shops or on farms or even on warships. They weren't left to create their own societies. They were junior members of adult societies.

Teenagers seem to have respected adults more then, because the adults were the visible experts in the skills they were trying to learn. Now most kids have little idea what their parents do in their distant offices, and see no connection (indeed, there is precious little) between schoolwork and the work they'll do as adults.

And if teenagers respected adults more, adults also had more use for teenagers. After a couple years' training, an apprentice could be a real help. Even the newest apprentice could be made to carry messages or sweep the workshop.

Now adults have no immediate use for teenagers. They would be in the way in an office. So they drop them off at school on their way to work, much as they might drop the dog off at a kennel if they were going away for the weekend.

What happened? We're up against a hard one here. The cause of this problem is the same as the cause of so many present ills: specialization. As jobs become more specialized, we have to train longer for them. Kids in pre-industrial times started working at about 14 at the latest; kids on farms, where most people lived, began far earlier. Now kids who go to college don't start working full-time till 21 or 22. With some degrees, like MDs and PhDs, you may not finish your training till 30.

Teenagers now are useless, except as cheap labor in industries like fast food, which evolved to exploit precisely this fact. In almost any other kind of work, they'd be a net loss. But they're also too young to be left unsupervised. Someone has to watch over them, and the most efficient way to do this is to collect them together in one place. Then a few adults can watch all of them.

If you stop there, what you're describing is literally a prison, albeit a part-time one. The problem is, many schools practically do stop there. The stated purpose of schools is to educate the kids. But there is no external pressure to do this well. And so most schools do such a bad job of teaching that the kids don't really take it seriously—not even the smart kids. Much of the time we were all, students and teachers both, just going through the motions.

In my high school French class we were supposed to read Hugo's *Les Miserables*. I don't think any of us knew French well enough to make our way through this enormous book. Like the rest of the class, I just skimmed the Cliff's Notes. When we were given a test on the book, I noticed that the questions sounded odd. They were full of long words that our teacher wouldn't have used. Where had these questions come from? From the Cliff's Notes, it turned out. The teacher was using them too. We were all just pretending.

There are certainly great public school teachers. The energy and imagination of my fourth grade teacher, Mr. Mihalko, made that year something his students still talk about, thirty years later. But teachers like him were individuals swimming upstream. They couldn't fix the system.

In almost any group of people you'll find hierarchy. When groups of adults form in the real world, it's generally for some common purpose, and the leaders end up being those who are best at it. The problem with most schools is, they have no purpose. But hierarchy there must be. And so the kids make one out of nothing.

We have a phrase to describe what happens when rankings have to be created without any meaningful criteria. We say that the situation *degenerates into a popularity contest.* And that's exactly what happens in most American schools. Instead of depending on some real test, one's rank depends mostly on one's ability to increase one's rank. It's like the court of Louis XIV. There is no external opponent, so the kids become one another's opponents.

When there is some real external test of skill, it isn't painful to be at the bottom of the hierarchy. A rookie on a football team doesn't resent the skill of the veteran; he hopes to be like him one day and is happy to have the chance to learn from him. The veteran may in turn feel a sense of *noblesse oblige.* And most importantly, their status depends on how well they do against opponents, not on whether they can push the other down.

Court hierarchies are another thing entirely. This type of society debases anyone who enters it. There is neither admiration at the bottom, nor *noblesse oblige* at the top. It's kill or be killed.

This is the sort of society that gets created in American secondary schools. And it happens because these schools have no real purpose beyond keeping the kids all in one place for a certain number of hours each day. What I didn't realize at the time, and in fact didn't realize till very recently, is that the twin horrors of school life, the cruelty and the boredom, both have the same cause.

The mediocrity of American public schools has worse consequences than just making kids unhappy for six years. It breeds a rebelliousness that actively drives kids away from the things they're supposed to be learning.

Like many nerds, probably, it was years after high school before I could bring myself to read anything we'd been assigned then. And I lost more than books. I mistrusted words like "character" and "integrity" because they had been so debased by adults. As they were used then, these words all seemed to mean the same thing: obedience. The kids who got praised for these qualities tended to be at best dull-witted prize bulls, and at worst facile schmoozers. If that was what character and integrity were, I wanted no part of them.

The word I most misunderstood was "tact." As used by adults, it seemed to mean keeping your mouth shut. I assumed it was derived from the same root as "tacit" and "taciturn," and that it literally meant being quiet. I vowed that I would never be tactful; they were never going to shut me up. In fact, it's derived from the same root as "tactile," and what it means is to have a deft touch. Tactful is the opposite of clumsy. I don't think I learned this until college.

Nerds aren't the only losers in the popularity rat race. Nerds are unpopular because they're distracted. There are other kids who deliberately opt out because they're so disgusted with the whole process.

Teenage kids, even rebels, don't like to be alone, so when kids opt out of the system, they tend to do it as a group. At the schools I went to, the focus of rebellion was drug use, specifically marijuana. The kids in this tribe wore black concert t-shirts and were called "freaks."

Freaks and nerds were allies, and there was a good deal of overlap between them. Freaks were on the whole smarter than other kids, though never studying (or at least never appearing to) was an important tribal value. I was more in the nerd camp, but I was friends with a lot of freaks.

They used drugs, at least at first, for the social bonds they created. It was something to do together, and because the drugs were illegal, it was a shared badge of rebellion.

I'm not claiming that bad schools are the whole reason kids get into trouble with drugs. After a while, drugs have their own momentum. No doubt some of the freaks ultimately used drugs to escape from other problems—trouble at home, for example. But, in my school at least, the reason most kids *started* using drugs was rebellion. Fourteen-year-olds didn't start smoking pot because they'd heard it would help them forget their problems. They started because they wanted to join a different tribe.

Misrule breeds rebellion; this is not a new idea. And yet the authorities still for the most part act as if drugs were themselves the cause of the problem.

The real problem is the emptiness of school life. We won't see solutions till adults realize that. The adults who may realize it first are the ones who were themselves nerds in school. Do you want your kids to be as unhappy in eighth grade as you were? I wouldn't. Well, then, is there anything we can do to fix things? Almost certainly. There is nothing inevitable about the current system. It has come about mostly by default.[2]

Adults, though, are busy. Showing up for school plays is one thing. Taking on the educational bureaucracy is another. Perhaps a few will have the energy to try to change things. I suspect the hardest part is realizing that you can.

Nerds still in school should not hold their breath. Maybe one day a heavily armed force of adults will show up in helicopters to rescue you, but they probably won't be coming this month. Any immediate improvement in nerds' lives is probably going to have to come from the nerds themselves.

Merely understanding the situation they're in should make it less painful. Nerds aren't losers. They're just playing a different game, and a game much closer to the one played in the real world. Adults know this. It's hard to find successful adults now who don't claim to have been nerds in high school.

It's important for nerds to realize, too, that school is not life. School is a strange, artificial thing, half sterile and half feral. It's all-encompassing, like life, but it isn't the real thing. It's only temporary, and if you look, you can see beyond it even while you're still in it.

If life seems awful to kids, it's neither because hormones are turning you all into monsters (as your parents believe), nor because life actually is awful (as you believe). It's because the adults, who no longer have any economic use for you, have abandoned you to spend years cooped up together with nothing real to do. *Any society of that type is awful to live in.* You don't have to look any further to explain why teenage kids are unhappy.

I've said some harsh things in this essay, but really the thesis is an optimistic one—that several problems we take for granted are in fact not insoluble after all. Teenage kids are not inherently unhappy monsters. That should be encouraging news to kids and adults both.

Chapter 2

Hackers and Painters

When I finished grad school in computer science I went to art school to study painting. A lot of people seemed surprised that someone interested in computers would also be interested in painting. They seemed to think that hacking and painting were very different kinds of work—that hacking was cold, precise, and methodical, and that painting was the frenzied expression of some primal urge.

Both of these images are wrong. Hacking and painting have a lot in common. In fact, of all the different types of people I've known, hackers and painters are among the most alike.

What hackers and painters have in common is that they're both makers. Along with composers, architects, and writers, what hackers and painters are trying to do is make good things. They're not doing research per se, though if in the course of trying to make good things they discover some new technique, so much the better.

I've never liked the term "computer science." The main reason I don't like it is that there's no such thing. Computer science is a grab bag of tenuously related areas thrown together by an accident of history, like Yugoslavia. At one end you have people who are really mathematicians, but call what they're doing computer science so they can get DARPA grants. In the middle you have people working on something like the natural history of computers—studying the behavior of algorithms for routing data through networks, for example. And then at the other extreme you have the hackers, who are trying to write interesting software, and for whom computers are just a medium of expression, as concrete is for architects or paint for painters. It's as if mathematicians, physicists, and architects all had to be in the same department.

Sometimes what the hackers do is called "software engineering," but this term is just as misleading. Good software designers are no more engineers than architects are. The border between architecture and engineering is not sharply defined, but it's there. It falls between what and how: architects decide what to do, and engineers figure out how to do it.

What and how should not be kept too separate. You're asking for trouble if you try to decide what to do without understanding how to do it. But hacking can certainly be more than just deciding how to implement some spec. At its best, it's creating the spec—though it turns out the best way to do that is to implement it.

Perhaps one day "computer science" will, like Yugoslavia, get broken up into its component parts. That might be a good thing. Especially if it meant independence for my native land, hacking.

Bundling all these different types of work together in one department may be convenient administratively, but it's confusing intellectually. That's the other reason I don't like the name "computer science." Arguably the people in the middle are doing something like an experimental science. But the people at either end, the hackers and the mathematicians, are not actually doing science.

The mathematicians don't seem bothered by this. They happily set to work proving theorems like the other mathematicians over in the math department, and probably soon stop noticing that the building they work in says "computer science" on the outside. But for the hackers this label is a problem. If what they're doing is called science, it makes them feel they ought to be acting scientific. So instead of doing what they really want to do, which is to design beautiful software, hackers in universities and research labs feel they ought to be writing research papers.

In the best case, the papers are just a formality. Hackers write cool software, and then write a paper about it, and the paper becomes a proxy for the achievement represented by the software. But often this mismatch causes problems. It's easy to drift away from building beautiful things toward building ugly things that make more suitable subjects for research papers.

Unfortunately, beautiful things don't always make the best subjects for papers. Number one, research must be original—and as anyone who has written a PhD dissertation knows, the way to be sure you're exploring virgin territory is to to stake out a piece of ground that no one wants. Number two, research must be substantial—and awkward systems yield meatier papers, because you can write about the obstacles you have to overcome in order to get things done. Nothing yields meaty problems like starting with the wrong assumptions. Most of AI is an example of this rule; if you assume that knowledge can be represented as a list of predicate logic expressions whose arguments represent abstract concepts, you'll have a lot of papers to write about how to make this work. As Ricky Ricardo used to say, "Lucy, you got a lot of explaining to do."

The way to create something beautiful is often to make subtle tweaks to something that already exists, or to combine existing ideas in a slightly new way. This kind of work is hard to convey in a research paper.

So why do universities and research labs continue to judge hackers by publications? For the same reason that "scholastic aptitude" gets measured by simple-minded standardized tests, or the productivity of programmers by lines of code. These tests are easy to apply, and there is nothing so tempting as an easy test that kind of works.

Measuring what hackers are actually trying to do, designing beautiful software, would be much more difficult. You need a good sense of design to judge good design. And there is no correlation, except possibly a negative one, between people's ability to recognize good design and their confidence that they can.

The only external test is time. Over time, beautiful things tend to thrive, and ugly things tend to get discarded. Unfortunately, the amounts of time involved can be longer than human lifetimes. Samuel Johnson said it took a hundred years for a writer's reputation to converge.[1] You have to wait for the writer's influential friends to die, and then for all their followers to die.

I think hackers just have to resign themselves to having a large random component in their reputations. In this they are no different from other makers. In fact, they're lucky by comparison. The influence of fashion is not nearly so great in hacking as it is in painting.

There are worse things than having people misunderstand your work. A worse danger is that you will yourself misunderstand your work. Related fields are where you go looking for ideas. If you find yourself in the computer science department, there is a natural temptation to believe, for example, that hacking is the applied version of what theoretical computer science is the theory of. All the time I was in graduate school I had an uncomfortable feeling in the back of my mind that I ought to know more theory, and that it was very remiss of me to have forgotten all that stuff within three weeks of the final exam.

Now I realize I was mistaken. Hackers need to understand the theory of computation about as much as painters need to understand paint chemistry. You need to know how to calculate time and space complexity, and perhaps also the concept of a state machine, in case you want to write a parser. Painters have to remember a good deal more about paint chemistry than that.

I've found that the best sources of ideas are not the other fields that have the word "computer" in their names, but the other fields inhabited by makers. Painting has been a much richer source of ideas than the theory of computation.

For example, I was taught in college that one ought to figure out a program completely on paper before even going near a computer. I found that I did not program this way. I found that I liked to program sitting in front of a computer, not a piece of paper. Worse still, instead of patiently writing out a complete program and assuring myself it was correct, I tended to just spew out code that was hopelessly broken, and gradually beat it into shape. Debugging, I was taught, was a kind of final pass where you caught typos and oversights. The way I worked, it seemed like programming consisted of debugging.

For a long time I felt bad about this, just as I once felt bad that I didn't hold my pencil the way they taught me to in elementary school. If I had only looked over at the other makers, the painters or the architects, I would have realized that there was a name for what I was doing: sketching. As far as I can tell, the way they taught me to program in college was all wrong. You should figure out programs as you're writing them, just as writers and painters and architects do.

Realizing this has real implications for software design. It means that a programming language should, above all, be malleable. A programming language is for thinking of programs, not for expressing programs you've already thought of. It should be a pencil, not a pen. Static typing would be a fine idea if people actually did write programs the way they taught me to in college. But that's not how any of the hackers I know write programs. We need a language that lets us scribble and smudge and smear, not a language where you have to sit with a teacup of types balanced on your knee and make polite conversation with a strict old aunt of a compiler.

While we're on the subject of static typing, identifying with the makers will save us from another problem that afflicts the sciences: math envy. Everyone in the sciences secretly believes that mathematicians are smarter than they are. I think mathematicians also believe this. At any rate, the result is that scientists tend to make their work look as mathematical as possible. In a field like physics this probably doesn't do much harm, but the further you get from the natural sciences, the more of a problem it becomes.

A page of formulas just looks so impressive. (Tip: for extra impressiveness, use Greek variables.) And so there is a great temptation to work on problems you can treat formally, rather than problems that are, say, important.

If hackers identified with other makers, like writers and painters, they wouldn't feel tempted to do this. Writers and painters don't suffer from math envy. They feel as if they're doing something completely unrelated. So are hackers, I think.

If universities and research labs keep hackers from doing the kind of work they want to do, perhaps the place for them is in companies. Unfortunately, most companies won't let hackers do what they want either. Universities and research labs force hackers to be scientists, and companies force them to be engineers.

I only discovered this myself quite recently. When Yahoo bought Viaweb, they asked me what I wanted to do. I had never liked business much, and said that I just wanted to hack. When I got to Yahoo, I found that what hacking meant to them was implementing software, not designing it. Programmers were seen as technicians who translated the visions (if that is the word) of product managers into code.

This seems to be the default plan in big companies. They do it because it decreases the standard deviation of the outcome. Only a small percentage of hackers can actually design software, and it's hard for the people running a company to pick these out. So instead of entrusting the future of the software to one brilliant hacker, most companies set things up so that it is designed by committee, and the hackers merely implement the design.

If you want to make money at some point, remember this, because this is one of the reasons startups win. Big companies want to decrease the standard deviation of design outcomes because they want to avoid disasters. But when you damp oscillations, you lose the high points as well as the low. This is not a problem for big companies, because they don't win by making great products. Big companies win by sucking less than other big companies.

So if you can figure out a way to get in a design war with a company big enough that its software is designed by product managers, they'll never be able to keep up with you. These opportunities are not easy to find, though. It's hard to engage a big company in a design war, just as it's hard to engage an opponent inside a castle in hand-to-hand combat. It would be pretty easy to write a better word processor than Microsoft Word, for example, but Microsoft, within the castle of their operating system monopoly, probably wouldn't even notice if you did.

The place to fight design wars is in new markets, where no one has yet managed to establish any fortifications. That's where you can win big by taking the bold approach to design, and having the same people both design and implement the product. Microsoft themselves did this at the start. So did Apple. And Hewlett-Packard. I suspect almost every successful startup has.

So one way to build great software is to start your own startup. There are two problems with this, though. One is that in a startup you have to do so much besides write software. At Viaweb I considered myself lucky if I got to hack a quarter of the time. And the things I had to do the other three quarters of the time ranged from tedious to terrifying. I have a benchmark for this, because I once had to leave a board meeting to have some cavities filled. I remember sitting back in the dentist's chair, waiting for the drill, and feeling like I was on vacation.

The other problem with startups is that there is not much overlap between the kind of software that makes money and the kind that's interesting to write. Programming languages are interesting to write, and Microsoft's first product was one, in fact, but no one will pay for programming languages now. If you want to make money, you tend to be forced to work on problems that are too nasty for anyone to solve for free.

All makers face this problem. Prices are determined by supply and demand, and there is just not as much demand for things that are fun to work on as there is for things that solve the mundane problems of individual customers. Acting in off-Broadway plays doesn't pay as well as wearing a gorilla suit in someone's booth at a trade show. Writing novels doesn't pay as well as writing ad copy for garbage disposals. And hacking programming languages doesn't pay as well as figuring out how to connect some company's legacy database to their web server.

I think the answer to this problem, in the case of software, is a concept known to nearly all makers: the day job. This phrase began with musicians, who perform at night. More generally, it means you have one kind of work you do for money, and another for love.

Nearly all makers have day jobs early in their careers. Painters and writers notoriously do. If you're lucky you can get a day job closely related to your real work. Musicians often seem to work in record stores. A hacker working on some programming language or operating system might likewise be able to get a day job using it.[2]

When I say that the answer is for hackers to have day jobs, and work on beautiful software on the side, I'm not proposing this as a new idea. This is what open source hacking is all about. What I'm saying is that open source is probably the right model, because it has been independently confirmed by all the other makers.

It seems surprising to me that any employer would be reluctant to let hackers work on open source projects. At Viaweb, we would have been reluctant to hire anyone who didn't. When we interviewed programmers, the main thing we cared about was what kind of software they wrote in their spare time. You can't do anything really well unless you love it, and if you love to hack you'll inevitably be working on projects of your own.[3]

Because hackers are makers rather than scientists, the right place to look for metaphors is not in the sciences, but among other kinds of makers. What else can painting teach us about hacking?

One thing we can learn, or at least confirm, from the example of painting is how to learn to hack. You learn to paint mostly by doing it. Ditto for hacking. Most hackers don't learn to hack by taking college courses in programming. They learn by writing programs of their own at age thirteen. Even in college classes, you learn to hack mostly by hacking.[4]

Because painters leave a trail of work behind them, you can watch them learn by doing. If you look at the work of a painter in chronological order, you'll find that each painting builds on things learned in previous ones. When there's something in a painting that works especially well, you can usually find version 1 of it in a smaller form in some earlier painting.

I think most makers work this way. Writers and architects seem to as well. Maybe it would be good for hackers to act more like painters, and regularly start over from scratch, instead of continuing to work for years on one project, and trying to incorporate all their later ideas as revisions.

The fact that hackers learn to hack by doing it is another sign of how different hacking is from the sciences. Scientists don't learn science by doing it, but by doing labs and problem sets. Scientists start out doing work that's perfect, in the sense that they're just trying to reproduce work someone else has already done for them. Eventually, they get to the point where they can do original work. Whereas hackers, from the start, are doing original work; it's just very bad. So hackers start original, and get good, and scientists start good, and get original.

The other way makers learn is from examples. To a painter, a museum is a reference library of techniques. For hundreds of years it has been part of the traditional education of painters to copy the works of the great masters, because copying forces you to look closely at the way a painting is made.

Writers do this too. Benjamin Franklin learned to write by summarizing the points in the essays of Addison and Steele and then trying to reproduce them. Raymond Chandler did the same thing with detective stories.

Hackers, likewise, can learn to program by looking at good programs—not just at what they do, but at the source code. One of the less publicized benefits of the open source movement is that it has made it easier to learn to program. When I learned to program, we had to rely mostly on examples in books. The one big chunk of code available then was Unix, but even this was not open source. Most of the people who read the source read it in illicit photocopies of John Lions' book, which though written in 1977 was not allowed to be published until 1996.

Another example we can take from painting is the way that paintings are created by gradual refinement. Paintings usually begin with a sketch. Gradually the details get filled in. But it is not merely a process of filling in. Sometimes the original plans turn out to be mistaken. Countless paintings, when you look at them in x-rays, turn out to have limbs that have been moved or facial features that have been readjusted.

Here's a case where we can learn from painting. I think hacking should work this way too. It's unrealistic to expect that the specifications for a program will be perfect. You're better off if you admit this up front, and write programs in a way that allows specifications to change on the fly.

(The structure of large companies makes this hard for them to do, so here is another place where startups have an advantage.)

Everyone by now presumably knows about the danger of premature optimization. I think we should be just as worried about premature design—deciding too early what a program should do.

The right tools can help us avoid this danger. A good programming language should, like oil paint, make it easy to change your mind. Dynamic typing is a win here because you don't have to commit to specific data representations up front. But the key to flexibility, I think, is to make the language very abstract. The easiest program to change is one that's short.

Leonardo's *Ginevra de' Benci*, 1474.

This sounds like a paradox, but a great painting has to be better than it has to be. For example, when Leonardo painted the portrait of Ginevra de' Benci in the National Gallery, he put a juniper bush behind her head. In it he carefully painted each individual leaf. Many painters might have thought, this is just something to put in the background to frame her head. No one will look that closely at it.

Not Leonardo. How hard he worked on part of a painting didn't depend at all on how closely he expected anyone to look at it. He was like Michael Jordan. Relentless.

Relentlessness wins because, in the aggregate, unseen details become visible. When people walk by the portrait of Ginevra de'

28

Benci, their attention is often immediately arrested by it, even be-fore they look at the label and notice that it says Leonardo da Vinci. All those unseen details combine to produce something that's just stunning, like a thousand barely audible voices all singing in tune.

Great software, likewise, requires a fanatical devotion to beau-ty. If you look inside good software, you find that parts no one is ever supposed to see are beautiful too. When it comes to code I behave in a way that would make me eligible for prescription drugs if I approached everyday life the same way. It drives me crazy to see code that's badly indented, or that uses ugly variable names.

If a hacker were a mere implementor, turning a spec into code, then he could just work his way through it from one end to the other like someone digging a ditch. But if the hacker is a creator, we have to take inspiration into account.

In hacking, like painting, work comes in cycles. Sometimes you get excited about a new project and you want to work sixteen hours a day on it. Other times nothing seems interesting.

To do good work you have to take these cycles into account, because they're affected by how you react to them. When you're driving a car with a manual transmission on a hill, you have to back off the clutch sometimes to avoid stalling. Backing off can likewise prevent ambition from stalling. In both painting and hacking there are some tasks that are terrifyingly ambitious, and others that are comfortingly routine. It's a good idea to save some easy tasks for moments when you would otherwise stall.

In hacking, this can literally mean saving up bugs. I like de-bugging: it's the one time that hacking is as straightforward as people think it is. You have a totally constrained problem, and all you have to do is solve it. Your program is supposed to do x. Instead it does y. Where does it go wrong? You know you're going to win in the end. It's as relaxing as painting a wall.

The example of painting can teach us not only how to manage our own work, but how to work together. A lot of the great art of the past is the work of multiple hands, though there may only be one name on the wall next to it in the museum. Leonardo was an apprentice in the workshop of Verrocchio and painted one of the angels in his *Baptism of Christ*. This sort of thing was the rule, not the exception. Michelangelo was considered especially dedicated for insisting on painting all the figures on the ceiling of the Sistine Chapel himself.

As far as I know, when painters worked together on a painting, they never worked on the same parts. It was common for the master to paint the principal figures and for assistants to paint the others and the background. But you never had one guy painting over the work of another.

I think this is the right model for collaboration in software too. Don't push it too far. When a piece of code is being hacked by three or four different people, no one of whom really owns it, it will end up being like a common-room. It will tend to feel bleak and abandoned, and accumulate cruft. The right way to collaborate, I think, is to divide projects into sharply defined modules, each with a definite owner, and with interfaces between them that are as carefully designed and, if possible, as articulated as programming languages.

Like painting, most software is intended for a human audience. And so hackers, like painters, must have empathy to do really great work. You have to be able to see things from the user's point of view.

When I was a kid I was constantly being told to look at things from someone else's point of view. What this always meant in practice was to do what someone else wanted, instead of what I wanted. This of course gave empathy a bad name, and I made a point of not cultivating it.

Boy, was I wrong. It turns out that looking at things from other people's point of view is practically the secret of success.

Empathy doesn't necessarily mean being self-sacrificing. Far from it. Understanding how someone else sees things doesn't imply that you'll act in his interest; in some situations—in war, for example— you want to do exactly the opposite.[5]

Most makers make things for a human audience. And to engage an audience you have to understand what they need. Nearly all the greatest paintings are paintings of people, for example, because people are what people are interested in.

Empathy is probably the single most important difference between a good hacker and a great one. Some hackers are quite smart, but practically solipsists when it comes to empathy. It's hard for such people to design great software, because they can't see things from the user's point of view.[6]

One way to tell how good people are at empathy is to watch them explain a technical matter to someone without a technical background. We probably all know people who, though otherwise smart, are just comically bad at this. If someone asks them at a dinner party what a programming language is, they'll say something like "Oh, a high-level language is what the compiler uses as input to generate object code." High-level language? Compiler? Object code? Someone who doesn't know what a programming language is obviously doesn't know what these things are, either.

Part of what software has to do is explain itself. So to write good software you have to understand how little users understand. They're going to walk up to the software with no preparation, and it had better do what they guess it will, because they're not going to read the manual. The best system I've ever seen in this respect was the original Macintosh, in 1984. It did what software almost never does: it just worked.[7]

Source code, too, should explain itself. If I could get people to remember just one quote about programming, it would be the one at the beginning of *Structure and Interpretation of Computer Programs.*[8]

Programs should be written for people to read, and only incidentally for machines to execute.

Piero della Francesca's *Federico da Montefeltro*, 1465-66 (detail).

You need to have empathy not just for your users, but for your readers. It's in your interest, because you'll be one of them. Many a hacker has written a program only to find on returning to it six months later that he has no idea how it works. I know several people who've sworn off Perl after such experiences.[9]

Lack of empathy is associated with intelligence, to the point that there is even something of a fashion for it in some places. But I don't think there's any correlation. You can do well in math and the natural sciences without having to learn empathy, and people in these fields tend to be smart, so the two qualities have come to be associated. But there are plenty of dumb people who are bad at empathy too.

So, if hacking works like painting and writing, is it as cool? After all, you only get one life. You might as well spend it working on something great.

Unfortunately, the question is hard to answer. There is always a big time lag in prestige. It's like light from a distant star. Painting has prestige now because of great work people did five hundred years ago. At the time, no one thought these paintings were as important as we do today. It would have seemed very odd to people in 1465 that Federico da Montefeltro, the Duke of Urbino, would one day be known mostly as the guy with the strange nose in a painting by Piero della Francesca.

So while I admit that hacking doesn't seem as cool as painting now, we should remember that painting itself didn't seem as cool in its glory days as it does now.

What we can say with some confidence is that these are the glory days of hacking. In most fields the great work is done early on. The paintings made between 1430 and 1500 are still unsurpassed. Shakespeare appeared just as professional theater was being born, and pushed the medium so far that every playwright since has had to live in his shadow. Albrecht Dürer did the same thing with engraving, and Jane Austen with the novel.

Over and over we see the same pattern. A new medium appears, and people are so excited about it that they explore most of its possibilities in the first couple generations. Hacking seems to be in this phase now.

Painting was not, in Leonardo's time, as cool as his work helped make it. How cool hacking turns out to be will depend on what we can do with this new medium.

Chapter 3

What You Can't Say

Have you ever seen an old photo of yourself and been embarrassed at the way you looked? *Did we actually dress like that?* We did. And we had no idea how silly we looked. It's the nature of fashion to be invisible, in the same way the movement of the earth is invisible to all of us riding on it.

What scares me is that there are moral fashions too. They're just as arbitrary, and just as invisible to most people. But they're much more dangerous. Fashion is mistaken for good design; moral fashion is mistaken for good. Dressing oddly gets you laughed at. Violating moral fashions can get you fired, ostracized, imprisoned, or even killed.

If you could travel back in a time machine, one thing would be true no matter where you went: you'd have to watch what you said. Opinions we consider harmless could have gotten you in big trouble. I've already said at least one thing that would have gotten me in big trouble in most of Europe in the seventeenth century, and did get Galileo in big trouble when he said it—that the earth moves.[1]

Nerds are always getting in trouble. They say improper things for the same reason they dress unfashionably and have good ideas. Convention has less hold over them.

It seems to be a constant throughout history: in every period, people believed things that were just ridiculous, and believed them so strongly that you would have gotten in terrible trouble for saying otherwise.

Is our time any different? To anyone who has read any amount of history, the answer is almost certainly no. It would be a remarkable coincidence if ours were the first era to get everything just right.

It's tantalizing to think we believe things that people in the future will find ridiculous. What *would* someone coming back to visit us in a time machine have to be careful not to say? That's what I want to study here. But I want to do more than just shock everyone with the heresy du jour. I want to find general recipes for discovering what you can't say, in any era.

The Conformist Test

Let's start with a test: do you have any opinions that you would be reluctant to express in front of a group of your peers?

If the answer is no, you might want to stop and think about that. If everything you believe is something you're supposed to believe, could that possibly be a coincidence? Odds are it isn't. Odds are you just think whatever you're told.

The other alternative would be that you independently considered every question and came up with the exact same answers that are now considered acceptable. That seems unlikely, because you'd also have to make the same mistakes. Mapmakers deliberately put slight mistakes in their maps so they can tell when someone copies them. If another map has the same mistake, that's very convincing evidence.

Like every other era in history, our moral map almost certainly contains mistakes. And anyone who makes the same mistakes probably didn't do it by accident. It would be like someone claiming they had independently decided in 1972 that bell-bottom jeans were a good idea.

If you believe everything you're supposed to now, how can you be sure you wouldn't also have believed everything you were supposed to if you had grown up among the plantation owners of the pre-Civil War South, or in Germany in the 1930s—or among the Mongols in 1200, for that matter? Odds are you would have.

Back in the era of terms like "well-adjusted," the idea seemed to be that there was something wrong with you if you thought

things you didn't dare say out loud. This seems backward. Almost
certainly, there is something wrong with you if you *don't* think
things you don't dare say out loud.

Trouble

What can't we say? One way to find these ideas is simply to look
at things people do say, and get in trouble for.[2]

Of course, we're not just looking for things we can't say. We're
looking for things we can't say that are true, or at least have enough
chance of being true that the question should remain open. But
many of the things people get in trouble for saying probably do
make it over this second, lower threshold. No one gets in trouble
for saying that 2 + 2 is 5, or that people in Pittsburgh are ten feet
tall. Such obviously false statements might be treated as jokes, or
at worst as evidence of insanity, but they are not likely to make
anyone mad. The statements that make people mad are the ones
they worry might be believed. I suspect the statements that make
people maddest are those they worry might be true.

If Galileo had said that people in Padua were ten feet tall, he
would have been regarded as a harmless eccentric. Saying the earth
orbited the sun was another matter. The church knew this would
set people thinking.

Certainly, as we look back on the past, this rule of thumb works
well. A lot of the statements that got people in trouble seem harmless now. So it's likely that visitors from the future would agree
with at least some of the statements that get people in trouble
today. Do we have no Galileos? Not likely.

To find them, keep track of opinions that get people in trouble,
and start asking, could this be true? Ok, it may be heretical (or
whatever modern equivalent), but might it also be true?

Heresy

This won't get us all the answers, though. What if no one happens
to have gotten in trouble for a particular idea yet? What if some

idea would be so radioactively controversial that no one would dare express it in public? How can we find these too?

Another approach is to follow that word, heresy. In every period of history, there seem to have been labels that got applied to statements to shoot them down before anyone had a chance to ask if they were true or not. "Blasphemy," "sacrilege," and "heresy" were such labels for a good part of Western history, as in more recent times "indecent," "improper," and "un-American" have been. By now these labels have lost their sting. They always do. By now they're mostly used ironically. But in their time, they had real force.

The word "defeatist," for example, has no particular political connotations now. But in Germany in 1917 it was a weapon, used by Ludendorff in a purge of those who favored a negotiated peace. At the start of World War II it was used extensively by Churchill and his supporters to silence their opponents. In 1940, any argument against Churchill's aggressive policy was "defeatist." Was it right or wrong? Ideally, no one got far enough to ask that.

We have such labels today, of course, quite a lot of them, from the all-purpose "inappropriate" to the dreaded "divisive." In any period, it should be easy to figure out what such labels are, simply by looking at what people call ideas they disagree with besides untrue. When a politician says his opponent is mistaken, that's a straightforward criticism, but when he attacks a statement as "divisive" or "racially insensitive" instead of arguing that it's false, we should start paying attention.

So another way to figure out which of our taboos future generations will laugh at is to start with the labels. Take a label—"sexist," for example—and try to think of some ideas that would be called that. Then for each ask, might this be true?

Just start listing ideas at random? Yes, because they won't really be random. The ideas that come to mind first will be the most plausible ones. They'll be things you've already noticed but didn't let yourself think.

In 1989 some clever researchers tracked the eye movements of radiologists as they scanned chest images for signs of lung cancer.[3]

They found that even when the radiologists missed a cancerous lesion, their eyes had usually paused at the site of it. Part of their brain knew there was something there; it just didn't percolate up into conscious knowledge. I think many interesting heretical thoughts are already mostly formed in our minds. If we turn off our self-censorship temporarily, those will be the first to emerge.

Time and Space

If we could look into the future it would be obvious which of our ideas they'd laugh at. We can't do that, but we can do something almost as good: we can look into the past. Another way to figure out what we're getting wrong is to look at what used to be acceptable and is now unthinkable.

Changes between the past and the present sometimes do represent progress. In a field like physics, if we disagree with past generations it's because we're right and they're wrong. But this becomes rapidly less true as you move away from the certainty of the hard sciences. By the time you get to social questions, many changes are just fashion. The age of consent fluctuates like hemlines.

We may imagine that we are a great deal smarter and more virtuous than past generations, but the more history you read, the less likely this seems. People in past times were much like us. Not heroes, not barbarians. Whatever their ideas were, they were ideas reasonable people could believe.

So here is another source of interesting heresies. Diff present ideas against those of various past cultures, and see what you get.[4] Some will be shocking by present standards. Ok, fine; but which might also be true?

You don't have to look into the past to find big differences. In our own time, different societies have wildly varying ideas of what's ok and what isn't. So you can try diffing other cultures' ideas against ours as well. (The best way to do that is to visit them.)

WHAT YOU CAN'T SAY

You might find contradictory taboos. In one culture it might seem shocking to think x, while in another it was shocking not to. But I think usually the shock is on one side. In one culture x is ok, and in another it's considered shocking. My hypothesis is that the side that's shocked is most likely to be the mistaken one.[5]

I suspect the only taboos that are more than taboos are the ones that are universal, or nearly so. Murder for example. But any idea that's considered harmless in a significant percentage of times and places, and yet is taboo in ours, is a good candidate for something we're mistaken about.

For example, at the high-water mark of political correctness in the early 1990s, Harvard distributed to its faculty and staff a brochure saying, among other things, that it was inappropriate to compliment a colleague's or student's clothes. No more "nice shirt." I think this principle is rare among the world's cultures, past or present. There are probably more where it's considered especially polite to compliment someone's clothing than where it's considered improper. So odds are this is, in a mild form, an example of one of the taboos a visitor from the future would have to be careful to avoid if he happened to set his time machine for Cambridge, Massachusetts, 1992.

Prigs

Of course, if they have time machines in the future they'll probably have a separate reference manual just for Cambridge. This has always been a fussy place, a town of i dotters and t crossers, where you're liable to get both your grammar and your ideas corrected in the same conversation. And that suggests another way to find taboos. Look for prigs, and see what's inside their heads.

Kids' heads are repositories of all our taboos. It seems fitting to us that kids' ideas should be bright and clean. The picture we give them of the world is not merely simplified, to suit their developing minds, but sanitized as well, to suit our ideas of what kids should think.[6]

You can see this on a small scale in the matter of dirty words. A lot of my friends are starting to have children now, and they're all trying not to use words like "fuck" and "shit" within baby's hearing, lest baby start using these words too. But these words are part of the language, and adults use them all the time. So parents are giving their kids an inaccurate idea of the language by not using them. Why do they do this? Because they don't think it's fitting that kids should use the whole language. We like children to seem innocent.[7]

Most adults, likewise, deliberately give kids a misleading view of the world. One of the most obvious examples is Santa Claus. We think it's cute for little kids to believe in Santa Claus. I myself think it's cute for little kids to believe in Santa Claus. But one wonders, do we tell them this stuff for their sake, or for ours?

I'm not arguing for or against this idea here. It is probably inevitable that parents should want to dress up their kids' minds in cute little baby outfits. I'll probably do it myself. The important thing for our purposes is that, as a result, a well brought-up teenage kid's brain is a more or less complete collection of all our taboos— and in mint condition, because they're untainted by experience. Whatever we think that will later turn out to be ridiculous, it's almost certainly inside that head.

How do we get at these ideas? By the following thought experiment. Imagine a kind of latter-day Conrad character who has worked for a time as a mercenary in Africa, for a time as a doctor in Nepal, for a time as the manager of a nightclub in Miami. The specifics don't matter—just someone who has seen a lot. Now imagine comparing what's inside this guy's head with what's inside the head of a well-behaved sixteen-year-old girl from the suburbs. What does he think that would shock her? He knows the world; she knows, or at least embodies, present taboos. Subtract one from the other, and the result is what we can't say.

Mechanism

I can think of one more way to figure out what we can't say: to look at how taboos are created. How do moral fashions arise, and why are they adopted? If we can understand this mechanism, we may be able to see it at work in our own time.

Moral fashions don't seem to be created the way ordinary fashions are. Ordinary fashions seem to arise by accident when everyone imitates the whim of some influential person. The fashion for broad-toed shoes in late fifteenth-century Europe began because Charles VIII of France had six toes on one foot. The fashion for the name Gary began when the actor Frank Cooper adopted the name of a tough mill town in Indiana. Moral fashions more often seem to be created deliberately. When there's something we can't say, it's often because some group doesn't want us to.

The prohibition will be strongest when the group is nervous. The irony of Galileo's situation was that he got in trouble for repeating Copernicus's ideas. Copernicus himself didn't. In fact, Copernicus was a canon of a cathedral, and dedicated his book to the pope. But by Galileo's time the church was in the throes of the Counter-Reformation and was much more worried about unorthodox ideas.

To launch a taboo, a group has to be poised halfway between weakness and power. A confident group doesn't need taboos to protect it. It's not considered improper to make disparaging remarks about Americans, or the English. And yet a group has to be powerful enough to enforce a taboo. Coprophiles, as of this writing, don't seem to be numerous or energetic enough to have had their interests promoted to a lifestyle.

I suspect the biggest source of moral taboos will turn out to be power struggles in which one side barely has the upper hand. That's where you'll find a group powerful enough to enforce taboos, but weak enough to need them.

Most struggles, whatever they're really about, will be cast as struggles between competing ideas. The English Reformation was at bottom a struggle for wealth and power, but it ended up being cast as a struggle to preserve the souls of Englishmen from the corrupting influence of Rome. It's easier to get people to fight for an idea. And whichever side wins, their ideas will also be considered to have triumphed, as if God wanted to signal his agreement by selecting that side as the victor.

We often like to think of World War II as a triumph of freedom over totalitarianism. We conveniently forget that the Soviet Union was also one of the winners.

I'm not saying that struggles are never about ideas, just that they will always be made to seem to be about ideas, whether they are or not. And just as there is nothing so unfashionable as the last, discarded fashion, there is nothing so wrong as the principles of the most recently defeated opponent. Representational art is only now recovering from the approval of both Hitler and Stalin.[8]

Although fashions in ideas tend to arise from different sources than fashions in clothing, the mechanism of their adoption seems much the same. The early adopters will be driven by ambition: self-consciously cool people who want to distinguish themselves from the common herd. As the fashion becomes established they'll be joined by a second, much larger group, driven by fear.[9] This second group adopt the fashion not because they want to stand out but because they are afraid of standing out.

So if you want to figure out what we can't say, look at the machinery of fashion and try to predict what it would make unsayable. What groups are powerful but nervous, and what ideas would they like to suppress? What ideas were tarnished by association when they ended up on the losing side of a recent struggle? If a self-consciously cool person wanted to differentiate himself from preceding fashions (e.g. from his parents), which of their ideas would he tend to reject? What are conventional-minded people afraid of saying?

This technique won't find us all the things we can't say. I can think of some that aren't the result of any recent struggle. Many of our taboos are rooted deep in the past. But this approach, combined with the preceding four, will turn up a good number of unthinkable ideas.

Why

Some would ask, why would one want to do this? Why deliberately go poking around among nasty, disreputable ideas? Why look under rocks?

I do it, first of all, for the same reason I did look under rocks as a kid: plain curiosity. And I'm especially curious about anything that's forbidden. Let me see and decide for myself.

Second, I do it because I don't like the idea of being mistaken. If, like other eras, we believe things that will later seem ridiculous, I want to know what they are so that I, at least, can avoid believing them.

Third, I do it because it's good for the brain. To do good work you need a brain that can go anywhere. And you especially need a brain that's in the habit of going where it's not supposed to.

Great work tends to grow out of ideas that others have overlooked, and no idea is so overlooked as one that's unthinkable. Natural selection, for example. It's so simple. Why didn't anyone think of it before? Well, that is all too obvious. Darwin himself was careful to tiptoe around the implications of his theory. He wanted to spend his time thinking about biology, not arguing with people who accused him of being an atheist.

In the sciences, especially, it's a great advantage to be able to question assumptions. The m.o. of scientists, or at least of the good ones, is precisely that: look for places where conventional wisdom is broken, and then try to pry apart the cracks and see what's underneath. That's where new theories come from.

A good scientist, in other words, does not merely ignore conventional wisdom, but makes a special effort to break it. Scientists go looking for trouble. This should be the m.o. of any scholar, but scientists seem much more willing to look under rocks.

Why? It could be that the scientists are simply smarter; most physicists could, if necessary, make it through a PhD program in French literature, but few professors of French literature could make it through a PhD program in physics.[10] Or it could be cause it's clearer in the sciences whether theories are true or false, and this makes scientists bolder. (Or it could be that, because it's clearer in the sciences whether theories are true or false, you have to be smart to get jobs as a scientist, rather than just a good politician.)

Whatever the reason, there seems a clear correlation between intelligence and willingness to consider shocking ideas. This isn't just because smart people actively work to find holes in conventional thinking. Conventions also have less hold over them to start with. You can see that in the way they dress.

It's not only in the sciences that heresy pays off. In any competitive field, you can win big by seeing things that others daren't. And in every field there are probably heresies few dare utter. Within the US car industry there is a lot of hand-wringing about declining market share. Yet the cause is so obvious that any observant outsider could explain it in a second: they make bad cars. And they have for so long that by now the US car brands are antibrands—something you'd buy a car despite, not because of. Cadillac stopped being the Cadillac of cars in about 1970. And yet I suspect no one dares say this." Otherwise these companies would have tried to fix the problem.

Training yourself to think unthinkable thoughts has advantages beyond the thoughts themselves. It's like stretching. When you stretch before running, you put your body into positions much more extreme than any it will assume during the run. If you can think things so outside the box that they'd make people's hair stand on end, you'll have no trouble with the small trips outside the box that people call innovative.

Pensieri Stretti

When you find something you can't say, what do you do with it? My advice is, don't say it. Or at least, pick your battles.

Suppose in the future there is a movement to ban the color yellow. Proposals to paint anything yellow are denounced as "yellowist," as is anyone suspected of liking the color. People who like orange are tolerated but viewed with suspicion. Suppose you realize there is nothing wrong with yellow. If you go around saying so, you'll be denounced as a yellowist too, and you'll find yourself having a lot of arguments with anti-yellowists. If your aim in life is to rehabilitate the color yellow, that may be what you want. But if you're mostly interested in other questions, being labelled as a yellowist will just be a distraction. Argue with idiots, and you become an idiot.

The most important thing is to be able to think what you want, not to say what you want. And if you feel you have to say everything you think, it may inhibit you from thinking improper thoughts. I think it's better to follow the opposite policy. Draw a sharp line between your thoughts and your speech. Inside your head, anything is allowed. Within my head I make a point of encouraging the most outrageous thoughts I can imagine. But, as in a secret society, nothing that happens within the building should be told to outsiders. The first rule of Fight Club is, you do not talk about Fight Club.

When Milton was going to visit Italy in the 1630s, Sir Henry Wootton, who had been ambassador to Venice, told him that his motto should be *"i pensieri stretti & il viso sciolto."* Closed thoughts and an open face. Smile at everyone, and don't tell them what you're thinking. This was wise advice. Milton was an argumentative fellow, and the Inquisition was a bit restive at that time. But the difference between Milton's situation and ours is only a matter of degree. Every era has its heresies, and if you don't get imprisoned for them, you will at least get in enough trouble that it becomes a complete distraction.

I admit it seems cowardly to keep quiet. When I read about the harassment to which the Scientologists subject their critics,[12] or people branded as anti-Semitic for speaking out against Israeli human-rights abuses,[13] or researchers threatened with lawsuits under the DMCA,[14] part of me wants to say, "All right, you bastards, bring it on." The problem is, there are so many things you can't say. If you said them all you'd have no time left for your real work. You'd have to turn into Noam Chomsky.[15]

45

The trouble with keeping your thoughts secret, though, is that you lose the advantages of discussion. Talking about an idea leads to more ideas. So the optimal plan, if you can manage it, is to have a few trusted friends you can speak openly to. This is not just a way to develop ideas; it's also a good rule of thumb for choosing friends. The people you can say heretical things to without getting jumped on are also the most interesting to know.

Viso Sciolto?

Perhaps the best policy is to make it plain that you don't agree with whatever zealotry is current in your time, but not to be too specific about what you disagree with. Zealots will try to draw you out, but you don't have to answer them. If they try to force you to treat a question on their terms by asking "are you with us or against us?" you can always just answer "neither."

Better still, answer "I haven't decided." That's what Larry Summers did when a group tried to put him in this position.[16] Explaining himself later, he said "I don't do litmus tests." A lot of the questions people get hot about are actually quite complicated. There is no prize for getting the answer quickly.

If the anti-yellowists seem to be getting out of hand and you want to fight back, there are ways to do it without getting yourself accused of yellowism. Like skirmishers in an ancient army, you want to avoid directly engaging the main body of the enemy's troops. Better to harass them with arrows from a distance.

One way to do this is to ratchet the debate up one level of abstraction. If you argue against censorship in general, you can avoid being accused of whatever heresy is contained in the book or film that someone is trying to censor. You can attack labels with meta-labels: labels that refer to the use of labels to prevent discussion. The spread of the term "political correctness" meant the beginning of the end of political correctness, because it enabled one to attack the phenomenon as a whole without being accused of any of the specific heresies it sought to suppress.

Another way to counterattack is with metaphor. Arthur Miller undermined the House Un-American Activities Committee by writing a play, *The Crucible*, about the Salem witch trials. He never referred directly to the committee and so gave them no way to reply. What could HUAC do, defend the Salem witch trials? And yet Miller's metaphor stuck so well that to this day the activities of the committee are often described as a "witch-hunt."

Best of all, probably, is humor. Zealots, whatever their cause, invariably lack a sense of humor. They can't reply in kind to jokes. They're as unhappy on the territory of humor as a mounted knight on a skating rink. Victorian prudishness, for example, seems to have been defeated mainly by treating it as a joke. Likewise its reincarnation as political correctness. "I am glad that I managed to write *The Crucible*," Arthur Miller wrote, "but looking back I have often wished I'd had the temperament to do an absurd comedy, which is what the situation deserved."[17]

Always Be Questioning

A Dutch friend says I should use Holland as an example of a tolerant society. It's true they have a long tradition of comparative open-mindedness. For centuries the low countries were the place to go to say things you couldn't say anywhere else, and this helped make the region a center of scholarship and industry (which have been closely tied for longer than most people realize). Descartes, though claimed by the French, did much of his thinking in Holland.

And yet, I wonder. The Dutch seem to live their lives up to their necks in rules and regulations. There's so much you can't do there; is there really nothing you can't say?

Certainly the fact that they value open-mindedness is no guarantee. Who thinks they're not open-minded? Our hypothetical prim miss from the suburbs thinks she's open-minded. Hasn't she been taught to be? Ask anyone, and they'll say the same thing: they're pretty open-minded, though they draw the line at things that are really wrong.[18] In other words, everything is ok except things that aren't.

When people are bad at math, they know it, because they get the wrong answers on tests. But when people are bad at open-mindedness, they don't know it. In fact they tend to think the opposite. Remember, it's the nature of fashion to be invisible. It wouldn't work otherwise. Fashion doesn't seem like fashion to someone in the grip of it. It just seems like the right thing to do. It's only by looking from a distance that we see oscillations in people's idea of the right thing to do, and can identify them as fashions.

Time gives us such distance for free. Indeed, the arrival of new fashions makes old fashions easy to see, because they seem so ridiculous by contrast. From one end of a pendulum's swing, the other end seems especially far away.

To see fashion in your own time, though, requires a conscious effort. Without time to give you distance, you have to create distance yourself. Instead of being part of the mob, stand as far away from it as you can and watch what it's doing. And pay especially close attention whenever an idea is being suppressed. Web filters for children and employees often ban sites containing pornography, violence, and hate speech. What counts as pornography and violence? And what, exactly, is "hate speech?" This sounds like a phrase out of *1984*.

Labels like that are probably the biggest external clue. If a statement is false, that's the worst thing you can say about it. You don't need to say that it's heretical. And if it isn't false, it shouldn't be suppressed. So when you see statements being attacked as x-ist or y-ic (substitute your current values of x and y), whether in 1630 or 2030, that's a sure sign that something is wrong. When you hear such labels being used, ask why.

Especially if you hear yourself using them. It's not just the mob you need to learn to watch from a distance. You need to be able to watch your own thoughts from a distance. That's not a radical idea, by the way; it's the main difference between children and adults. When a child gets angry because he's tired, he doesn't know what's happening. An adult can distance himself enough from the situation to say "never mind, I'm just tired." I don't see why one couldn't, by a similar process, learn to recognize and discount the effects of moral fashions.

You have to take that extra step if you want to think clearly. But it's harder, because now you're working against social customs instead of with them. Everyone encourages you to grow up to the point where you can discount your own bad moods. Few encourage you to continue to the point where you can discount society's bad moods.

How can you see the wave, when you're the water? Always be questioning. That's the only defence. What can't you say? And why?

Chapter 4

Good Bad Attitude

To the popular press, "hacker" means someone who breaks into computers. Among programmers it means a good programmer. But the two meanings are connected. To programmers, "hacker" connotes mastery in the most literal sense: someone who can make a computer do what he wants—whether the computer wants to or not.

To add to the confusion, the noun "hack" also has two senses. It can be either a compliment or an insult. It's called a hack when you do something in an ugly way. But when you do something so clever that you somehow beat the system, that's also called a hack. The word is used more often in the former than the latter sense, probably because ugly solutions are more common than brilliant ones.

Believe it or not, the two senses of "hack" are also connected. Ugly and imaginative solutions have something in common: they both break the rules. And there is a gradual continuum between rule breaking that's merely ugly (using duct tape to attach something to your bike) and rule breaking that is brilliantly imaginative (discarding Euclidean space).

Hacking predates computers. When he was working on the Manhattan Project, Richard Feynman used to amuse himself by breaking into safes containing secret documents. This tradition continues today. When we were in grad school, a hacker friend of mine who spent too much time around MIT had his own lock picking kit.[1] (He now runs a hedge fund, a not unrelated enterprise.)

It is sometimes hard to explain to authorities why one would want to do such things. Another friend of mine once got in trouble with the government for breaking into computers. This had only recently been declared a crime, and the FBI found that their usual investigative technique didn't work. Police investigation apparently begins with a motive. The usual motives are few: drugs, money, sex, revenge. Intellectual curiosity was not one of the motives on the FBI's list. Indeed, the whole concept seemed foreign to them.

Those in authority tend to be annoyed by hackers' general attitude of disobedience. But that disobedience is a byproduct of the qualities that make them good programmers. They may laugh at the CEO when he talks in generic corporate newspeech, but they also laugh at someone who tells them a certain problem can't be solved. Suppress one, and you suppress the other.

This attitude is sometimes affected. Sometimes young programmers notice the eccentricities of eminent hackers and decide to adopt some of their own in order to seem smarter. The fake version is not merely annoying; the prickly attitude of these posers can actually slow the process of innovation.

But even factoring in their annoying eccentricities, the disobedient attitude of hackers is a net win. I wish its advantages were better understood.

For example, I suspect people in Hollywood are simply mystified by hackers' attitudes toward copyrights. They are a perennial topic of heated discussion on Slashdot. But why should people who program computers be so concerned about copyrights, of all things?

Partly because some companies use *mechanisms* to prevent copying. Show any hacker a lock and his first thought is how to pick it. But there is a deeper reason that hackers are alarmed by measures like copyrights and patents. They see increasingly aggressive measures to protect "intellectual property" as a threat to the intellectual freedom they need to do their job. And they are right.

It is by poking about inside current technology that hackers get ideas for the next generation. No thanks, intellectual homeowners may say, we don't need any outside help. But they're wrong. The next generation of computer technology has often—perhaps more often than not—been developed by outsiders. In 1977 there was no

Jobs and Wozniak with a circumvention device, 1975.

doubt some group within IBM developing what they expected to be the next generation of business computer. They were mistaken. The next generation of business computer was being developed on entirely different lines by two long-haired guys called Steve in a garage in Los Altos. At about the same time, the powers that be were cooperating to develop the official next generation operating system, Multics. But two guys who thought Multics excessively complex went off and wrote their own. They gave it a name that was a joking reference to Multics: Unix.

The latest intellectual property laws impose unprecedented restrictions on the sort of poking around that leads to new ideas. In the past, a competitor might use patents to prevent you from selling a copy of something they made, but they couldn't prevent you from taking one apart to see how it worked. The latest laws make this a crime. How are we to develop new technology if we can't study current technology to figure out how to improve it?

Ironically, hackers have brought this on themselves. Computers are responsible for the problem. The control systems inside machines used to be physical: gears and levers and cams. Increasingly, the brains (and thus the value) of products is in software.[2] And by this I mean software in the general sense: i.e. data. A song on an LP is physically stamped into the plastic. A song on an iPod's disk is merely stored on it.

Data is by definition easy to copy. And the Internet makes copies easy to distribute. So it is no wonder companies are afraid. But, as so often happens, fear has clouded their judgement. The government has responded with draconian laws to protect intellectual property. They probably mean well. But they may not realize that such laws will do more harm than good.

Why are programmers so violently opposed to these laws? If I were a legislator, I'd be interested in this mystery—for the same reason that, if I were a farmer and suddenly heard a lot of squawking coming from my hen house one night, I'd want to go out and investigate. Hackers are not stupid, and unanimity is very rare in this world. So if they're all squawking, perhaps there is something amiss.

Could it be that such laws, though intended to protect America, will actually harm it? Think about it. There is something very *American* about Feynman breaking into safes during the Manhattan Project. It's hard to imagine the authorities having a sense of humor about such things over in Germany at that time. Maybe it's not a coincidence.

Hackers are unruly. That is the essence of hacking. And it is also the essence of American-ness. It is no accident that Silicon Valley is in America, and not France, or Germany, or England, or Japan. In those countries, people color inside the lines.

I lived for a while in Florence. But after I'd been there a few months I realized that what I'd been unconsciously hoping to find there was back in the place I'd just left. The reason Florence is famous is that in 1450, it was New York. In 1450 it was filled with the kind of turbulent and ambitious people you find now in America. (So I went back to America.)

It is greatly to America's advantage that it is a congenial atmosphere for the right sort of unruliness—that it is a home not just for the smart, but for smart-alecks. And hackers are invariably smart-alecks. If we had a national holiday, it would be April 1st. It says a great deal about our work that we use the same word for a brilliant or a horribly cheesy solution. When we cook one up we're not always 100% sure which kind it is. But as long as it has the right sort of wrongness, that's a promising sign. It's odd that people think of programming as precise and methodical. *Computers* are precise and methodical. Hacking is something you do with a gleeful laugh.

In our world some of the most characteristic solutions are not far removed from practical jokes. IBM was no doubt rather surprised by the consequences of the licensing deal for DOS, just as the hypothetical "adversary" must be when Michael Rabin solves a problem by redefining it as one that's easier to solve.

Smart-alecks have to develop a keen sense of how much they can get away with. And lately hackers have sensed a change in the atmosphere. Lately hackerliness seems rather frowned upon.

To hackers the recent contraction in civil liberties seems especially ominous. That must also mystify outsiders. Why should we care especially about civil liberties? Why programmers, more than dentists or salesmen or landscapers?

Let me put the case in terms a government official would appreciate. Civil liberties are not just an ornament, or a quaint American tradition. Civil liberties make countries rich. If you made a graph of GNP per capita vs. civil liberties, you'd notice a definite trend. Could civil liberties really be a cause, rather than just an effect? I think so. I think a society in which people can do and say what they want will also tend to be one in which the most efficient solutions win, rather than those sponsored by the most influential people. Authoritarian countries become corrupt; corrupt countries become poor; and poor countries are weak. It seems to me there is a Laffer curve for government power, just as for tax revenues.[3] At least, it seems likely enough that it would be stupid to try the experiment and find out. Unlike high tax rates, you can't repeal totalitarianism if it turns out to be a mistake.

This is why hackers worry. The government spying on people doesn't literally make programmers write worse code. It just leads eventually to a world in which bad ideas will win. And because this is so important to hackers, they're especially sensitive to it.

They can sense totalitarianism approaching from a distance, as animals can sense an approaching thunderstorm.

It would be ironic if, as hackers fear, recent measures intended to protect national security and intellectual property turned out to be a missile aimed right at what makes America successful. But it would not be the first time that measures taken in an atmosphere of panic had the opposite of the intended effect.

There is such a thing as American-ness. There's nothing like living abroad to teach you that. And if you want to know whether something will nurture or squash this quality, it would be hard to find a better focus group than hackers, because they come closest of any group I know to embodying it. Closer, probably, than the men running our government, who for all their talk of patriotism remind me more of Richelieu or Mazarin than Thomas Jefferson or George Washington.

When you read what the founding fathers had to say for themselves, they sound more like hackers. "The spirit of resistance to government," Jefferson wrote, "is so valuable on certain occasions, that I wish it always to be kept alive."

Imagine an American president saying that today. Like the remarks of an outspoken old grandmother, the sayings of the the founding fathers have embarrassed generations of their less confident successors. They remind us where we come from. They remind us that it is the people who break rules that are the source of America's wealth and power.

Those in a position to impose rules naturally want them to be obeyed. But be careful what you ask for. You might get it.

Chapter 5

The Other Road Ahead

IN THE SUMMER OF 1995, MY FRIEND ROBERT MORRIS AND I decided to start a startup. The PR campaign leading up to Netscape's IPO was running full blast then, and there was a lot of talk in the press about online commerce. At the time there might have been thirty actual stores on the Web, all made by hand. If there were going to be a lot of online stores, there would need to be software for making them, so we decided to write some.

For the first week or so we intended to make this an ordinary desktop application. Then one day we had the idea of making the software run on our web server, using the browser as an interface. We tried rewriting the software to work over the Web, and it was clear that this was the way to go. If we wrote our software to run on the server, it would be a lot easier for the users and for us as well.

This turned out to be a good plan. Now, as Yahoo Store, this software is the most popular online store builder, with over 20,000 users.

When we started Viaweb, hardly anyone understood what we meant when we said that the software ran on the server. It was not until Hotmail was launched a year later that people started to get it. Now everyone knows that this is a valid approach. There is a name now for what we were: an Application Service Provider, or ASP.

I think a lot of the next generation of software will be written on this model. Even Microsoft, who have the most to lose, seem to see the inevitability of moving some things off the desktop. If software moves off the desktop and onto servers, it will mean a very different world for developers. This essay describes the surprising things we saw, as some of the first visitors to this new world. To the extent software does move onto servers, what I'm describing here is the future.

The Next Thing?

When we look back on the desktop software era, I think we'll marvel at the inconveniences people put up with, just as we marvel now at what early car owners put up with. For the first twenty or thirty years, you had to be a car expert to own a car. But cars were such a big win that lots of people who weren't car experts wanted to have them as well.

Computers are in this phase now. When you own a desktop computer, you end up learning a lot more than you wanted to know about what's happening inside it. But more than half the households in the US own one. My mother has a computer that she uses for email and for keeping accounts. A couple years ago she was alarmed to receive a letter from Apple, offering her a discount on a new version of the operating system. There's something wrong when a sixty-five-year-old woman who wants to use a computer for email and accounts has to think about installing new operating systems. Ordinary users shouldn't even know the words "operating system," much less "device driver" or "patch."

There is now another way to deliver software that will save users from becoming system administrators. Web-based applications are programs that run on web servers and use web pages as the user interface. For the average user this new kind of software will be easier, cheaper, more mobile, more reliable, and often more powerful than desktop software.

With web-based software, most users won't have to think about anything except the applications they use. All the messy, changing stuff will be sitting on a server somewhere, maintained by the kind of people who are good at that kind of thing. And so you won't ordinarily need a computer, per se, to use software. All you'll need will be something with a keyboard, a screen, and a web browser. Maybe it will have wireless Internet access. Maybe it will also be your cell phone. Whatever it is, it will be consumer electronics:

something that costs about $200, and that people choose mostly based on how the case looks. You'll pay more for Internet services than you do for the hardware, just as you do now with telephones.[1]

It will take about a tenth of a second for a click to get to the server and back, so users of heavily interactive software, like Photoshop, will still want to have the computations happening on the desktop. But if you look at the kind of things most people use computers for, a tenth of a second latency would not be a problem. My mother doesn't really need a desktop computer, and there are a lot of people like her.

The Win for Users

Near my house there is a car with a bumper sticker that reads "death before inconvenience." Most people, most of the time, will take whatever choice requires least work. If web-based software wins, it will be because it's more convenient. And it looks as if it will be, for users and developers both.

To use a purely web-based application, all you need is a browser connected to the Internet. So you can use a web-based application anywhere. When you install software on your desktop computer, you can only use it on that computer. Worse still, your files are trapped on that computer. The inconvenience of this model becomes more and more evident as people get used to networks.

The thin end of the wedge here was web-based email. Millions of people now realize that you should have access to email messages no matter where you are. And if you can see your email, why not your calendar? If you can discuss a document with your colleagues, why can't you edit it? Why should any of your data be trapped on some computer sitting on a faraway desk?

The whole idea of "your computer" is going away, and being replaced with "your data." You should be able to get at your data from any computer. Or rather, any client, and a client doesn't have to be a computer.

Clients shouldn't store data; they should be like telephones. In fact they may become telephones, or vice versa. And as clients get smaller, you have another reason not to keep your data on them: something you carry around with you can be lost or stolen. Leaving your PDA in a taxi is like a disk crash, except your data is handed to someone else instead of being vaporized.

With purely web-based software, neither your data nor the applications are kept on the client. So you don't have to install anything to use it. And when there's no installation, you don't have to worry about installation going wrong. There can't be incompatibilities between the application and your operating system, because the software doesn't run on your operating system.

Because it needs no installation, it will be easy, and common, to try web-based software before you "buy" it. You should expect to be able to test-drive any web-based application for free, just by going to the site where it's offered. At Viaweb our whole site was like a big arrow pointing users to the test drive.

After trying the demo, signing up for the service should require nothing more than filling out a brief form. And that should be the last work the user has to do. With web-based software, you should get new releases without paying extra, or doing any work, or possibly even knowing about it.

Upgrades won't be the big shocks they are now. Over time applications will quietly grow more powerful. This will take some effort on the part of the developers. They will have to design software so it can be updated without confusing the users. That's a new problem, but there are ways to solve it.

With web-based applications, everyone uses the same version, and bugs can be fixed as soon as they're discovered. So web-based software should have far fewer bugs than desktop software. At Viaweb, I doubt we ever had ten known bugs at any one time. That's orders of magnitude better than desktop software.

Web-based applications can be used by several people at the same time. This is an obvious win for collaborative applications, but I bet users will start to want this in most applications once they realize it's possible. It will often be useful to let two people edit the same document, for example. Viaweb let multiple users edit a site simultaneously, more because that was the right way to write the software than because we expected users to want to, but it turned out many did.

When you use a web-based application, your data will be safer. Disk crashes won't be a thing of the past, but users won't hear about them anymore. They'll happen within server farms. And companies offering web-based applications will actually do backups— not only because they'll have real system administrators worrying about such things, but because an ASP that does lose people's data will be in big, big trouble. When people lose their own data in a disk crash, they can't get that mad, because they only have themselves to be mad at. When a company loses their data for them, they'll get a lot madder.

Finally, web-based software should be less vulnerable to viruses. If the client doesn't run anything except a browser, there's less chance of running viruses, and no data locally to damage. And a program that attacked the servers themselves should find them well defended.[2]

For users, web-based software will be *less stressful*. I think if you looked inside the average Windows user you'd find a huge and pretty much untapped desire for software meeting that description. Unleashed, it could be a powerful force.

City of Code

To developers, the most conspicuous difference between web-based and desktop software is that a web-based application is not a single piece of code. It will be a collection of programs of different types rather than a single big binary. And so designing web-based software is like designing a city rather than a building: as well as buildings you need roads, street signs, utilities, police and fire departments, and plans for both growth and various kinds of disasters.

At Viaweb, software included fairly big applications that users talked to directly, programs those programs used, programs that ran constantly in the background looking for problems, programs that tried to restart things if they broke, programs that ran occasionally to compile statistics or build indexes for searches, programs we ran explicitly to garbage-collect resources or to move or restore data, programs that pretended to be users (to measure performance or expose bugs), programs for diagnosing network troubles, programs for doing backups, interfaces to outside services, software that drove an impressive collection of dials displaying real-time server statistics (a hit with visitors, but indispensable for us too), modifications (including bug fixes) to open source software, and a great many configuration files and settings. Trevor Blackwell wrote a spectacular program for moving stores to new servers across the country, without shutting them down, after we were bought by Yahoo. Programs paged us, sent faxes and email to users, conducted transactions with credit card processors, and talked to one another through sockets, pipes, HTTP requests, SSH, UDP packets, shared memory, and files. Some of Viaweb even consisted of the absence of programs, since one of the keys to Unix security is not to run unnecessary utilities that people might use to break into your servers.

It did not end with software. We spent a lot of time thinking about server configurations. We built the servers ourselves, from components—partly to save money, and partly to get exactly what we wanted. We had to think about whether our upstream ISP had fast enough connections to all the backbones. We serially dated RAID suppliers.

But hardware is not just something to worry about. When you control it you can do more for users. With a desktop application, you can specify certain minimum hardware, but you can't add more. If you administer the servers, you can in one step enable all your users to page people, or send faxes, or send commands by phone, or process credit cards, etc, just by installing the relevant hardware. We always looked for new ways to add features with hardware, not just because it pleased users, but also as a way to distinguish ourselves from competitors who (either because they sold desktop software, or resold web-based applications through ISPs) didn't have direct control over the hardware.

Because the software in a web-based application will be a collection of programs rather than a single binary, it can be written in any number of different languages. When you're writing desktop software, you're practically forced to write the application in the same language as the underlying operating system—meaning C and C++. And so these languages (especially among nontechnical people like managers and VCs) got to be considered as the languages for "serious" software development. But that was just an artifact of the way desktop software had to be delivered. For server-based software you can use any language you want.[3] Today a lot of the top hackers are using languages far removed from C and C++: Perl, Python, and even Lisp.

With server-based software, no one can tell you what language to use, because you control the whole system, right down to the hardware. Different languages are good for different tasks. You can use whichever is best for each. And when you have competitors, "you can" means "you must" (we'll return to this later), because if you don't take advantage of this possibility, your competitors will.

Most of our competitors used C and C++, and this made their software visibly inferior because (among other things), they had no way around the statelessness of CGI scripts. If you were going to change something, all the changes had to happen on one page, with an Update button at the bottom. As I explain in Chapter 12, by using Lisp, which many people still consider a research language, we could make the Viaweb editor behave more like desktop software.

Releases

One of the most important changes in this new world is the way you do releases. In the desktop software business, doing a release is a huge trauma, in which the whole company sweats and strains to push out a single, giant piece of code. Obvious comparisons suggest themselves, both to the process and the resulting product.

With server-based software, you can make changes almost as you would in a program you were writing for yourself. You release software as a series of incremental changes instead of an occasional big explosion. A typical desktop software company might do one or two releases a year. At Viaweb we often did three to five releases a day.

When you switch to this new model, you realize how much software development is affected by the way it is released. Many of the nastiest problems you see in the desktop software business are due to the catastrophic nature of releases.

When you release only one new version a year, you tend to deal with bugs wholesale. Some time before the release date you assemble a new version in which half the code has been torn out and replaced, introducing countless bugs. Then a squad of QA people step in and start counting them, and the programmers work down the list, fixing them. They do not generally get to the end of the list, and indeed, no one is sure where the end is. It's like fishing rubble out of a pond. You never really know what's happening inside the software. At best you end up with a statistical sort of correctness.

With server-based software, most of the change is small and incremental. That in itself is less likely to introduce bugs. It also means you know what to test most carefully when you're about to release software: the last thing you changed. You end up with a much firmer grip on the code. As a general rule, you do know what's happening inside it. You don't have the source code memorized, of course, but when you read the source you do it like a pilot scanning the instrument panel, not like a detective trying to solve a mystery.

Desktop software breeds a certain fatalism about bugs. You know you're shipping something loaded with bugs, and you've even set up mechanisms to compensate for it (e.g. patch releases). So why worry about a few more? Soon you're releasing whole features you know are broken. Apple did this a few years ago. They felt under pressure to release their new OS, whose release date had already slipped four times, but some of the software (support for

CDs and DVDs) wasn't ready. The solution? They released the OS without the unfinished parts, and users had to install them later.

With web-based software, you never have to release software before it works, and you can release it as soon as it does work.

The industry veteran may be thinking: it's a fine-sounding idea to say that you never have to release software before it works, but what happens when you've promised to deliver a new version of your software by a certain date? With web-based software, you wouldn't make such a promise, because there are no versions. Your software changes gradually and continuously. Some changes might be bigger than others, but the idea of versions just doesn't naturally fit onto web-based software.

If anyone remembers Viaweb this might sound odd, because we were always announcing new versions. This was done entirely for PR purposes. The trade press, we learned, thinks in version numbers. They will give you major coverage for a major release, meaning a new first digit on the version number, and generally a paragraph at most for a point release, meaning a new digit after the decimal point.

Some of our competitors were offering desktop software and actually had version numbers. And for these releases, the mere fact of which seemed to us evidence of their backwardness, they would get all kinds of publicity. We didn't want to miss out, so we started giving version numbers to our software too. When we wanted some publicity, we'd make a list of all the features we'd added since the last "release," stick a new version number on the software, and issue a press release saying that the new version was available immediately. Amazingly, no one ever called us on it.

By the time we were bought, we had done this three times, so we were on Version 4. Version 4.1 if I remember correctly. Once Viaweb became Yahoo Store there was no longer such a desperate need for publicity, so although the software continued to evolve, the whole idea of version numbers was quietly dropped.

Bugs

The other major technical advantage of web-based software is that you can reproduce most bugs. You have the users' data right there on your disk. If someone breaks your software, you don't have to try to guess what's going on, as you would with desktop software: you should be able to reproduce the error while they're on the phone with you. You might even know about it already, if you have code for noticing errors built into your application.

Web-based software gets used round the clock, so everything you do is immediately put through the wringer. Bugs turn up quickly.

Software companies are sometimes accused of letting the users debug their software. And that is just what I'm advocating. For web-based software it's actually a good plan, because the bugs are fewer and transient. When you release software gradually you get far fewer bugs to start with. And when you can reproduce errors and release changes instantly, you can find and fix most bugs as soon as they appear. We never had enough bugs at any one time to bother with a formal bug-tracking system.

You should test changes before you release them, of course, so no major bugs should get released. Those few that inevitably slip through will involve borderline cases and will only affect the few users who encounter them before someone calls in to complain. As long as you fix bugs right away, the net effect, for the average user, is far fewer bugs. I doubt the average Viaweb user ever saw a bug.

Fixing fresh bugs is easier than fixing old ones. It's usually fairly quick to find a bug in code you just wrote. When it turns up you often know what's wrong before you even look at the source, because you were already worrying about it subconsciously. Fixing a bug in something you wrote six months ago (the average case if you release once a year) is a lot more work. And since you don't understand the code as well, you're more likely to fix it in an ugly way, or even introduce more bugs.[4]

When you catch bugs early, you also get fewer compound bugs. Compound bugs are two separate bugs that interact: you trip going downstairs, and when you reach for the handrail it comes off in your hand. In software this kind of bug is the hardest to find, and also tends to have the worst consequences.[5] The traditional "break everything and then filter out the bugs" approach inherently yields a lot of compound bugs. And software released in a series of small changes inherently tends not to. The floors are constantly being swept clean of any loose objects that might later get stuck in something.

It helps if you use a technique called functional programming. Functional programming means avoiding side effects. It's something you're more likely to see in research papers than commercial software, but for web-based applications it turns out to be really useful. It's hard to write entire programs as purely functional code, but you can write substantial chunks this way. It makes those parts of your software easier to test, because they have no state, and that is very convenient in a situation where you are constantly making and testing small modifications. I wrote much of Viaweb's editor in this style, and we made our scripting language, RTML, a purely functional language.

People from the desktop software business will find this hard to credit, but at Viaweb bugs became almost a game. Since most released bugs involved borderline cases, the users who encountered them were likely to be advanced users, pushing the envelope. Advanced users are more forgiving about bugs, especially since you probably introduced them in the course of adding some feature they were asking for. In fact, because bugs were rare and you had to be doing sophisticated things to see them, advanced users were often proud to catch one. They would call support in a spirit more of triumph than anger, as if they had scored points off us.

Support

When you can reproduce errors, it changes your approach to customer support. At most software companies, support is offered as a way to make customers feel better. They're either calling you about a known bug, or they're just doing something wrong and you have to figure out what. In either case there's not much you can learn from them. And so you tend to view support calls as a pain in the ass that you want to isolate from your developers as much as possible.

This was not how things worked at Viaweb. At Viaweb, support was free, because we wanted to hear from customers. If someone had a problem, we wanted to know about it right away so we could reproduce the error and release a fix.

So at Viaweb the developers were always in close contact with support. The customer support people were about thirty feet away from the programmers, and knew they could always interrupt anything with a report of a genuine bug. We would leave a board meeting to fix a serious bug.

Our approach to support made everyone happier. The customers were delighted. Just imagine how it would feel to call a support line and be treated as someone bringing important news. The customer support people liked it because it meant they could help the users, instead of reading scripts at them. And the programmers liked it because they could reproduce bugs instead of just hearing vague second-hand reports about them.

Our policy of fixing bugs on the fly changed the relationship between customer support people and hackers. At most software companies, support people are underpaid human shields, and hackers are little copies of God the Father, creators of the world. Whatever the procedure for reporting bugs, it is likely to be one-directional: support people who hear about bugs fill out some form that eventually gets passed on (possibly via QA) to programmers, who put it on their list of things to do. It was different at Viaweb. Within a minute of hearing about a bug from a customer, the support people could be standing next to a programmer hearing him say "Shit, you're right, it's a bug." It delighted the support people to hear that "you're right" from the hackers. They used to bring us bugs with the same expectant air as a cat bringing you a mouse it has just killed. It also made them more careful in judging the seriousness of a bug, because now their honor was on the line.

After we were bought by Yahoo, the customer support people were moved far away from the programmers. It was only then that we realized they were effectively QA and to some extent marketing as well. In addition to catching bugs, they were the keepers of the knowledge of vaguer, buglike things, like features that confused users.[6] They were also a kind of proxy focus group; we could ask them which of two new features users wanted more, and they were always right.

Morale

Being able to release software immediately is a big motivator. Often as I was walking to work I would think of some change I wanted to make to the software, and do it that day. This worked for bigger features as well. Even if something was going to take two weeks to write (few projects took longer), I knew I could see the effect in the software as soon as it was done.

If I'd had to wait a year for the next release, I would have shelved most of these ideas, for a while at least. The thing about ideas, though, is that they lead to more ideas. Have you ever noticed that when you sit down to write something, half the ideas that end up in it are ones you thought of while writing? The same thing happens with software. Working to implement one idea gives you more ideas. So shelving an idea costs you not only that delay in implementing it, but also all the ideas that implementing it would have led to. In fact, shelving an idea probably even inhibits new ideas: as you start to think of some new feature, you catch sight of the shelf and think, "but I already have a lot of new things I want to do for the next release."

What big companies do instead of implementing features is plan them. At Viaweb we sometimes ran into trouble on this account. Investors and analysts would ask us what we had planned for the future. The truthful answer would have been, we didn't have any plans. We had general ideas about things we wanted to improve, but if we knew how we would have done it already. What were we going to do in the next six months? Whatever looked like the biggest win. I don't know if I ever dared give this answer, but that was the truth. Plans are just another word for ideas on the shelf. When we thought of good ideas, we implemented them.

At Viaweb, as at many software companies, most code had one definite owner. But when you owned something you really owned it: no one except the owner of a piece of software had to approve (or even know about) a release. There was no protection against breakage except the fear of looking like an idiot to one's peers, and that was more than enough. I may have given the impression that we just blithely plowed forward writing code. We did go fast, but we thought very carefully before we released software onto those servers. And paying attention is more important to reliability than moving slowly. Because he pays close attention, a Navy pilot can land a 40,000 lb. aircraft at 140 miles per hour on a pitching carrier deck, at night, more safely than the average teenager can cut a bagel.

This way of writing software is a double-edged sword of course. It works a lot better for a small team of good, trusted programmers than it would for a big company of mediocre ones, where bad ideas are caught by committees instead of the people who had them.

Brooks in Reverse

Fortunately, web-based software does require fewer programmers. I once worked for a medium-sized desktop software company that had over 100 people working in engineering as a whole. Only 13 of these were in product development. All the rest were working on releases, ports, and so on. With web-based software, all you need (at most) are the 13 people, because there are no releases, ports, and so on.

Viaweb was written by just three people.[7] I was always under pressure to hire more, because we wanted to get bought, and we knew that buyers would have a hard time paying a high price for a company with only three programmers. (Solution: we hired more, but created new projects for them.)

When you can write software with fewer programmers, it saves you more than money. As Fred Brooks pointed out in *The Mythical Man-Month*, adding people to a project tends to slow it down. The number of possible connections between developers grows exponentially with the size of the group.[8] The larger the group, the more time they'll spend in meetings negotiating how their software will work together, and the more bugs they'll get from unforeseen interactions. Fortunately, this process also works in reverse: as groups get smaller, software development gets exponentially more efficient. I can't remember the programmers at Viaweb ever having an actual meeting. We never had more to say at any one time than we could say as we were walking to lunch.

If there is a downside here, it is that all the programmers have to be to some degree system administrators as well. When you're hosting software, someone has to be watching the servers, and in practice the only people who can do this properly are the ones who wrote the software. At Viaweb our system had so many components and changed so frequently that there was no definite border between software and infrastructure. Arbitrarily declaring such a border would have constrained our design choices. And so although we were constantly hoping that one day ("in a couple months") everything would be stable enough that we could hire someone whose job was just to worry about the servers, it never happened.

I don't think it could be any other way, as long as you're still actively developing the product. Web-based software is never going to be something you write, check in, and go home. It's a live thing, running on your servers right now. A bad bug might not just crash one user's process; it could crash them all. If a bug in your code corrupts some data on disk, you have to fix it. And so on. We found that you don't have to watch the servers every minute (after the first year or so), but you definitely want to keep an eye on things you've changed recently. You don't release code late at night and then go home.

Watching Users

With server-based software, you're in closer touch with your code. You can also be in closer touch with your users. Intuit is famous for introducing themselves to customers at retail stores and asking to follow them home. If you've ever watched someone use your software for the first time, you know what surprises must have awaited them.

Software should do what users think it will. But you can't have any idea what users will be thinking, believe me, until you watch them. And server-based software gives you unprecedented information about their behavior. You're not limited to small, artificial focus groups. You can see every click made by every user. You have to consider carefully what you're going to look at, because you don't want to violate users' privacy, but even the most general statistical sampling can be very useful.

When you have the users on your server, you don't have to rely on benchmarks, for example. Benchmarks are simulated users. With server-based software, you can watch actual users. To decide what to optimize, just log into a server and see what's consuming all the CPU. And you know when to stop optimizing too: we eventually got the Viaweb editor to the point where it was memory-bound rather than CPU-bound, and since there was nothing we could do to decrease the size of users' data (well, nothing easy), we knew we might as well stop there.

Efficiency matters for server-based software, because you're paying for the hardware. The number of users you can support per server is the divisor of your capital cost, so if you can make your software very efficient, you can undersell competitors and still make a profit. At Viaweb we got the capital cost per user down to about $5. It would be less now, probably less than the cost of sending them the first month's bill. Hardware is free now, if your software is reasonably efficient.

Watching users can guide you in design as well as optimization. Viaweb had a scripting language called RTML that let advanced users define their own page styles. We found that RTML became a kind of suggestion box, because users only used it when the predefined page styles couldn't do what they wanted. Originally the editor put button bars across the page, for example, but after a number of users used RTML to put buttons down the left side, we made that the default in the predefined page styles.

Finally, by watching users you can often tell when they're in trouble. And since the customer is always right, that's a sign of something you need to fix. At Viaweb the key to getting users was the online test drive. It was not just a series of slides built by marketing people. In our test drive, users actually used the software. It took about five minutes, and at the end of it they had built a real, working store.

The test drive was the way we got nearly all our new users. I think it will be the same for most web-based applications. If users can get through a test drive successfully, they'll like the product. If they get confused or bored, they won't. So anything we could do to get more people through the test drive would increase our growth rate.

I studied click trails of people taking the test drive and found that at a certain step they would get confused and click on the browser's Back button. (If you try writing web-based applications, you'll find the Back button becomes one of your most interesting philosophical problems.) So I added a message at that point, telling users they were nearly finished, and reminding them not to click on the Back button. Another great thing about web-based software is that you get instant feedback from changes: the number of people completing the test drive rose immediately from 60% to 90%. And since the number of new users was a function of the number of completed test drives, our revenue growth increased by 50%, just from that change.

Money

In the early 1990s I read an article that described software as a "subscription business." At first this seemed a very cynical statement. But later I realized that it reflects reality: software devel-

THE OTHER ROAD AHEAD

opment is an ongoing process. I think it's cleaner if you openly charge subscription fees, instead of forcing people to keep buying and installing new versions so they'll keep paying you. And fortunately, subscriptions are the natural way to bill for web-based applications.

Hosting applications is an area where companies will play a role that is not likely to be filled by freeware. Hosting applications is a lot of stress, and has real expenses. No one will want to do it for free.

For companies, web-based applications are an ideal source of revenue. Instead of starting each quarter with a blank slate, you have a recurring revenue stream. Because your software evolves gradually, you don't have to worry that a new model will flop. There never need be a new model, per se, and if you do something to the software that users hate, you'll know right away. You have no trouble with uncollectible bills; if someone won't pay, you can just turn off the service. And there is no possibility of piracy.

That last "advantage" may turn out to be a problem. Some amount of piracy is to the advantage of software companies. If some user would never have bought your software at any price, you haven't lost anything if he uses a pirated copy. In fact you gain, because he is one more user helping to make your software the standard—or who might buy a copy later, when he graduates from high school.

When they can, companies like to do something called price discrimination, which means charging each customer as much as they can afford.[9] Software is particularly suitable for price discrimination, because the marginal cost is close to zero. This is why some software costs more to run on Suns than on Intel boxes: a company that uses Suns is not interested in saving money and can safely be charged more. Piracy is effectively the lowest tier of price discrimination. I think software companies understand this and deliberately turn a blind eye to some kinds of piracy.[10] With server-based software they will have to come up with some other solution.

Web-based software sells well, especially in comparison to desktop software, because it's easy to buy. You might think that people decide to buy something, and then buy it, as two separate steps. That's what I thought before Viaweb, to the extent I thought about the question at all. In fact the second step can propagate back into the first: if something is hard to buy, people will change their mind about whether they wanted it. And vice versa: you'll sell more of something when it's easy to buy. I buy more new books because Amazon exists. Web-based software is just about the easiest thing in the world to buy, especially if you have just done an online demo. Users should not have to do much more than enter a credit card number. (Make them do more at your peril.)

Sometimes web-based software is offered through ISPs acting as resellers. This is a bad idea. You have to be administering the servers, because you need to be constantly improving both hardware and software. If you give up direct control of the servers, you give up most of the advantages of developing web-based applications.

Several of our competitors shot themselves in the foot this way—usually, I think, because they were overrun by suits who were excited about this huge potential channel, and didn't realize that it would ruin the product they hoped to sell through it. Selling web-based software through ISPs is like selling sushi through vending machines.

Customers

Who will the customers be? At Viaweb they were initially individuals and smaller companies, and I think this will be the rule with web-based applications. These are the users who are ready to try new things, partly because they're more flexible, and partly because they want the lower costs of new technology.

Web-based applications will often be the best thing for big companies too (though they'll be slow to realize it). The best intranet is the Internet. If a company uses true web-based applications, the software will work better, the servers will be better administered, and employees will have access to the system from anywhere.

The argument against this approach usually hinges on security: if access is easier for employees, it will be for bad guys too. Some larger merchants were reluctant to use Viaweb because they thought customers' credit card information would be safer on their own servers. It was not easy to make this point diplomatically, but in fact the data was almost certainly safer in our hands than theirs. Who can hire better people to manage security, a technology startup whose whole business is running servers, or a clothing retailer? Not only did we have better people worrying about security, we worried more about it. If someone broke into the clothing retailer's servers, it would affect at most one merchant, could probably be hushed up, and in the worst case might get one person fired. If someone broke into ours, it could affect thousands of merchants, would probably end up as news on CNet, and could put us out of business.

If you want to keep your money safe, do you keep it under your mattress at home, or put it in a bank? This argument applies to every aspect of server administration: not just security, but uptime, bandwidth, load management, backups, etc. Our existence depended on doing these things right. Server problems were the big no-no for us, like a dangerous toy would be for a toy maker, or a salmonella outbreak for a food processor.

A big company that uses web-based applications is to that extent outsourcing IT. Drastic as it sounds, I think this is generally a good idea. Companies are likely to get better service this way than they would from in-house system administrators. System administrators can become cranky and unresponsive because they're not directly exposed to competitive pressure. A salesman has to deal with customers, and a developer has to deal with competitors' software, but a system administrator, like an old bachelor, has few external forces to keep him in line.[11] At Viaweb we had external forces in plenty to keep us in line. The people calling us were customers, not just co-workers. If a server got wedged, we jumped. Just thinking about it gives me a jolt of adrenaline, years later.

So web-based applications will ordinarily be the right answer for big companies too. They will be the last to realize it, however, just as they were with desktop computers. And partly for the same reason: it will be worth a lot of money to convince big companies that they need something more expensive.

There is always a tendency for rich customers to buy expensive solutions, even when cheap solutions are better, because the people offering expensive solutions can spend more to sell them. At Viaweb we were always up against this. We lost several high-end merchants to web consulting firms who convinced them they'd be better off if they paid half a million dollars for a custom-made online store on their own server. They were, as a rule, not better off, as more than one discovered when Christmas shopping season came around and loads rose on their server. Viaweb was a lot more sophisticated than what most of these merchants got, but we couldn't afford to tell them. At $300 a month, we couldn't afford to send a team of well-dressed and authoritative-sounding people to make presentations to customers.

At times we toyed with the idea of a new service called Viaweb Gold. It would have exactly the same features as our regular service, but would cost ten times as much would be sold in person by a man in a suit. We never got around to offering this variant, but I'm sure we could have signed up a few merchants for it.

A large part of what big companies pay extra for is the cost of selling expensive things to them. (If the Defense Department pays a thousand dollars for toilet seats, it's partly because it costs a lot to sell toilet seats for a thousand dollars.) And this is one reason intranet software will continue to thrive, even though it is probably a bad idea. It's simply more expensive. There is nothing you can do about this conundrum, so the best plan is to go for the smaller customers first. The rest will come in time.

Son of Server

Running software on the server is nothing new. In fact it's the old model: mainframe applications are all server-based. If server-based software is such a good idea, why did it lose last time? Why did desktop computers eclipse mainframes?

At first desktop computers didn't look like much of a threat. The first users were all hackers—or hobbyists, as they were called then. They liked microcomputers because they were cheap. For the first time, you could have your own computer. The phrase "personal computer" is part of the language now, but when it was first used it had a deliberately audacious sound, like the phrase "personal satellite" would today.

Why did desktop computers take over? Mainly because they had better software. And the reason microcomputer software was better was that it could be written by small companies.

I don't think many people realize how fragile and tentative startups are in the earliest stage. Many startups begin almost by accident—as a couple guys, either with day jobs or in school, writing a prototype of something that might, if it looks promising, turn into a company. At this larval stage, any significant obstacle will stop the startup dead in its tracks. Writing mainframe software required too much commitment up front. Development machines were expensive, and because the customers would be big companies, you'd need an impressive-looking sales force to sell it to them. Starting a startup to write mainframe software would be a much more serious undertaking than just hacking something together on your Apple II in the evenings. And so you didn't get a lot of startups writing mainframe applications.

The arrival of desktop computers inspired a lot of new software, because writing applications for them seemed an attainable goal to larval startups. Development was cheap, and the customers would be individual people that you could reach through computer stores or even by mail-order.

The application that pushed desktop computers out into the mainstream was VisiCalc, the first spreadsheet. It was written by two guys working in an attic, and yet did things no mainframe software could do.[12] VisiCalc was such an advance, in its time, that people bought Apple IIs just to run it. And this was the beginning of a trend: desktop computers won because startups wrote software for them.

It looks as if server-based software will be good this time around, because startups will write it. Computers are so cheap now that you can get started, as we did, using a desktop computer as a server. Inexpensive processors have eaten the workstation market (you rarely even hear the word now) and are most of the way through the server market; Yahoo's servers, which deal with loads as high as any on the Internet, all have the same inexpensive Intel processors that you have in your desktop machine. And once you've written the software, all you need to sell it is a web site. Nearly all our users came direct to our site through word of mouth and references in the press.[13]

Viaweb was a typical larval startup. We were terrified of starting a company, and for the first few months comforted ourselves by treating the whole thing as an experiment that we might call off at any moment. Fortunately, there were few obstacles except technical ones. While we were writing the software, our web server was the same desktop machine we used for development, connected to the outside world by a dialup line. Our only expenses in that phase were food and rent.

There is all the more reason for startups to write web-based software now, because writing desktop software has become a lot less fun. If you want to write desktop software now, you do it on Microsoft's terms, calling their APIs and working around their buggy OS. And if you manage to write something that takes off, you may find that you were merely doing market research for Microsoft.

If a company wants to make a platform that startups will build on, they have to make it something that hackers themselves will want to use. That means it has to be inexpensive and well-designed. The Mac was popular with hackers when it first came out, and a lot of them wrote software for it.[14] You see this less with

Windows, because hackers don't use it. The kind of people who are good at writing software tend to be running Linux or FreeBSD now.

I don't think we would have started a startup to write desktop software, because desktop software has to run on Windows, and before we could write software for Windows we'd have to *use* it. The Web let us do an end-run around Windows, and deliver software running on Unix direct to users through the browser. That is a liberating prospect, a lot like the arrival of PCs twenty-five years ago.

Microsoft

Back when desktop computers arrived, IBM was the giant that everyone feared. It's hard to imagine now, but I remember the feeling well. Now the frightening giant is Microsoft, and I don't think they are as blind to the threat facing them as IBM was. After all, Microsoft deliberately built their business in IBM's blind spot.

I mentioned earlier that my mother doesn't really need a desktop computer. Most users probably don't. That's a problem for Microsoft, and they know it. If applications run on remote servers, no one needs Windows. What will Microsoft do? Will they be able to use their control of the desktop to prevent, or constrain, this new generation of software?

I expect Microsoft will develop some kind of server/desktop hybrid, where the operating system works together with servers they control. At a minimum, files will be centrally available for users who want that. I don't expect Microsoft to go all the way to the extreme of doing the computations on the server, with only a browser for a client, if they can avoid it. If you only need a browser for a client, you don't need Microsoft on the client, and if Microsoft doesn't control the client, they can't push users towards their server-based applications.

I think Microsoft will have a hard time keeping the genie in the bottle. There will be too many different types of clients for them to control them all. And if Microsoft's applications only work with some clients, competitors will be able to trump them by offering applications that work from any client.[15]

In a world of web-based applications, there is no automatic place for Microsoft. They may succeed in making themselves a place, but I don't think they'll dominate this new world as they did the world of desktop applications.

It's not so much that a competitor will trip them up as that they will trip over themselves. With the rise of web-based software, they will be facing not just technical problems but their own wishful thinking. What they need to do is cannibalize their existing business, and I can't see them facing that. The same single-mindedness that has brought them this far will now be working against them. IBM was in exactly the same situation, and they couldn't master it. IBM made a late and half-hearted entry into the microcomputer business because they were ambivalent about threatening their cash cow, mainframe computing. Microsoft will likewise be hampered by wanting to save the desktop. A cash cow can be a heavy monkey on your back.

I'm not saying that no one will dominate server-based applications. Someone probably will eventually. But I think there will be a good long period of cheerful chaos, just as there was in the early days of microcomputers. That was a good time for startups. Lots of small companies flourished, and did it by making cool things.

Startups but More So

The classic startup is fast and informal, with few people and little money. Those few people work very hard, and technology magnifies the effect of the decisions they make. If they win, they win big.

In a startup writing web-based applications, everything you associate with startups is taken to an extreme. You can write and launch a product with even fewer people and even less money. You have to be even faster, and you can get away with being more informal. You can literally launch your product as three guys operating out of an apartment, with a server collocated at an ISP. We did.

Over time the teams have gotten smaller, faster, and more informal. In 1960, software development meant a roomful of men with horn-rimmed glasses and narrow black neckties, industriously writing ten lines of code a day on IBM coding forms. In 1980, it was a team of eight to ten people wearing jeans to the office and typing into VT100s. Now it's a couple of guys sitting in a living room with laptops. (And jeans turn out not to be the last word in informality.)

Startups are stressful, and this, unfortunately, is also taken to an extreme with web-based applications. Many software companies, especially at the beginning, have periods where the developers slept under their desks and so on. The alarming thing about web-based software is that there is nothing to prevent this becoming the default. The stories about sleeping under desks usually end: then at last we shipped it, and we all went home and slept for a week. Web-based software never ships. You can work 16-hour days for as long as you want to. And because you can, and your competitors can, you tend to be forced to. You can, so you must. It's Parkinson's Law running in reverse.

The worst thing is not the hours but the responsibility. Programmers and system administrators traditionally each have their own separate worries. Programmers worry about bugs, and system administrators worry about infrastructure. Programmers may spend a long day up to their elbows in source code, but at some point they get to go home and forget about it. System administrators never quite leave the job behind, but when they do get paged at 4:00 AM, they don't usually have to do anything very complicated. With web-based applications, these two kinds of stress get combined. The programmers become system administrators, but without the sharply defined limits that ordinarily make the job bearable.

At Viaweb we spent the first six months just writing software. We worked the usual long hours of an early startup. In a desktop software company, this would have been the hard part, but it felt like a vacation compared to the next phase, when we took users onto our server. The second biggest benefit of selling Viaweb to Yahoo (after the money) was to be able to dump ultimate responsibility for the whole thing onto the shoulders of a big company.

Desktop software forces users to become system administrators. Web-based software forces programmers to. There is less stress in total, but more for the programmers. That's not necessarily bad news. If you're a startup competing with a big company, it's good news.[16] Web-based applications offer a straightforward way to outwork your competitors. No startup asks for more.

Just Good Enough

One thing that might deter you from writing web-based applications is the lameness of web pages as a UI. That is a problem, I admit. There were a few things we would have *really* liked to add to HTML and HTTP. What matters, though, is that web pages are just good enough.

There is a parallel here with the first microcomputers. The processors in those machines weren't intended to be the CPUs of computers. They were designed to be used in things like traffic lights. But guys like Ed Roberts, who designed the Altair, realized that they were just good enough. You could combine one of these chips with some memory (256 bytes in the first Altair), and front panel switches, and you'd have a working computer. Being able to have your own computer was so exciting that there were plenty of people who wanted to buy them, however limited.

Web pages weren't designed to be a UI for applications, but they're just good enough. And for a significant number of users, software you can use from any browser will be enough of a win in itself to outweigh any awkwardness in the UI. Maybe you can't write the best-looking spreadsheet using HTML, but you can write a spreadsheet that several people can use simultaneously from different locations without special client software, or that can incorporate live data feeds, or that can page you when certain conditions are triggered. More importantly, you can write new kinds of ap-

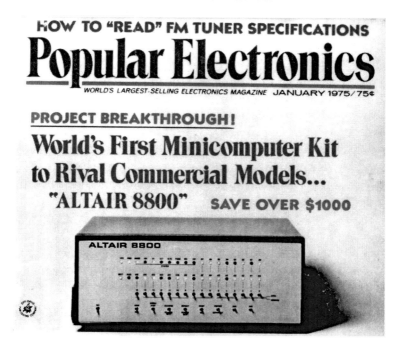

Popular Electronics, January 1975 (detail).

plications that don't even have names yet. VisiCalc was not merely a microcomputer version of a mainframe application, after all—it was a new type of application.

Of course, server-based applications don't have to be web-based. You could have some other kind of client. But I'm pretty sure that's a bad idea. It would be very convenient if you could assume that everyone would install your client—so convenient that you could easily convince yourself that they all would. But if they don't, you're hosed.

Because web-based software assumes nothing about the client, it will work anywhere the Web works. That's a big advantage already, and the advantage will grow as new web devices proliferate. Users will like you because your software just works, and your life will be easier because you won't have to tweak it for every new client.[17]

I feel like I've watched the evolution of the Web as closely as anyone, and I can't predict what's going to happen with clients. Convergence is probably coming, but where?

How will it all play out? I don't know. And you don't have to know if you bet on web-based applications. No one can break that without breaking browsing. The Web may not be the only way to deliver software, but it's one that works now and will continue to work for a long time. Web-based applications are cheap to develop, and easy for even the smallest startup to deliver. They're a lot of work, and of a particularly stressful kind, but that only makes the odds better for startups.

Why Not?

E. B. White was amused to learn from a farmer friend that many electrified fences don't have any current running through them. The cows apparently learn to stay away from them, and after that you don't need the current. "Rise up, cows!" he wrote. "Take your liberty while despots snore!"

If you're a hacker who has thought of one day starting a startup, there are probably two things keeping you from doing it. One is that you don't know anything about business. The other is that you're afraid of competition. Neither of these fences have any current in them.

There are only two things you have to know about business: build something users love, and make more than you spend. If you get these two right, you'll be ahead of most startups. You can figure out the rest as you go.

You may not at first make more than you spend, but as long as the gap is closing fast enough you'll be ok. If you start out underfunded, it will at least encourage a habit of frugality. The less you spend, the easier it is to make more than you spend. Fortunately, it can be very cheap to launch a web-based application. We launched on under $10,000, and it would be even cheaper today. We had to spend thousands on a server, and thousands more to get SSL. (The only company selling SSL software at the time was Netscape.) Now you can rent a much more powerful server, with SSL included, for less than we paid for bandwidth alone. You could launch a web-based application now for less than the cost of a fancy office chair.

As for building something users love, here are some general tips. Start by making something clean and simple that you would want to use yourself. Get a version 1.0 out fast, then continue to improve the software, listening closely to users as you do. The customer is always right, but different customers are right about different things; the least sophisticated users show you what you need to simplify and clarify, and the most sophisticated tell you what features you need to add. The best thing software can be is easy, but the way to do this is to get the defaults right, not to limit users' choices. Don't get complacent if your competitors' software is lame; the standard to compare your software to is what it could be, not what your current competitors happen to have. Use your software yourself, all the time. Viaweb was supposed to be an online store builder, but we used it to make our own site too. Don't listen to marketing people or designers or product managers just because of their job titles. If they have good ideas, use them, but it's up to you to decide; software has to be designed by hackers who understand design, not designers who know a little about software. If you can't design software as well as implement it, don't start a startup.

Now let's talk about competition. What you're afraid of is not presumably groups of hackers like you, but actual companies, with offices and business plans and salesmen and so on, right? Well, they are more afraid of you than you are of them, and they're right. It's a lot easier for a couple of hackers to figure out how to rent office space or hire sales people than it is for a company of any size to get software written. I've been on both sides, and I know. When Viaweb was bought by Yahoo, I suddenly found myself working for a big company, and it was like trying to run through waist-deep water.

I don't mean to disparage Yahoo. They had some good hackers, and the top management were real butt-kickers. For a big com-

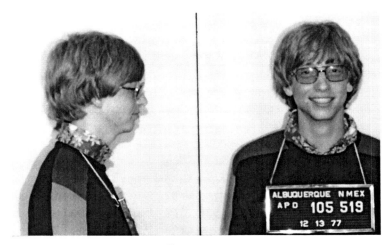

Bill Gates, 1977.

pany, they were exceptional. But they were still only about a tenth as productive as a small startup. No big company can do much better than that. What's scary about Microsoft is that a company so big can develop software at all. They're like a mountain that can walk.

Don't be intimidated. You can do as much that Microsoft can't as they can do that you can't. And no one can stop you. You don't have to ask anyone's permission to develop web-based applications. You don't have to do licensing deals, or get shelf space in retail stores, or grovel to have your application bundled with the OS. You can deliver software right to the browser, and no one can get between you and potential users without preventing them from browsing the Web.

You may not believe it, but I promise you, Microsoft is scared of you. The complacent middle managers may not be, but Bill is, because he was you once, back in 1975, the last time a new way of delivering software appeared.

Chapter 6

How to Make Wealth

IF YOU WANTED TO GET RICH, HOW WOULD YOU DO IT? I THINK your best bet would be to start or join a startup. That's been a reliable way to get rich for hundreds of years. The word "startup" dates from the 1960s, but what happens in one is very similar to the venture-backed trading voyages of the Middle Ages.

Startups usually involve technology, so much so that the phrase "high-tech startup" is almost redundant. A startup is a small company that takes on a hard technical problem.

Lots of people get rich knowing nothing more than that. You don't have to know physics to be a good pitcher. But I think it could give you an edge to understand the underlying principles. Why do startups have to be small? Will a startup inevitably stop being a startup as it grows larger? And why do they so often work on developing new technology? Why are there so many startups selling new drugs or computer software, and none selling corn oil or laundry detergent?

The Proposition

Economically, you can think of a startup as a way to compress your whole working life into a few years. Instead of working at a low intensity for forty years, you work as hard as you possibly can for four. This pays especially well in technology, where you earn a premium for working fast.

Here is a brief sketch of the economic proposition. If you're a good hacker in your mid twenties, you can get a job paying about $80,000 per year. So on average such a hacker must be able to do at least $80,000 worth of work per year for the company just to break even. You could probably work twice as many hours as a corporate employee, and if you focus you can probably get three times as much done in an hour.[1] You should get another multiple of two, at least, by eliminating the drag of the pointy-haired middle manager who would be your boss in a big company. Then there is one more multiple: how much smarter are you than your job description expects you to be? Suppose another multiple of three. Combine all these multipliers, and I'm claiming you could be 36 times more productive than you're expected to be in a random corporate job.[2] If a fairly good hacker is worth $80,000 a year at a big company, then a smart hacker working very hard without any corporate bullshit to slow him down should be able to do work worth about $3 million a year.

Like all back-of-the-envelope calculations, this one has a lot of wiggle room. I wouldn't try to defend the actual numbers. But I stand by the structure of the calculation. I'm not claiming the multiplier is precisely 36, but it is certainly more than 10, and probably rarely as high as 100.

If $3 million a year seems high, remember that we're talking about the limit case: the case where you not only have zero leisure time but indeed work so hard that you endanger your health.

Startups are not magic. They don't change the laws of wealth creation. They just represent a point at the far end of the curve. There is a conservation law at work here: if you want to make a million dollars, you have to endure a million dollars' worth of pain. For example, one way to make a million dollars would be to work for the Post Office your whole life, and save every penny of your salary. Imagine the stress of working for the Post Office for fifty years. In a startup you compress all this stress into three or four years. You do tend to get a certain bulk discount if you buy the economy-size pain, but you can't evade the fundamental conservation law. If starting a startup were easy, everyone would do it.

Millions, not Billions

If $3 million a year seems high to some people, it will seem low to others. Three *million?* How do I get to be a billionaire, like Bill Gates?

So let's get Bill Gates out of the way right now. It's not a good idea to use famous rich people as examples, because the press only write about the very richest, and these tend to be outliers. Bill Gates is a smart, determined, and hardworking man, but you need more than that to make as much money as he has. You also need to be very lucky.

There is a large random factor in the success of any company. So the guys you end up reading about in the papers are the ones who are very smart, totally dedicated, *and* win the lottery. Certainly Bill is smart and dedicated, but Microsoft also happens to have been the beneficiary of one of the most spectacular blunders in the history of business: the licensing deal for DOS. No doubt Bill did everything he could to steer IBM into making that blunder, and he has done an excellent job of exploiting it, but if there had been one person with a brain on IBM's side, Microsoft's future would have been very different. Microsoft at that stage had little leverage over IBM. They were effectively a component supplier. If IBM had required an exclusive license, as they should have, Microsoft would still have signed the deal. It would still have meant a lot of money for them, and IBM could easily have gotten an operating system elsewhere.

Instead IBM ended up using all its power in the market to give Microsoft control of the PC standard. From that point, all Microsoft had to do was execute. They never had to bet the company on a bold decision. All they had to do was play hardball with licensees and copy more innovative products reasonably promptly.

If IBM hadn't made this mistake, Microsoft would still have been a successful company, but it could not have grown so big so fast. Bill Gates would be rich, but he'd be somewhere near the bottom of the Forbes 400 with the other guys his age.

There are a lot of ways to get rich, and this essay is about only one of them. This essay is about how to make money by creating wealth and getting paid for it. There are plenty of other ways to get money, including chance, speculation, marriage, inheritance, theft, extortion, fraud, monopoly, graft, lobbying, counterfeiting, and prospecting. Most of the greatest fortunes have probably involved several of these.

The advantage of creating wealth, as a way to get rich, is not just that it's more legitimate (many of the other methods are now illegal) but that it's more *straightforward*. You just have to do something people want.

Money Is Not Wealth

If you want to create wealth, it will help to understand what it is. Wealth is not the same thing as money.[3] Wealth is as old as human history. Far older, in fact; ants have wealth. Money is a comparatively recent invention.

Wealth is the fundamental thing. Wealth is stuff we want: food, clothes, houses, cars, gadgets, travel to interesting places, and so on. You can have wealth without having money. If you had a magic machine that could on command make you a car or cook you dinner or do your laundry, or do anything else you wanted, you wouldn't need money. Whereas if you were in the middle of Antarctica, where there is nothing to buy, it wouldn't matter how much money you had.

Wealth is what you want, not money. But if wealth is the important thing, why does everyone talk about making money? It is a kind of shorthand: money is a way of moving wealth, and in practice they are usually interchangeable. But they are not the same thing, and unless you plan to get rich by counterfeiting, talking about *making money* can make it harder to understand how to make money.

Money is a side effect of specialization. In a specialized society, most of the things you need, you can't make for yourself. If you want a potato or a pencil or a place to live, you have to get it from someone else.

How do you get the person who grows the potatoes to give you some? By giving him something he wants in return. But you can't get very far by trading things directly with the people who need them. If you make violins, and none of the local farmers wants one, how will you eat?

The solution societies find, as they get more specialized, is to make the trade into a two-step process. Instead of trading violins directly for potatoes, you trade violins for, say, silver, which you can then trade again for anything else you need. The intermediate stuff—the *medium of exchange*—can be anything that's rare and portable. Historically metals have been the most common, but recently we've been using a medium of exchange, called the *dollar*, that doesn't physically exist. It works as a medium of exchange, however, because its rarity is guaranteed by the U.S. Government.

The advantage of a medium of exchange is that it makes trade work. The disadvantage is that it tends to obscure what trade really means. People think that what a business does is make money. But money is just the intermediate stage—just a shorthand—for whatever people want. What most businesses really do is make wealth. They do something people want.[4]

The Pie Fallacy

A surprising number of people retain from childhood the idea that there is a fixed amount of wealth in the world. There is, in any normal family, a fixed amount of *money* at any moment. But that's not the same thing.

When wealth is talked about in this context, it is often described as a pie. "You can't make the pie larger," say politicians. When you're talking about the amount of money in one family's bank account, or the amount available to a government from one year's tax revenue, this is true. If one person gets more, someone else has to get less.

I can remember believing, as a child, that if a few rich people had all the money, it left less for everyone else. Many people seem to continue to believe something like this well into adulthood. This fallacy is usually there in the background when you hear someone talking about how x percent of the population have y percent of the wealth. If you plan to start a startup, then whether you realize it or not, you're planning to disprove the Pie Fallacy.

What leads people astray here is the abstraction of money. Money is not wealth. It's just something we use to move wealth around. So although there may be, in certain specific moments (like your family, this month) a fixed amount of money available to trade with other people for things you want, there is not a fixed amount of wealth in the world. *You can make more wealth.* Wealth has been getting created and destroyed (but on balance, created) for all of human history.

Suppose you own a beat-up old car. Instead of sitting on your butt next summer, you could spend the time restoring your car to pristine condition. In doing so you create wealth. The world is—and you specifically are—one pristine old car the richer. And not just in some metaphorical way. If you sell your car, you'll get more for it.

In restoring your old car you have made yourself richer. You haven't made anyone else poorer. So there is obviously not a fixed pie. And in fact, when you look at it this way, you wonder why anyone would think there was.[5]

Kids know, without knowing they know, that they can create wealth. If you need to give someone a present and don't have any money, you make one. But kids are so bad at making things that they consider home-made presents to be a distinct, inferior, sort of thing to store-bought ones—a mere expression of the proverbial thought that counts. And indeed, the lumpy ashtrays we made for our parents did not have much of a resale market.

Craftsmen

The people most likely to grasp that wealth can be created are the ones who are good at making things, the craftsmen. Their hand-made objects become store-bought ones. But with the rise of industrialization there are fewer and fewer craftsmen. One of the biggest remaining groups is computer programmers.

A programmer can sit down in front of a computer and *create wealth*. A good piece of software is, in itself, a valuable thing. There is no manufacturing to confuse the issue. Those characters you type are a complete, finished product. If someone sat down and wrote a web browser that didn't suck (a fine idea, by the way), the world would be that much richer.

Everyone in a company works together to create wealth, in the sense of making more things people want. Many of the employees (e.g. the people in the mailroom or the personnel department) work at one remove from the actual making of stuff. Not the programmers. They literally think the product, one line at a time. And so it's clearer to programmers that wealth is something that's made, rather than being distributed, like slices of a pie, by some imaginary Daddy.

It's also obvious to programmers that there are huge variations in the rate at which wealth is created. At Viaweb we had one programmer who was a sort of monster of productivity. I remember watching what he did one long day and estimating that he had added several hundred thousand dollars to the market value of the company. A great programmer, on a roll, could create a million dollars worth of wealth in a couple weeks. A mediocre programmer over the same period will generate zero or even negative wealth (e.g. by introducing bugs).

This is why so many of the best programmers are libertarians. In our world, you sink or swim, and there are no excuses. When those far removed from the creation of wealth—undergraduates, reporters, politicians—hear that the richest 5% of the people have half the total wealth, they tend to think *injustice!* An experienced

93

programmer would be more likely to think *is that all?* The top 5% of programmers probably write 99% of the good software.

Wealth can be created without being sold. Scientists, till recently at least, effectively donated the wealth they created. We are all richer for knowing about penicillin, because we're less likely to die from infections. Wealth is whatever people want, and not dying is certainly something we want. Hackers often donate their work by writing open source software that anyone can use for free. I am much the richer for the operating system FreeBSD, which I'm running on the computer I'm using now, and so is Yahoo, which runs it on all their servers.

What a Job Is

In industrialized countries, people belong to one institution or another at least until their twenties. After all those years you get used to the idea of belonging to a group of people who all get up in the morning, go to some set of buildings, and do things that they do not, ordinarily, enjoy doing. Belonging to such a group becomes part of your identity: name, age, role, institution. If you have to introduce yourself, or someone else describes you, it will be as something like, John Smith, age 10, a student at such and such elementary school, or John Smith, age 20, a student at such and such college.

When John Smith finishes school he is expected to get a job. And what getting a job seems to mean is joining another institution. Superficially it's a lot like college. You pick the companies you want to work for and apply to join them. If one likes you, you become a member of this new group. You get up in the morning and go to a new set of buildings, and do things that you do not, ordinarily, enjoy doing. There are a few differences: life is not as much fun, and you get paid, instead of paying, as you did in college. But the similarities feel greater than the differences. John Smith is now John Smith, 22, a software developer at such and such corporation.

In fact John Smith's life has changed more than he realizes. Socially, a company looks much like college, but the deeper you go into the underlying reality, the more different it gets.

What a company does, and has to do if it wants to continue to exist, is earn money. And the way most companies make money is by creating wealth. Companies can be so specialized that this similarity is concealed, but it is not only manufacturing companies that create wealth. A big component of wealth is location. Remember that magic machine that could make you cars and cook you dinner and so on? It would not be so useful if it delivered your dinner to a random location in central Asia. If wealth means what people want, companies that move things also create wealth. Ditto for many other kinds of companies that don't make anything physical. Nearly all companies exist to do something people want.

And that's what you do, as well, when you go to work for a company. But here there is another layer that tends to obscure the underlying reality. In a company, the work you do is averaged together with a lot of other people's. You may not even be aware you're doing something people want. Your contribution may be indirect. But the company as a whole must be giving people something they want, or they won't make any money. And if they are paying you x dollars a year, then on average you must be contributing at least x dollars a year worth of work, or the company will be spending more than it makes, and will go out of business.

Someone graduating from college thinks, and is told, that he needs to get a job, as if the important thing were becoming a member of an institution. A more direct way to put it would be: you need to start doing something people want. You don't need to join a company to do that. All a company is is a group of people working together to do something people want. It's doing something people want that matters, not joining the group.[6]

For most people the best plan probably is to go to work for some existing company. But it is a good idea to understand what's happening when you do this. A job means doing something people want, averaged together with everyone else in that company.

Working Harder

That averaging gets to be a problem. I think the single biggest problem afflicting large companies is the difficulty of assigning a value to each person's work. For the most part they punt. In a big company you get paid a fairly predictable salary for working fairly hard. You're expected not to be obviously incompetent or lazy, but you're not expected to devote your whole life to your work.

It turns out, though, that there are economies of scale in how much of your life you devote to your work. In the right kind of business, someone who really devoted himself to work could generate ten or even a hundred times as much wealth as an average employee. A programmer, for example, instead of chugging along maintaining and updating an existing piece of software, could write a whole new piece of software, and with it create a new source of revenue.

Companies are not set up to reward people who want to do this. You can't go to your boss and say, I'd like to start working ten times as hard, so will you please pay me ten times as much? For one thing, the official fiction is that you are already working as hard as you can. But a more serious problem is that the company has no way of measuring the value of your work.

Salesmen are an exception. It's easy to measure how much revenue they generate, and they're usually paid a percentage of it. If a salesman wants to work harder, he can just start doing it, and he will automatically get paid proportionally more.

There is one other job besides sales where big companies can hire first-rate people: in the top management jobs. And for the same reason: their performance can be measured. The top managers are held responsible for the performance of the entire company. Because an ordinary employee's performance can't usually be measured, he is not expected to do more than put in a solid effort. Whereas top management, like salespeople, have to actually come up with the numbers. The CEO of a company that tanks cannot plead that he put in a solid effort. If the company does badly, he's done badly.

A company that could pay all its employees so straightforwardly would be enormously successful. Many employees would work harder if they could get paid for it. More importantly, such a company would attract people who wanted to work especially hard. It would crush its competitors.

Unfortunately, companies can't pay everyone like salesmen. Salesmen work alone. Most employees' work is tangled together. Suppose a company makes some kind of consumer gadget. The engineers build a reliable gadget with all kinds of new features; the industrial designers design a beautiful case for it; and then the marketing people convince everyone that it's something they've got to have. How do you know how much of the gadget's sales are due to each group's efforts? Or, for that matter, how much is due to the creators of past gadgets that gave the company a reputation for quality? There's no way to untangle all their contributions. Even if you could read the minds of the consumers, you'd find these factors were all blurred together.

If you want to go faster, it's a problem to have your work tangled together with a large number of other people's. In a large group, your performance is not separately measurable—and the rest of the group slows you down.

Measurement and Leverage

To get rich you need to get yourself in a situation with two things, measurement and leverage. You need to be in a position where your performance can be measured, or there is no way to get paid more by doing more. And you have to have leverage, in the sense that the decisions you make have a big effect.

Measurement alone is not enough. An example of a job with measurement but not leverage is doing piecework in a sweatshop. Your performance is measured and you get paid accordingly, but you have no scope for decisions. The only decision you get to make is how fast you work, and that can probably only increase your earnings by a factor of two or three.

An example of a job with both measurement and leverage would be lead actor in a movie. Your performance can be measured in the gross of the movie. And you have leverage in the sense that your performance can make or break it.

CEOs also have both measurement and leverage. They're measured, in that the performance of the company is their performance. And they have leverage in that their decisions set the whole company moving in one direction or another.

I think everyone who gets rich by their own efforts will be found to be in a situation with measurement and leverage. Everyone I can think of does: CEOs, movie stars, hedge fund managers, professional athletes. A good hint to the presence of leverage is the possibility of failure. Upside must be balanced by downside, so if there is big potential for gain there must also be a terrifying possibility of loss. CEOs, stars, fund managers, and athletes all live with the sword hanging over their heads; the moment they start to suck, they're out. If you're in a job that feels safe, you are not going to get rich, because if there is no danger there is almost certainly no leverage.

But you don't have to become a CEO or a movie star to be in a situation with measurement and leverage. All you need to do is be part of a small group working on a hard problem.

Smallness = Measurement

If you can't measure the value of the work done by individual employees, you can get close. You can measure the value of the work done by small groups.

One level at which you can accurately measure the revenue generated by employees is at the level of the whole company. When the company is small, you are thereby fairly close to measuring the contributions of individual employees. A viable startup might only have ten employees, which puts you within a factor of ten of measuring individual effort.

Starting or joining a startup is thus as close as most people can get to saying to one's boss, I want to work ten times as hard, so please pay me ten times as much. There are two differences: you're not saying it to your boss, but directly to the customers (for whom your boss is only a proxy after all), and you're not doing it individually, but along with a small group of other ambitious people.

It will, ordinarily, be a group. Except in a few unusual kinds of work, like acting or writing books, you can't be a company of one person. And the people you work with had better be good, because it's their work that yours is going to be averaged with.

A big company is like a giant galley driven by a thousand rowers. Two things keep the speed of the galley down. One is that individual rowers don't see any result from working harder. The other is that, in a group of a thousand people, the average rower is likely to be pretty average.

If you took ten people at random out of the big galley and put them in a boat by themselves, they could probably go faster. They would have both carrot and stick to motivate them. An energetic rower would be encouraged by the thought that he could have a visible effect on the speed of the boat. And if someone was lazy, the others would be more likely to notice and complain.

But the real advantage of the ten-man boat shows when you take the ten *best* rowers out of the big galley and put them in a boat together. They will have all the extra motivation that comes from being in a small group. But more importantly, by selecting that small a group you can get the best rowers. Each one will be in the top 1%. It's a much better deal for them to average their work together with a small group of their peers than to average it with everyone.

That's the real point of startups. Ideally, you are getting together with a group of other people who also want to work a lot harder, and get paid a lot more, than they would in a big company. And because startups tend to get founded by self-selecting groups of ambitious people who already know one another (at least by reputation), the level of measurement is more precise than you get from smallness alone. A startup is not merely ten people, but ten people like you.

Steve Jobs once said that the success or failure of a startup depends on the first ten employees. I agree. If anything, it's more like the first five. Being small is not, in itself, what makes startups kick butt, but rather that small groups can be select. You don't want small in the sense of a village, but small in the sense of an all-star team.

The larger a group, the closer its average member will be to the average for the population as a whole. So all other things being equal, a very able person in a big company is probably getting a bad deal, because his performance is dragged down by the overall lower performance of the others. Of course, all other things often are not equal: the able person may not care about money, or may prefer the stability of a large company. But a very able person who does care about money will ordinarily do better to go off and work with a small group of peers.

Technology = Leverage

Startups offer anyone a way to be in a situation with measurement and leverage. They allow measurement because they're small, and they offer leverage because they make money by inventing new technology.

What is technology? It's *technique*. It's the way we all do things. And when you discover a new way to do things, its value is multiplied by all the people who use it. It is the proverbial fishing rod, rather than the fish. That's the difference between a startup and a restaurant or a barber shop. You fry eggs or cut hair one customer at a time. Whereas if you solve a technical problem that a lot of people care about, you help everyone who uses your solution. That's leverage.

If you look at history, it seems that most people who got rich by creating wealth did it by developing new technology. You just can't fry eggs or cut hair fast enough. What made the Florentines rich in 1200 was the discovery of new techniques for making the high-tech product of the time, fine woven cloth. What made the Dutch rich in

1600 was the discovery of shipbuilding and navigation techniques that enabled them to dominate the seas of the Far East.

Fortunately there is a natural fit between smallness and solving hard problems. The leading edge of technology moves fast. Technology that's valuable today could be worthless in a couple years. Small companies are more at home in this world, because they don't have layers of bureaucracy to slow them down. Also, technical advances tend to come from unorthodox approaches, and small companies are less constrained by convention.

Big companies can develop technology. They just can't do it quickly. Their size makes them slow and prevents them from rewarding employees for the extraordinary effort required. So in practice big companies only get to develop technology in fields where large capital requirements prevent startups from competing with them, like microprocessors, power plants, or passenger aircraft. And even in those fields they depend heavily on startups for components and ideas.

It's obvious that biotech or software startups exist to solve hard technical problems, but I think it will also be found to be true in businesses that don't seem to be about technology. McDonald's, for example, grew big by designing a system, the McDonald's franchise, that could then be reproduced at will all over the face of the earth. A McDonald's franchise is controlled by rules so precise that it is practically a piece of software. Write once, run everywhere. Ditto for Wal-Mart. Sam Walton got rich not by being a retailer, but by designing a new kind of store.

Use difficulty as a guide not just in selecting the overall aim of your company, but also at decision points along the way. At Viaweb one of our rules of thumb was *run upstairs*. Suppose you are a little, nimble guy being chased by a big, fat, bully. You open a door and find yourself in a staircase. Do you go up or down? I say up. The bully can probably run downstairs as fast as you can. Going upstairs his bulk will be more of a disadvantage. Running upstairs is hard for you but even harder for him.

What this meant in practice was that we deliberately sought hard problems. If there were two features we could add to our software, both equally valuable in proportion to their difficulty, we'd always take the harder one. Not just because it was more valuable, but *because it was harder.* We delighted in forcing bigger, slower competitors to follow us over difficult ground. Like guerillas, startups prefer the difficult terrain of the mountains, where the troops of the central government can't follow. I can remember times when we were just exhausted after wrestling all day with some horrible technical problem. And I'd be delighted, because something that was hard for us would be impossible for our competitors.

This is not just a good way to run a startup. It's what a startup is. Venture capitalists know about this and have a phrase for it: *barriers to entry.* If you go to a VC with a new idea and ask him to invest in it, one of the first things he'll ask is, how hard would this be for someone else to develop? That is, how much difficult ground have you put between yourself and potential pursuers?[7] And you had better have a convincing explanation of why your technology would be hard to duplicate. Otherwise as soon as some big company becomes aware of it, they'll make their own, and with their brand name, capital, and distribution clout, they'll take away your market overnight. You'd be like guerillas caught in the open field by regular army forces.

One way to put up barriers to entry is through patents. But patents may not provide much protection. Competitors commonly find ways to work around a patent. And if they can't, they may simply violate it and invite you to sue them. A big company is not afraid to be sued; it's an everyday thing for them. They'll make sure that suing them is expensive and takes a long time. Ever heard of Philo Farnsworth? He invented television. The reason you've never heard of him is that his company was not the one to make money from it.[8] The company that did was RCA, and Farnsworth's reward for his efforts was a decade of patent litigation.

Here, as so often, the best defense is a good offense. If you can develop technology that's simply too hard for competitors to duplicate, you don't need to rely on other defenses. Start by picking a hard problem, and then at every decision point, take the harder choice.[9]

The Catch(es)

If it were simply a matter of working harder than an ordinary employee and getting paid proportionately, it would obviously be a good deal to start a startup. Up to a point it would be more fun. I don't think many people like the slow pace of big companies, the interminable meetings, the water-cooler conversations, the clueless middle managers, and so on.

Unfortunately there are a couple catches. One is that you can't choose the point on the curve that you want to inhabit. You can't decide, for example, that you'd like to work just two or three times as hard, and get paid that much more. When you're running a startup, your competitors decide how hard you work. And they pretty much all make the same decision: as hard as you possibly can.

The other catch is that the payoff is only on average proportionate to your productivity. There is, as I said before, a large random multiplier in the success of any company. So in practice the deal is not that you're 30 times as productive and get paid 30 times as much. It is that you're 30 times as productive, and get paid between zero and a thousand times as much. If the mean is 30x, the median is probably zero. Most startups tank, and not just the dogfood portals we all heard about during the Internet Bubble. It's common for a startup to be developing a genuinely good product, take slightly too long to do it, run out of money, and have to shut down.

A startup is like a mosquito. A bear can absorb a hit and a crab is armored against one, but a mosquito is designed for one thing: to score. No energy is wasted on defense. The defense of mosquitos, as a species, is that there are a lot of them, but this is little consolation to the individual mosquito.

Startups, like mosquitos, tend to be an all-or-nothing proposition. And you don't generally know which of the two you're going to get till the last minute. Viaweb came close to tanking several times. Our trajectory was like a sine wave. Fortunately we got bought at the top of the cycle, but it was damned close. While we were visiting Yahoo in California to talk about selling the company to them, we had to borrow a conference room to reassure an investor who was about to back out of a new round of funding that we needed to stay alive.

The all-or-nothing aspect of startups was not something we wanted. Viaweb's hackers were all extremely risk-averse. If there had been some way just to work super hard and get paid for it, without having a lottery mixed in, we would have been delighted. We would have much preferred a 100% chance of $1 million to a 20% chance of $10 million, even though theoretically the second is worth twice as much. Unfortunately, there is not currently any space in the business world where you can get the first deal.

The closest you can get is by selling your startup in the early stages, giving up upside (and risk) for a smaller but guaranteed pay-off. We had a chance to do this, and stupidly, as we then thought, let it slip by. After that we became comically eager to sell. For the next year or so, if anyone expressed the slightest curiosity about Viaweb we would try to sell them the company. But there were no takers, so we had to keep going.

It would have been a bargain to buy us at an early stage, but companies doing acquisitions are not looking for bargains. A company big enough to acquire startups will be big enough to be fairly conservative, and within the company the people in charge of acquisitions will be among the more conservative, because they are likely to be business school types who joined the company late. They would rather overpay for a safe choice. So it is easier to sell an established startup, even at a large premium, than an early-stage one.

Get Users

I think it's a good idea to get bought, if you can. Running a business is different from growing one. It is just as well to let a big company take over once you reach cruising altitude. It's also financially wiser, because selling allows you to diversify. What would you think of a financial advisor who put all his client's assets into one volatile stock?

How do you get bought? Mostly by doing the same things you'd do if you didn't intend to sell the company. Being profitable, for example. But getting bought is also an art in its own right, and one that we spent a lot of time trying to master.

Potential buyers will always delay if they can. The hard part about getting bought is getting them to act. For most people, the most powerful motivator is not the hope of gain, but the fear of loss. For potential acquirers, the most powerful motivator is the prospect that one of their competitors will buy you. This, as we found, causes CEOs to take red-eyes. The second biggest is the worry that, if they don't buy you now, you'll continue to grow rapidly and will cost more to acquire later, or even become a competitor.

In both cases, what it all comes down to is users. You'd think that a company about to buy you would do a lot of research and decide for themselves how valuable your technology was. Not at all. What they go by is the number of users you have.

In effect, acquirers assume the customers know who has the best technology. And this is not as stupid as it sounds. Users are the only real proof that you've created wealth. Wealth is what people want, and if people aren't using your software, maybe it's not just because you're bad at marketing. Maybe it's because you haven't made what they want.

Venture capitalists have a list of danger signs to watch out for. Near the top is the company run by techno-weenies who are obsessed with solving interesting technical problems, instead of making users happy. In a startup, you're not just trying to solve problems. You're trying to solve problems *that users care about.*

So I think you should make users the test, just as acquirers do. Treat a startup as an optimization problem in which performance is measured by number of users. As anyone who has tried to optimize software knows, the key is measurement. When you try to guess where your program is slow, and what would make it faster, you almost always guess wrong.

Number of users may not be the perfect test, but it will be very close. It's what acquirers care about. It's what revenues depend on. It's what makes competitors unhappy. It's what impresses reporters, and potential new users. Certainly it's a better test than your a priori notions of what problems are important to solve, no matter how technically adept you are.

Among other things, treating a startup as an optimization problem will help you avoid another pitfall that VCs worry about, and rightly—taking a long time to develop a product. Now we can recognize this as something hackers already know to avoid: premature optimization. Get a version 1.0 out there as soon as you can. Until you have some users to measure, you're optimizing based on guesses.

The ball you need to keep your eye on here is the underlying principle that wealth is what people want. If you plan to get rich by creating wealth, you have to know what people want. So few businesses really pay attention to making customers happy. How often do you walk into a store, or call a company on the phone, with a feeling of dread in the back of your mind? When you hear "your call is important to us, please stay on the line," do you think, oh good, now everything will be all right?

A restaurant can afford to serve the occasional burnt dinner. But in technology, you cook one thing and that's what everyone eats. So any difference between what people want and what you deliver is multiplied. You please or annoy customers wholesale. The closer you can get to what they want, the more wealth you generate.

Wealth and Power

Making wealth is not the only way to get rich. For most of human history it has not even been the most common. Until a few centuries ago, the main sources of wealth were mines, slaves and serfs, land, and cattle, and the only ways to acquire these rapidly were by inheritance, marriage, conquest, or confiscation. Naturally wealth had a bad reputation.

Two things changed. The first was the rule of law. For most of the world's history, if you did somehow accumulate a fortune, the ruler or his henchmen would find a way to steal it. But in medieval Europe something new happened. A new class of merchants and manufacturers began to collect in towns.[10] Together they were able to withstand the local feudal lord. So for the first time in our history, the bullies stopped stealing the nerds' lunch money. This was naturally a great incentive, and possibly indeed the main cause of the second big change, industrialization.

A great deal has been written about the causes of the Industrial Revolution. But surely a necessary, if not sufficient, condition was that people who made fortunes be able to enjoy them in peace.[11] One piece of evidence is what happened to countries that tried to return to the old model, like the Soviet Union, and to a lesser extent Britain under the labor governments of the 1960s and early 1970s. Take away the incentive of wealth, and technical innovation grinds to a halt.

Remember what a startup is, economically: a way of saying, I want to work faster. Instead of accumulating money slowly by being paid a regular wage for fifty years, I want to get it over with as soon as possible. So governments that forbid you to accumulate wealth are in effect decreeing that you work slowly. They're willing to let you earn $3 million over fifty years, but they're not willing to let you work so hard that you can do it in two. They are like the corporate boss that you can't go to and say, I want to work ten times as hard, so please pay me ten times a much. Except this is not a boss you can escape by starting your own company.

The problem with working slowly is not just that technical innovation happens slowly. It's that it tends not to happen at all. It's only when you're deliberately looking for hard problems, as a way to use speed to the greatest advantage, that you take on this kind of project. Developing new technology is a pain in the ass. It is, as Edison said, one percent inspiration and ninety-nine percent perspiration. Without the incentive of wealth, no one wants to do it. Engineers will work on sexy projects like fighter planes and moon rockets for ordinary salaries, but more mundane technologies like light bulbs or semiconductors have to be developed by entrepreneurs.

Startups are not just something that happened in Silicon Valley in the last couple decades. Since it became possible to get rich by creating wealth, everyone who has done it has used essentially the same recipe: measurement and leverage, where measurement comes from working with a small group, and leverage from developing new techniques. The recipe was the same in Florence in 1200 as it is in Santa Clara today.

Understanding this may help to answer an important question: why Europe grew so powerful. Was it something about the geography of Europe? Was it that Europeans are somehow racially superior? Was it their religion? The answer (or at least the proximate cause) may be that the Europeans rode on the crest of a powerful new idea: allowing those who made a lot of money to keep it.

Once you're allowed to do that, people who want to get rich can do it by generating wealth instead of stealing it. The resulting technological growth translates not only into wealth but into military power. The theory that led to the stealth plane was developed by a Soviet mathematician. But because the Soviet Union didn't have a computer industry, it remained for them a theory; they didn't have hardware capable of executing the calculations fast enough to design an actual airplane.

In that respect the Cold War teaches the same lesson as World War II and, for that matter, most wars in recent history. Don't let a ruling class of warriors and politicians squash the entrepreneurs. The same recipe that makes individuals rich makes countries powerful. Let the nerds keep their lunch money, and you rule the world.

Chapter 7

Mind the Gap

WHEN PEOPLE CARE ENOUGH ABOUT SOMETHING TO DO IT well, those who do it best tend to be far better than everyone else. There's a huge gap between Leonardo and second-rate contemporaries like Borgognone. You see the same gap between Raymond Chandler and the average writer of detective novels. A top-ranked professional chess player could play ten thousand games against an ordinary club player without losing once.

Like chess or painting or writing novels, making money is a very specialized skill. But for some reason we treat this skill differently. No one complains when a few people surpass all the rest at playing chess or writing novels, but when a few people make more money than the rest, we get editorials saying this is wrong.

Why? The pattern of variation seems no different than for any other skill. What causes people to react so strongly when the skill is making money?

I think there are three reasons we treat making money as different: the misleading model of wealth we learn as children; the disreputable way in which, till recently, most fortunes were accumulated; and the worry that great variations in income are somehow bad for society. As far as I can tell, the first is mistaken, the second outdated, and the third empirically false. Could it be that, in a modern democracy, variation in income is actually a sign of health?

The Daddy Model of Wealth

When I was five I thought electricity was created by electric sockets. I didn't realize there were power plants out there generating it. Likewise, it doesn't occur to most kids that wealth is something that has to be generated. It seems to be something that flows from parents.

Because of the circumstances in which they encounter it, children tend to misunderstand wealth. They confuse it with money. They think that there is a fixed amount of it. And they think of it as something that's distributed by authorities (and so should be distributed equally), rather than something that has to be created (and might be created unequally).

In fact, wealth is not money. Money is just a convenient way of trading one form of wealth for another. Wealth is the underlying stuff—the goods and services we buy. When you travel to a rich or poor country, you don't have to look at people's bank accounts to tell which kind you're in. You can *see* wealth—in buildings and streets, in the clothes and the health of the people.

Where does wealth come from? People make it. This was easier to grasp when most people lived on farms, and made many of the things they wanted with their own hands. Then you could see in the house, the herds, and the granary the wealth that each family created. It was obvious then too that the wealth of the world was not a fixed quantity that had to be shared out, like slices of a pie. If you wanted more wealth, you could make it.

This is just as true today, though few of us create wealth directly for ourselves (except for a few vestigial domestic tasks). Mostly we create wealth for other people in exchange for money, which we then trade for the forms of wealth we want.[1]

Because kids are unable to create wealth, whatever they have has to be given to them. And when wealth is something you're given, then of course it seems that it should be distributed equally.[2] As in most families it is. The kids see to that. "Unfair," they cry, when one sibling gets more than another.

In the real world, you can't keep living off your parents. If you want something, you either have to make it, or do something of equivalent value for someone else, in order to get them to give you enough money to buy it. In the real world, wealth is (except for a few specialists like thieves and speculators) something you have to create, not something that's distributed by Daddy. And since the ability and desire to create it vary from person to person, it's not made equally.

You get paid by doing or making something people want, and those who make more money are often simply better at doing what people want. Top actors make a lot more money than B-list actors. The B-list actors might be almost as charismatic, but when people go to the theater and look at the list of movies playing, they want that extra oomph that the big stars have.

Doing what people want is not the only way to get money, of course. You could also rob banks, or solicit bribes, or establish a monopoly. Such tricks account for some variation in wealth, and indeed for some of the biggest individual fortunes, but they are not the root cause of variation in income. The root cause of variation in income, as Occam's Razor implies, is the same as the root cause of variation in every other human skill.

In the United States, the CEO of a large public company makes about 100 times as much as the average person.[3] Basketball players make about 128 times as much, and baseball players 72 times as much. Editorials quote this kind of statistic with horror. But I have no trouble imagining that one person could be 100 times as productive as another. In ancient Rome the price of *slaves* varied by a factor of 50 depending on their skills.[4] And that's without considering motivation, or the extra leverage in productivity that you can get from modern technology.

Editorials about athletes' or CEOs' salaries remind me of early Christian writers, arguing from first principles about whether the Earth was round, when they could just walk outside and check.[5] How much someone's work is worth is not a policy question. It's something the market already determines.

"Are they really worth 100 of us?" editorialists ask. Depends on what you mean by worth. If you mean worth in the sense of what people will pay for their skills, the answer is yes, apparently.

A few CEOs' incomes reflect some kind of wrongdoing. But are there not others whose incomes really do reflect the wealth they generate? Steve Jobs saved a company that was in a terminal decline. And not merely in the way a turnaround specialist does, by cutting costs; he had to decide what Apple's next products should be. Few others could have done it. And regardless of the case with CEOs, it's hard to see how anyone could argue that the salaries of professional basketball players don't reflect supply and demand.

It may seem unlikely in principle that one individual could really generate so much more wealth than another. The key to this mystery is to revisit that question, are they really worth 100 of us? *Would* a basketball team trade one of their players for 100 random people? What would Apple's next product look like if you replaced Steve Jobs with a committee of 100 random people?[6] These things don't scale linearly. Perhaps the CEO or the professional athlete has only ten times (whatever that means) the skill and determination of an ordinary person. But it makes all the difference that it's concentrated in one individual.

When we say that one kind of work is overpaid and another underpaid, what are we really saying? In a free market, prices are determined by what buyers want. People like baseball more than poetry, so baseball players make more than poets. To say that a certain kind of work is underpaid is thus identical with saying that people want the wrong things.

Well, of course people want the wrong things. It seems odd to be surprised by that. And it seems even odder to say that it's *unjust* that certain kinds of work are underpaid.[7] Then you're saying that it's unjust that people want the wrong things. It's lamentable that people prefer reality TV and corndogs to Shakespeare and steamed vegetables, but unjust? That seems like saying that blue is heavy, or that up is circular.

The appearance of word "unjust" here is the unmistakable spectral signature of the Daddy Model. Why else would this idea occur in this odd context? Whereas if the speaker were still operating on the Daddy Model, and saw wealth as something that flowed from a common source and had to be shared out, rather than something generated by doing what other people wanted, this is exactly what you'd get on noticing that some people made much more than others.

When we talk about "unequal distribution of income," we should also ask, where does that income come from?[8] Who made the wealth it represents? Because to the extent that income varies simply according to how much wealth people create, the distribution may be unequal, but it's hardly unjust.

Stealing It

The second reason we tend to find great disparities of wealth alarming is that for most of human history the usual way to accumulate a fortune was to steal it: in pastoral societies by cattle raiding; in agricultural societies by appropriating others' estates in times of war, and taxing them in times of peace.

In conflicts, those on the winning side would receive the estates confiscated from the losers. In England in the 1060s, when William the Conqueror distributed the estates of the defeated Anglo-Saxon nobles to his followers, the conflict was military. By the 1530s, when Henry VIII distributed the estates of the monasteries to his followers,[9] it was mostly political. But the principle was the same. Indeed, the same principle is at work now in Zimbabwe.

In more organized societies, like China, the ruler and his officials used taxation instead of confiscation. But here too we see the same principle: the way to get rich was not to create wealth, but to serve a ruler powerful enough to appropriate it.

This started to change in Europe with the rise of the middle class. Now we think of the middle class as people who are neither rich nor poor, but originally they were a distinct group. In a feudal society, there are just two classes: a warrior aristocracy, and the serfs who work their estates. The middle class were a new, third group who lived in towns and supported themselves by manufacturing and trade.

Starting in the tenth and eleventh centuries, petty nobles and former serfs banded together in towns that gradually became powerful enough to ignore the local feudal lords.[10] Like serfs, the middle class made a living largely by creating wealth. (In port cities like Genoa and Pisa, they also engaged in piracy.) But unlike serfs they had an incentive to create a lot of it. Any wealth a serf created belonged to his master. There was not much point in making more than you could hide. Whereas the independence of the townsmen allowed them to keep whatever wealth they created.

Once it became possible to get rich by creating wealth, society as a whole started to get richer very rapidly. Nearly everything we have was created by the middle class. Indeed, the other two classes have effectively disappeared in industrial societies, and their names been given to either end of the middle class. (In the original sense of the word, Bill Gates is middle class.)

But it was not till the Industrial Revolution that wealth creation definitively replaced corruption as the best way to get rich. In England, at least, corruption only became unfashionable (and in fact only started to be called "corruption") when there started to be other, faster ways to get rich.

Seventeenth-century England was much like the third world today, in that government office was a recognized route to wealth. The great fortunes of that time still derived more from what we would now call corruption than from commerce.[11] By the nineteenth century that had changed. There continued to be bribes, as there still are everywhere, but politics had by then been left to men who were driven more by vanity than greed. Technology had made it possible to create wealth faster than you could steal it. The prototypical rich man of the nineteenth century was not a courtier but an industrialist.

With the rise of the middle class, wealth stopped being a zero-sum game. Jobs and Wozniak didn't have to make us poor to make themselves rich. Quite the opposite: they created things that made our lives materially richer. They had to, or we wouldn't have paid for them.

But since for most of the world's history the main route to wealth was to steal it, we tend to be suspicious of rich people. Idealistic undergraduates find their unconsciously preserved child's model of wealth confirmed by eminent writers of the past. It is a case of the mistaken meeting the outdated.

"Behind every great fortune, there is a crime," Balzac wrote. Except he didn't. What he actually said was that a great fortune with no apparent cause was probably due to a crime well enough executed that it had been forgotten. If we were talking about Europe in 1000, or most of the third world today, the standard misquotation would be spot on. But Balzac lived in nineteenth-century France, where the Industrial Revolution was well advanced. He knew you could make a fortune without stealing it. After all, he did himself, as a popular novelist.[12]

Only a few countries (by no coincidence, the richest ones) have reached this stage. In most, corruption still has the upper hand. In most, the fastest way to get wealth is by stealing it. And so when we see increasing differences in income in a rich country, there is a tendency to worry that it's sliding back toward becoming another Venezuela. I think the opposite is happening. I think you're seeing a country a full step ahead of Venezuela.

The Lever of Technology

Will technology increase the gap between rich and poor? It will certainly increase the gap between the productive and the unproductive. That's the whole point of technology. With a tractor an energetic farmer could plow six times as much land in a day as he could with a team of horses. But only if he mastered a new kind of farming.

I've seen the lever of technology grow visibly in my own time. In high school I made money by mowing lawns and scooping ice cream at Baskin-Robbins. This was the only kind of work available at the time. Now high school kids could write software or design web sites. But only some of them will; the rest will still be scooping ice cream.

I remember very vividly when in 1985 improved technology made it possible for me to buy a computer of my own. Within months I was using it to make money as a freelance programmer. A few years before, I couldn't have done this. A few years before, there was no such *thing* as a freelance programmer. But Apple created wealth, in the form of powerful, inexpensive computers, and programmers immediately set to work using it to create more.

As this example suggests, the rate at which technology increases our productive capacity is probably polynomial, rather than linear. So we should expect to see ever-increasing variation in individual productivity as time goes on. Will that increase the gap between rich and the poor? Depends which gap you mean.

Technology should increase the gap in income, but it seems to decrease other gaps. A hundred years ago, the rich led a different *kind* of life from ordinary people. They lived in houses full of servants, wore elaborately uncomfortable clothes, and travelled about in carriages drawn by teams of horses which themselves required their own houses and servants. Now, thanks to technology, the rich live more like the average person.

Cars are a good example of why. It's possible to buy expensive, handmade cars that cost hundreds of thousands of dollars. But there is not much point. Companies make more money by building a large number of ordinary cars than a small number of expensive ones. So a company making a mass-produced car can afford to spend a lot more on its design. If you buy a custom-made car, something will always be breaking. The only point of buying one now is to advertise that you can.

Or consider watches. Fifty years ago, by spending a lot of money on a watch you could get better performance. When watches had mechanical movements, expensive watches kept better time. Not any more. Since the invention of the quartz movement, an ordinary Timex is more accurate than a Patek Philippe costing hundreds of thousands of dollars.[13] Indeed, as with expensive cars, if you're determined to spend a lot of money on a watch, you have to put up with some inconvenience to do it: as well as keeping worse time, mechanical watches have to be wound.

The only thing technology can't cheapen is brand. Which is precisely why we hear ever more about it. Brand is the residue left as the substantive differences between rich and poor evaporate. But what label you have on your stuff is a much smaller matter than having it versus not having it. In 1900, if you kept a carriage, no one asked what year or brand it was. If you had one, you were rich. And if you weren't rich, you took the omnibus or walked. Now even the poorest Americans drive cars, and it is only because we're so well trained by advertising that we can even recognize the especially expensive ones.[14]

The same pattern has played out in industry after industry. If there is enough demand for something, technology will make it cheap enough to sell in large volumes,[15] and the mass-produced versions will be, if not better, at least more convenient. And there is nothing the rich like more than convenience. The rich people I know drive the same cars, wear the same clothes, have the same kind of furniture, and eat the same foods as my other friends. Their houses are in different neighborhoods, or if in the same neighborhood are different sizes, but within them life is similar. The houses are made using the same construction techniques and contain much the same objects. It's inconvenient to do something expensive and custom.

The rich spend their time more like everyone else too. Bertie Wooster seems long gone. Now, most people who are rich enough not to work do anyway. It's not just social pressure that makes them; idleness is lonely and demoralizing.

Nor do we have the social distinctions there were a hundred years ago. The novels and etiquette manuals of that period read now like descriptions of some strange tribal society. "With respect to the continuance of friendships..." hints *Mrs. Beeton's Book of Household Management* (1880), "it may be found necessary, in some cases, for a mistress to relinquish, on assuming the responsibility of a household, many of those commenced in the earlier part of her life." A woman who married a rich man was expected to drop friends who didn't. You'd seem a barbarian if you behaved that way today. You'd also have a very boring life. People still tend to segregate themselves somewhat, but much more on the basis of education than wealth.[16]

Materially and socially, technology seems to be decreasing the gap between the rich and the poor, not increasing it. If Lenin walked around the offices of a company like Yahoo or Intel or

Cisco, he'd think communism had won. Everyone would be wearing the same clothes, have the same kind of office (or rather, cubicle) with the same furnishings, and address one another by their first names instead of by honorifics. Everything would seem exactly as he'd predicted, until he looked at their bank accounts. Oops.

Is it a problem if technology increases that gap? It doesn't seem to be so far. As it increases the gap in income, it seems to decrease most other gaps.

Alternative to an Axiom

One often hears a policy criticized on the grounds that it would increase the income gap between rich and poor. As if it were an axiom that this would be bad. It might be true that increased variation in income would be bad, but I don't see how we can say it's *axiomatic.*

Indeed, it may even be false, in industrial democracies. In a society of serfs and warlords, certainly, variation in income is a sign of an underlying problem. But serfdom is not the only cause of variation in income. A 747 pilot doesn't make 40 times as much as a checkout clerk because he is a warlord who somehow holds her in thrall. His skills are simply much more valuable.

I'd like to propose an alternative idea: that in a modern society, increasing variation in income is a sign of health. Technology seems to increase the variation in productivity at faster than linear rates. If we don't see corresponding variation in income, there are three possible explanations: (a) that technical innovation has stopped, (b) that the people who would create the most wealth aren't doing it, or (c) that they aren't getting paid for it.

I think we can safely say that (a) and (b) would be bad. If you disagree, try living for a year using only the resources available to the average Frankish nobleman in 800, and report back to us. (I'll be generous and not send you back to the stone age.)

The only option, if you're going to have an increasingly prosperous society without increasing variation in income, seems to be (c), that people will create a lot of wealth without being paid for it. That Jobs and Wozniak, for example, will cheerfully work 20-hour days to produce the Apple computer for a society that allows them, after taxes, to keep just enough of their income to match what they would have made working 9 to 5 at a big company.

Will people create wealth if they can't get paid for it? Only if it's fun. People will write operating systems for free. But they won't install them, or take support calls, or train customers to use them. And at least 90% of the work that even the highest tech companies do is of this second, unedifying kind.

All the unfun kinds of wealth creation slow dramatically in a society that confiscates private fortunes. We can confirm this empirically. Suppose you hear a strange noise that you think may be due to a nearby fan. You turn the fan off, and the noise stops. You turn the fan back on, and the noise starts again. Off, quiet. On, noise. In the absence of other information, it would seem the noise is caused by the fan.

At various times and places in history, whether you could accumulate a fortune by creating wealth has been turned on and off. Northern Italy in 800, off (warlords would steal it). Northern Italy in 1100, on. Central France in 1100, off (still feudal). England in 1800, on. England in 1974, off (98% tax on investment income). United States in 1974, on. We've even had a twin study: West Germany, on; East Germany, off. In every case, the creation of wealth seems to appear and disappear like the noise of a fan as you switch on and off the prospect of keeping it.

There is some momentum involved. It probably takes at least a generation to turn people into East Germans (luckily for England). But if it were merely a fan we were studying, without all the extra baggage that comes from the controversial topic of wealth, no one would have any doubt that the fan was causing the noise.

If you suppress variations in income, whether by stealing private fortunes, as feudal rulers used to do, or by taxing them away, as some modern governments have done, the result always seems to be the same. Society as a whole ends up poorer.

If I had a choice of living in a society where I was materially much better off than I am now, but was among the poorest, or in one where I was the richest, but much worse off than I am now, I'd take the first option. If I had children, it would arguably be immoral not to. It's absolute poverty you want to avoid, not relative poverty. If, as the evidence so far implies, you have to have one or the other in your society, take relative poverty.

You need rich people in your society not so much because in spending their money they create jobs, but because of what they have to do to *get* rich. I'm not talking about the trickle-down effect here. I'm not saying that if you let Henry Ford get rich, he'll hire you as a waiter at his next party. I'm saying that he'll make you a tractor to replace your horse.

Chapter 8

A Plan for Spam

I THINK IT'S POSSIBLE TO STOP SPAM, AND THAT CONTENT-BASED filters are the way to do it. The Achilles heel of the spammers is their message. They can circumvent any other barrier you set up. They have so far, at least. But they have to deliver their message, whatever it is. If we can write software that recognizes their messages, there is no way they can get around that.[1]

To the recipient, spam is easily recognizable. If you hired someone to read your mail and discard the spam, they would have little trouble doing it. How much do we have to do, short of AI, to automate this process?

I think we will be able to solve the problem with fairly simple algorithms. In fact, I've found that you can filter present-day spam acceptably well using nothing more than a Bayesian combination of the spam probabilities of individual words. Using a slightly tweaked (as described below) Bayesian filter, we now miss less than 5 per 1000 spams, with 0 false positives.

The statistical approach is not usually the first one people try when they write spam filters. Most hackers' first instinct is to try to write software that recognizes individual properties of spam. You look at spams and you think, the gall of these guys to try sending me mail that begins "Dear Friend" or has a subject line that's all uppercase and ends in eight exclamation points. I can filter out that stuff with about one line of code.

And so you do, and in the beginning it works. A few simple rules will take a big bite out of your incoming spam. Merely looking for the word `click` will catch 79.7% of the emails in my spam corpus, with only 1.2% false positives.

I spent about six months writing software that looked for individual spam features before I tried the statistical approach. What I found was that recognizing that last few percent of spams got very hard, and that as I made the filters stricter I got more false positives.

False positives are innocent emails that get mistakenly identified as spams. For most users, missing legitimate email is an order of magnitude worse than receiving spam, so a filter that yields false positives is like an acne cure that carries a risk of death to the patient.

The more spam a user gets, the less likely he'll be to notice one innocent mail sitting in his spam folder. And strangely enough, the better your spam filters get, the more dangerous false positives become, because when the filters are really good, users will be more likely to ignore everything they catch.

I don't know why I avoided trying the statistical approach for so long. I think it was because I got addicted to trying to identify spam features myself, as if I were playing some kind of competitive game with the spammers. (Nonhackers don't often realize this, but most hackers are very competitive.) When I did try statistical analysis, I found immediately that it was much cleverer than I had been. It discovered, of course, that terms like `virtumundo` and `teens` were good indicators of spam. But it also discovered that `per` and `FL` and `ff0000` are good indicators of spam. In fact, `ff0000` (HTML for bright red) turns out to be as good an indicator of spam as any pornographic term.

Here's a sketch of how I do statistical filtering. I start with one corpus of spam and one of nonspam mail. At the moment each one has about 4000 messages in it. I scan the entire text, including headers and embedded HTML and Javascript, of each message in each corpus. I currently consider alphanumeric characters, dashes, apostrophes, and dollar signs to be part of tokens, and everything else to be a token separator. (There is probably room for improvement here.) I ignore tokens that are all digits, and I also ignore HTML comments, not even considering them as token separators.

I count the number of times each token (ignoring case, currently) occurs in each corpus. At this stage I end up with two large hash tables, one for each corpus, mapping tokens to number of occurrences.

Next I create a third hash table, this time mapping each token to the probability that an email containing it is a spam, $P_{spam|w}$ which I calculate as follows:

$$r_g = min(1, 2(good(w)/G)), \quad r_b = min(1, bad(w)/B)$$

$$P_{spam|w} = max(.01, min(.99, r_b/(r_g + r_b)))$$

where w is the token whose probability we're calculating, *good* and *bad* are the hash tables I created in the first step, and G and B are the number of nonspam and spam messages respectively.

I want to bias the probabilities slightly to avoid false positives, and by trial and error I've found that a good way to do it is to double all the numbers in *good*. This helps to distinguish between words that occasionally do occur in legitimate email and words that almost never do. I only consider words that occur more than five times in total (actually, because of the doubling, occurring three times in nonspam mail would be enough). And then there is the question of what probability to assign to words that occur in one corpus but not the other. Again by trial and error I chose .01 and .99. There may be room for tuning here, but as the corpus grows such tuning will happen automatically anyway.

The especially observant will notice that while I consider each corpus to be a single long stream of text for purposes of counting occurrences, I use the number of emails in each, rather than their combined length, as the divisor in calculating spam probabilities. This adds another slight bias to protect against false positives.

When new mail arrives, it is scanned into tokens, and the most interesting fifteen tokens, where interesting is measured by how far their spam probability is from a neutral .5, are used to calculate the probability that the mail is spam. If $w_1, \ldots, w_{15}$ are the fifteen

most interesting tokens, you calculate the combined probability
thus:

$$P_{spam} = \frac{\prod_{i=1}^{15} P_{spam|w_i}}{\prod_{i=1}^{15} P_{spam|w_i} + \prod_{i=1}^{15}(1 - P_{spam|w_i})}$$

One question that arises in practice is what probability to assign
to a word you've never seen, i.e. one that doesn't occur in the
hash table of word probabilities. I've found, again by trial and
error, that .4 is a good number to use. If you've never seen a word
before, it is probably fairly innocent; spam words tend to be all
too familiar.

I treat mail as spam if the algorithm above gives it a probability
of more than .9 of being spam. But in practice it would not matter
much where I put this threshold, because few probabilities end up
in the middle of the range.

One great advantage of the statistical approach is that you don't
have to read so many spams. Over the past six months, I've read
literally thousands of spams, and it is really kind of demoralizing.
Norbert Wiener said if you compete with slaves you become a slave,
and there is something similarly degrading about competing with
spammers. To recognize individual spam features you have to try
to get into the mind of the spammer, and frankly I want to spend
as little time inside the minds of spammers as possible.

But the real advantage of the Bayesian approach, of course, is
that you know what you're measuring. Feature-recognizing filters
like SpamAssassin assign a spam "score" to email. The Bayesian
approach assigns an actual probability. The problem with a "score"
is that no one knows what it means. The user doesn't know what it
means, but worse still, neither does the developer of the filter. How
many *points* should an email get for having the word sex in it? A
probability can of course be mistaken, but there is little ambiguity
about what it means, or how evidence should be combined to
calculate it. Based on my corpus, sex indicates a .97 probability
of the containing email being a spam, whereas sexy indicates .99

probability. And Bayes's Rule, equally unambiguous, says that an email containing both words would, in the (unlikely) absence of any other evidence, have a 99.97% chance of being a spam.

Because it is measuring probabilities, the Bayesian approach considers all the evidence in the email, both good and bad. Words that occur disproportionately rarely in spam (like though or tonight or apparently) contribute as much to decreasing the probability as bad words like unsubscribe and opt-in do to increasing it. So an otherwise innocent email that happens to include the word sex is not going to get tagged as spam.

Ideally, of course, the probabilities should be calculated individually for each user. I get a lot of email containing the word Lisp, and (so far) no spam that does. So a word like that is effectively a kind of password for sending mail to me. In my earlier spam-filtering software, the user could set up a list of such words and mail containing them would automatically get past the filters. On my list I put words like Lisp and also my zipcode, so that (otherwise rather spammy-sounding) receipts from online orders would get through. I thought I was being very clever, but I found that the Bayesian filter did the same thing for me, and moreover discovered of a lot of words I hadn't thought of.

When I said at the start that our filters let through less than 5 spams per 1000 with 0 false positives, I'm talking about filtering my mail based on a corpus of my mail. But these numbers are not misleading, because that is the approach I'm advocating: filter each user's mail based on the spam and nonspam mail he receives. Essentially, each user should have two delete buttons, ordinary delete and delete-as-spam. Anything deleted as spam goes into the spam corpus, and everything else goes into the nonspam corpus.

You could start users with a seed filter, but ultimately each user should have his own per-word probabilities based on the actual mail he receives. This (a) makes the filters more effective, (b) lets each user decide their own precise definition of spam, and (c) perhaps best of all makes it hard for spammers to tune mails to get through the filters. If a lot of the brain of the filter is in the individual databases, then merely tuning spams to get through the seed filters won't guarantee anything about how well they'll get through individual users' varying and much more trained filters.

Content-based spam filtering is often combined with a white-list, a list of senders whose mail can be accepted with no filtering. One easy way to build such a whitelist is to keep a list of every address the user has ever sent mail to. If a mail reader has a delete-as-spam button then you could also add the from address of every email the user has deleted as ordinary trash.

I'm an advocate of whitelists, but more as a way to save com-putation than as a way to improve filtering. I used to think that whitelists would make filtering easier, because you'd only have to filter email from people you'd never heard from, and someone sending you mail for the first time is constrained by convention in what they can say to you. Someone you already know might send you an email talking about sex, but someone sending you mail for the first time would not be likely to. The problem is, people can have more than one email address, so a new from-address doesn't guarantee that the sender is writing to you for the first time. It is not unusual for an old friend (especially if he is a hacker) to suddenly send you an email with a new from-address, so you can't risk false positives by filtering mail from unknown addresses especially stringently.

In a sense, though, my filters do themselves embody a kind of whitelist (and blacklist) because they are based on entire messages, including the headers. So to that extent they "know" the email addresses of trusted senders and even the routes by which mail gets from them to me. And they know the same about spam, including the server names, mailer versions, and protocols.

If I thought that I could keep up current rates of spam filtering, I would consider this problem solved. But it doesn't mean much to be able to filter out most present-day spam, because spam evolves. Indeed, most antispam techniques so far have been like pesticides that do nothing more than create a new, resistant strain of bugs.

I'm more hopeful about Bayesian filters, because they evolve with the spam. So as spammers start using v1agra instead of viagra to evade simple-minded spam filters based on individual words, Bayesian filters automatically notice. Indeed, v1agra is far more damning evidence than viagra, and Bayesian filters know precisely how much more.

Still, anyone who proposes a plan for spam filtering has to be able to answer the question: if the spammers knew exactly what you were doing, how well could they get past you? For example, I think that if checksum-based spam filtering becomes a serious obstacle, the spammers will just switch to mad-lib techniques for generating message bodies.

To beat Bayesian filters, it would not be enough for spammers to make their emails unique or to stop using individual naughty words. They'd have to make their mails indistinguishable from your ordinary mail. And this I think would severely constrain them. Spam is mostly sales pitches, so unless your regular mail is all sales pitches, spams will inevitably have a different character. And the spammers would also, of course, have to change (and keep changing) their whole infrastructure, because otherwise the headers would look as bad to the Bayesian filters as ever, no matter what they did to the message body. I don't know enough about the infrastructure that spammers use to know how hard it would be to make the headers look innocent, but my guess is that it would be even harder than making the message look innocent.

Assuming they could solve the problem of the headers, the spam of the future will probably look something like this:

```
Hey there. Check out the following:
http://www.27meg.com/foo
```

because that is about as much sales pitch as content-based filtering will leave the spammer room to make. (Indeed, it will be hard even to get this past filters, because if everything else in the email is neutral, the spam probability will hinge on the URL, and it will take some effort to make that look neutral.)

Spammers range from businesses running so-called opt-in lists who don't even try to conceal their identities, to guys who hijack mail servers to send out spams promoting porn sites. If we use filtering to whittle their options down to mails like the one above, that should pretty much put the spammers on the "legitimate" end of the spectrum out of business; they feel obliged by various state laws to include boilerplate about why their spam is not spam, and how to cancel your "subscription," and that kind of text is easy to recognize.

(I used to think it was naive to believe that stricter laws would decrease spam. Now I think that while stricter laws may not decrease the amount of spam that spammers send, they can certainly help filters to decrease the amount of spam that recipients actually see.)

All along the spectrum, if you restrict the sales pitches spammers can make, you will inevitably tend to put them out of business. That word business is an important one to remember. The spammers are businessmen. They send spam because it works. It works because although the response rate is abominably low (at best 15 per million, vs. 3000 per million for a catalog mailing), the cost, to them, is practically nothing. The cost is enormous for the recipients, about 5 man-weeks for each million recipients who spend a second to delete the spam, but the spammer doesn't have to pay that.

Sending spam does cost the spammer something, though.[2] So the lower we can get the response rate—whether by filtering, or by using filters to force spammers to dilute their pitches—the fewer businesses will find it worth their while to send spam.

The reason the spammers use the kinds of sales pitches that they do is to increase response rates. This is possibly even more disgusting than getting inside the mind of a spammer, but let's take a quick look inside the mind of someone who responds to a spam. This person is either astonishingly credulous or deeply in denial about their sexual interests. In either case, repulsive or idiotic as the spam seems to us, it is exciting to them. The spammers wouldn't say these things if they didn't sound exciting. And "check out the following" is just not going to have nearly the pull with the spam recipient as the kinds of things that spammers say now. Result: if it can't contain exciting sales pitches, spam becomes less effective as a marketing vehicle, and fewer businesses want to use it.

That is the big win in the end. I started writing spam filtering software because I didn't want have to look at the stuff anymore. But if we get good enough at filtering out spam, it will stop working, and the spammers will actually stop sending it.

Of all the approaches to fighting spam, from software to laws, I believe Bayesian filtering will be the single most effective. But I also think that the more different kinds of antispam efforts we undertake, the better, because any measure that constrains spammers will tend to make filtering easier. And even within the world of content-based filtering, I think it will be a good thing if there are many different kinds of software being used simultaneously. The more different filters there are, the harder it will be for spammers to tune spams to get through them.

Chapter 9

Taste for Makers

Copernicus' aesthetic objections to [equants] provided one essential motive for his rejection of the Ptolemaic system. . . .

THOMAS KUHN, *The Copernican Revolution*

All of us had been trained by Kelly Johnson and believed fanatically in his insistence that an airplane that looked beautiful would fly the same way.

BEN RICH, *Skunk Works*

Beauty is the first test: there is no permanent place in this world for ugly mathematics.

G. H. HARDY, *A Mathematician's Apology*

I WAS TALKING RECENTLY TO A FRIEND WHO TEACHES AT MIT. His field is hot now and every year he is inundated by applications from would-be graduate students. "A lot of them seem smart," he said. "What I can't tell is whether they have any kind of taste."

Taste. You don't hear that word much now. And yet we still need the underlying concept, whatever we call it. What my friend meant was that he wanted students who were not just good technicians, but who could use their technical knowledge to design beautiful things.

Mathematicians call good work "beautiful," and so, either now or in the past, have scientists, engineers, musicians, architects, designers, writers, and painters. Is it just a coincidence that they used the same word, or is there some overlap in what they meant? If there is an overlap, can we use one field's discoveries about beauty to help us in another?

For those of us who design things, these are not just theoretical questions. If there is such a thing as beauty, we need to be able to recognize it. We need good taste to make good things. Instead of treating beauty as an airy abstraction, to be either blathered about or avoided depending on how one feels about airy abstractions, let's try considering it as a practical question: *how do you make good stuff?*

If you mention taste nowadays, a lot of people will tell you that "taste is subjective." They believe this because it really feels that way to them. When they like something, they have no idea why. It could be because it's beautiful, or because their mother had one, or because they saw a movie star with one in a magazine, or because they know it's expensive. Their thoughts are a tangle of unexamined impulses.

Most of us were encouraged, as children, to leave this tangle unexamined. If you made fun of your little brother for coloring people green in his coloring book, your mother was likely to tell you something like "you like to do it your way and he likes to do it his way."

Your mother at this point was not trying to teach you important truths about aesthetics. She was trying to get the two of you to stop bickering.

Like many of the half-truths adults tolds us, this one contradicts other things they told us. After dinning into you that taste is merely a matter of personal preference, they took you to the museum and told you that you should pay attention because Leonardo is a great artist.

What goes through the kid's head at this point? What does he think "great artist" means? After having been told for years that everyone just likes to do things their own way, he is unlikely to head straight for the conclusion that a great artist is someone whose work is *better* than the others'. A far more likely theory, in his Ptolemaic model of the universe, is that a great artist is something that's good for you, like broccoli, because someone said so in a book.

Saying that taste is just personal preference is a good way to prevent disputes. The trouble is, it's not true. You feel this when you start to design things.

Whatever job people do, they naturally want to do better. Football players like to win games. CEOs like to increase earnings. It's a matter of pride, and a real pleasure, to get better at your job. But if your job is to design things, and there is no such thing as beauty, then there is *no way to get better at your job*. If taste is just personal preference, then everyone's is already perfect: you like whatever you like, and that's it.

As in any job, as you continue to design things, you'll get better at it. Your tastes will change. And, like anyone who gets better at their job, you'll know you're getting better. If so, your old tastes were not merely different, but worse. Poof goes the axiom that taste can't be wrong.

Relativism is fashionable at the moment, and that may hamper you from thinking about taste, even as yours grows. But if you come out of the closet and admit, at least to yourself, that there is such a thing as good design, then you can start to study it in detail. How has your taste changed? When you made mistakes, what caused you to make them? What have other people learned about design?

Once you start to examine the question, it's surprising how much different fields' ideas of beauty have in common. The same principles of good design crop up again and again.

GOOD DESIGN IS SIMPLE. You hear this from math to painting. In math it means that a shorter proof tends to be a better one.

Where axioms are concerned, especially, less is more. It means much the same thing in programming. For architects and designers, it means that beauty should depend on a few carefully chosen structural elements rather than a profusion of superficial ornament. (Ornament is not in itself bad, only when it's camouflage on insipid form.) Similarly, in painting, a still life of a few carefully observed and solidly modelled objects will tend to be more interesting than a stretch of flashy but mindlessly repetitive painting of, say, a lace collar. In writing it means: say what you mean and say it briefly.

It seems strange to have to emphasize simplicity. You'd think simple would be the default. Ornate is more work. But something seems to come over people when they try to be creative. Beginning writers adopt a pompous tone that doesn't sound anything like the way they speak. Designers trying to be artistic resort to swooshes and curlicues. Painters discover that they're expressionists. It's all evasion. Underneath the long words or the "expressive" brush strokes, there's not much going on, and that's frightening.

When you're forced to be simple, you're forced to face the real problem. When you can't deliver ornament, you have to deliver substance.

GOOD DESIGN IS TIMELESS. In math, every proof is timeless unless it contains a mistake. So what does Hardy mean when he says there is no permanent place for ugly mathematics? He means the same thing Kelly Johnson did: if something is ugly, it can't be the best solution. There must be a better one, and eventually someone else will discover it.

Aiming at timelessness is a way to make yourself find the best answer: if you can imagine someone surpassing you, you should do it yourself. Some of the greatest masters did this so well that they left little room for those who came after. Every engraver since Dürer suffers by comparison.

Aiming at timelessness is also a way to evade the grip of fashion. Fashions almost by definition change with time, so if you can make something that will still look good far into the future, then its appeal must derive more from merit than fashion.

Strangely enough, if you want to make something that will appeal to future generations, one way to do it is to try to appeal to past generations. It's hard to guess what the future will be like, but we can be sure it will be like the past in caring nothing for present fashions. So if you can make something that appeals to people today and would also have appealed to people in 1500, there is a good chance it will appeal to people in 2500.

GOOD DESIGN SOLVES THE RIGHT PROBLEM. The typical stove has four burners arranged in a square, and a dial to control each. How do you arrange the dials? The simplest answer is to put them in a row. But this is a simple answer to the wrong question. The dials are for humans to use, and if you put them in a row, the unlucky human will have to stop and think each time about which dial matches which burner. Better to arrange the dials in a square like the burners.

A lot of bad design is industrious, but misguided. In the mid twentieth century there was a vogue for setting text in sans-serif fonts. These fonts are closer to the pure, underlying letterforms. But in text that's not the problem you're trying to solve. For legibility it's more important that letters be easy to tell apart. It may look Victorian, but a Times Roman lowercase g is easy to tell from a lowercase y.

Problems can be improved as well as solutions. In software, an intractable problem can usually be replaced by an equivalent one that's easy to solve. Physics progressed faster as the problem became predicting observable behavior, instead of reconciling it with scripture.

GOOD DESIGN IS SUGGESTIVE. Jane Austen's novels contain almost no description; instead of telling you how everything looks, she tells her story so well that you envision the scene for yourself.

1973 Porsche 911E.

Likewise, a painting that suggests is usually more engaging than one that tells. Everyone makes up their own story about the *Mona Lisa.*

In architecture and design, this principle means that a building or object should let you use it as you want: a good building, for example, will serve as a backdrop for whatever life people want to lead in it, instead of making them live as if they were executing a program written by the architect.

In software, it means you should give users a few basic elements that they can combine as they wish, like Lego. In math it means a proof that becomes the basis for a lot of new work is preferable to one that was difficult, but doesn't lead to future discoveries. In the sciences generally, citation is considered a rough indicator of merit.

GOOD DESIGN IS OFTEN SLIGHTLY FUNNY. This one may not always be true. But Dürer's engravings and Saarinen's Womb Chair and the Pantheon and the original Porsche 911 all seem to me slightly funny. Gödel's incompleteness theorem seems like a practical joke.

I think it's because humor is related to strength. To have a sense of humor is to be strong: to keep one's sense of humor is to shrug off misfortunes, and to lose one's sense of humor is to be wounded by them. And so the mark—or at least the prerogative—of strength is not to take oneself too seriously. The confident will often, like swallows, seem to be making fun of the whole process slightly, as Hitchcock does in his films or Bruegel in his paintings (or Shakespeare, for that matter).

Good design may not have to be funny, but it's hard to imagine something that could be called humorless also being good design.

GOOD DESIGN IS HARD. If you look at the people who've done great work, one thing they all seem to have in common is that they worked very hard. If you're not working hard, you're probably wasting your time.

Hard problems call for great efforts. In math, difficult proofs require ingenious solutions, and these tend to be interesting. Ditto in engineering.

When you have to climb a mountain you toss everything unnecessary out of your pack. And so an architect who has to build on a difficult site, or a small budget, will find that he's forced to produce an elegant design. Fashions and flourishes get knocked aside by the difficult business of solving the problem at all.

Not every kind of hard is good. There is good pain and bad pain. You want the kind of pain you get from going running, not the kind you get from stepping on a nail. A difficult problem could be good for a designer, but a fickle client or unreliable materials would not be.

In art, the highest place has traditionally been given to paintings of people. There's something to this tradition, and not just because pictures of faces press buttons in our brains that other pictures don't. We are so good at looking at faces that we force anyone who draws them to work hard to satisfy us. If you draw a tree and you change the angle of a branch five degrees, no one will know. When you change the angle of someone's eye five degrees, people notice.

When Bauhaus designers adopted Sullivan's "form follows function," what they meant was, form *should* follow function.[1] And if function is hard enough, form is forced to follow it, because there is no effort to spare for error. Wild animals are beautiful because they have hard lives.

GOOD DESIGN LOOKS EASY. Like great athletes, great designers make it look easy. Mostly this is an illusion. The easy, conversational tone of good writing comes only on the eighth rewrite.

In science and engineering, some of the greatest discoveries seem so simple that you say to yourself, I could have thought of that. The discoverer is entitled to reply, why didn't you?

Some Leonardo heads are just a few lines. You look at them and you think, all you have to do is get eight or ten lines in the right place and you've made this beautiful portrait. Well, yes, but you have to get them in *exactly* the right place. The slightest error will make the whole thing collapse.

Line drawings are in fact the most difficult visual medium, because they demand near perfection. In math terms, they are a closed-form solution; lesser artists literally solve the same problems by successive approximation. One of the reasons kids give up drawing at age ten or so is that they decide to start drawing like grownups, and one of the first things they try is a line drawing of a face.

In most fields the appearance of ease seems to come with practice. Perhaps what practice does is train your unconscious mind to handle tasks that used to require conscious thought. In some cases you literally train your body. An expert pianist can play notes faster than the brain can send signals to his hand. Likewise an artist, after a while, can make visual perception flow in through his eye and out through his hand as automatically as someone tapping his foot to a beat.

When people talk about being in "the zone," I think what they mean is that the spinal cord has the situation under control. Your spinal cord is less hesitant, and it frees conscious thought for the hard problems.

GOOD DESIGN USES SYMMETRY. Symmetry may just be one way to achieve simplicity, but it's important enough to be mentioned on its own. Nature uses it a lot, which is a good sign.

There are two kinds of symmetry, repetition and recursion. Recursion means repetition in subelements, like the pattern of veins in a leaf.

Symmetry is unfashionable in some fields now, in reaction to excesses in the past. Architects started consciously making buildings asymmetric in Victorian times, and by the 1920s asymmetry was an explicit premise of modernist architecture. Even these buildings only tended to be asymmetric about major axes, though; there were hundreds of minor symmetries.

In writing you find symmetry at every level, from the phrases in a sentence to the plot of a novel. You find the same in music and art. Mosaics (and some Cézannes) have extra visual punch because the whole picture is made out of the same atoms. Compositional symmetry yields some of the most memorable paintings, especially when two halves react to one another, as in the *Creation of Adam* or *American Gothic*.

In math and engineering, recursion, especially, is a big win. Inductive proofs are wonderfully short. In software, a problem that can be solved by recursion is nearly always best solved that way. The Eiffel Tower looks striking partly because it is a recursive solution, a tower on a tower.

The danger of symmetry, and repetition especially, is that it can be used as a substitute for thought.

GOOD DESIGN RESEMBLES NATURE. It's not so much that resembling nature is intrinsically good as that nature has had a long time

Eiffel Tower, 1889. A tower on a tower.

to work on the problem. So it's a good sign when your answer resembles nature's.

It's not cheating to copy. Few would deny that a story should be like life. Working from life is a valuable tool in painting too, though its role has often been misunderstood. The aim is not simply to make a record. The point of painting from life is that it gives your mind something to chew on: when your eyes are looking at something, your hand will do more interesting work.

Imitating nature also works in engineering. Boats have long had spines and ribs like an animal's ribcage. In other cases we may have to wait for better technology. Early aircraft designers were mistaken to design aircraft that looked like birds, because they didn't have materials or power sources light enough, or control systems sophisticated enough, for machines that flew like birds.[2] But I could imagine little unmanned reconnaissance planes flying like birds in fifty years.

Leonardo da Vinci, study of a rearing horse, 1481-99.

Now that we have enough computer power, we can imitate nature's method as well as its results. Genetic algorithms may let us create things too complex to design in the ordinary sense.

GOOD DESIGN IS REDESIGN. It's rare to get things right the first time. Experts expect to throw away some early work. They plan for plans to change.

It takes confidence to throw work away. You have to be able to think, *there's more where that came from.* When people first start drawing, for example, they're often reluctant to redo parts that aren't right. They feel they've been lucky to get that far, and if they try to redo something, it will turn out worse. Instead they convince themselves that the drawing is not that bad, really—in fact, maybe they meant it to look that way.

Dangerous territory, that. If anything, you should cultivate dissatisfaction. In Leonardo's drawings there are often five or six attempts to get a line right. The distinctive back of the Porsche 911 only appeared in the redesign of an awkward prototype. In Wright's early plans for the Guggenheim, the right half was a ziggurat; he inverted it to get the present shape.

Mistakes are natural. Instead of treating them as disasters, make them easy to acknowledge and easy to fix. Leonardo more or less invented the sketch, as a way to make drawing bear a greater weight of exploration. Open source software has fewer bugs because it admits the possibility of bugs.

It helps to have a medium that makes change easy. When oil paint replaced tempera in the fifteenth century, it helped painters to deal with difficult subjects like the human figure because, unlike tempera, oil can be blended and overpainted.

GOOD DESIGN CAN COPY. Attitudes to copying often make a round trip. A novice imitates without knowing it; next he tries consciously to be original; finally, he decides it's more important to be right than original.

Unknowing imitation is almost a recipe for bad design. If you don't know where your ideas are coming from, you're probably imitating an imitator. Raphael so pervaded mid-nineteenth century taste that almost anyone who tried to draw was imitating him, often at several removes. It was this, more than Raphael's own work, that bothered the Pre-Raphaelites.

The ambitious are not content to imitate. The second phase in the growth of taste is a conscious attempt at originality.

I think the greatest masters go on to achieve a kind of self-lessness. They just want to get the right answer, and if part of the right answer has already been discovered by someone else, that's no reason not to use it. They're confident enough to take from anyone without feeling that their own vision will be lost in the process.

Lockheed SR-71, 1964.

GOOD DESIGN IS OFTEN STRANGE. Some of the very best work has an uncanny quality: Euler's Formula, Bruegel's *Hunters in the Snow*, the SR-71, Lisp. They're not just beautiful, but strangely beautiful.

I'm not sure why. It may just be my own stupidity. A can-opener must seem miraculous to a dog. Maybe if I were smart enough it would seem the most natural thing in the world that $e^{i\pi} = -1$. It is after all necessarily true.

Most of the qualities I've mentioned are things that can be cultivated, but I don't think it works to cultivate strangeness. The best you can do is not squash it if it starts to appear. Einstein didn't try to make relativity strange. He tried to make it true, and the truth turned out to be strange.

At an art school where I once studied, the students wanted most of all to develop a personal style. But if you just try to make good things, you'll inevitably do it in a distinctive way, just as each person walks in a distinctive way. Michelangelo was not trying to paint like Michelangelo. He was just trying to paint well; he couldn't help painting like Michelangelo.

The only style worth having is the one you can't help. And this is especially true for strangeness. There is no shortcut to it. The Northwest Passage that the Mannerists, the Romantics, and two generations of American high school students have searched for

Bruegel's *Hunters in the Snow*, 1565.

does not seem to exist. The only way to get there is to go through good and come out the other side.

GOOD DESIGN HAPPENS IN CHUNKS. The inhabitants of fifteenth century Florence included Brunelleschi, Ghiberti, Donatello, Masaccio, Filippo Lippi, Fra Angelico, Verrocchio, Botticelli, Leonardo, and Michelangelo. Milan at the time was as big as Florence. How many fifteenth century Milanese artists can you name?

Something was happening in Florence in the fifteenth century. And it can't have been genetic, because it isn't happening now. You have to assume that whatever inborn ability Leonardo and Michelangelo had, there were people born in Milan with just as much. What happened to the Milanese Leonardo?

There are roughly a thousand times as many people alive in the US right now as lived in Florence during the fifteenth century. A thousand Leonardos and a thousand Michelangelos walk among us. If DNA ruled, we should be greeted daily by artistic marvels.

We aren't, and the reason is that to make Leonardo you need more than his innate ability. You also need Florence in 1450.

Nothing is more powerful than a community of talented people working on related problems. Genes count for little by comparison: being a genetic Leonardo was not enough to compensate for having been born near Milan instead of Florence. Today we move around more, but great work still comes disproportionately from a few hotspots: the Bauhaus, the Manhattan Project, *The New Yorker*, Lockheed's Skunk Works, Xerox Parc.

At any given time there are a few hot topics and a few groups doing great work on them, and it's nearly impossible to do good work yourself if you're too far removed from one of these centers. You can push or pull these trends to some extent, but you can't break away from them. (Maybe *you* can, but the Milanese Leonardo couldn't.)

GOOD DESIGN IS OFTEN DARING. At every period of history, people have believed things that were just ridiculous, and believed them so strongly that you risked ostracism or even violence by saying otherwise.

If our own time were any different, that would be remarkable. As far as I can tell it isn't.

This problem afflicts not just every era, but in some degree every field. Much Renaissance art was in its time considered shockingly secular: according to Vasari, Botticelli repented and gave up painting, and Fra Bartolommeo and Lorenzo di Credi actually burned some of their work. Einstein's theory of relativity offended many contemporary physicists, and was not fully accepted for decades—in France, not until the 1950s.[3]

Today's experimental error is tomorrow's new theory. If you want to discover great new things, then instead of turning a blind eye to the places where conventional wisdom and truth don't quite meet, you should pay particular attention to them.

In practice I think it's easier to see ugliness than to imagine beauty. Most of the people who've made beautiful things seem to have done it by fixing something they thought ugly. Great work usually seems to happen because someone sees something and thinks, *I could do better than that.* Giotto saw traditional Byzantine madonnas painted according to a formula that had satisfied everyone for centuries, and to him they looked wooden and unnatural. Copernicus was so troubled by a hack that all his contemporaries could tolerate that he felt there must be a better solution.

Intolerance for ugliness is not in itself enough. You have to understand a field well before you develop a good nose for what needs fixing. You have to do your homework. But as you become expert in a field, you'll start to hear little voices saying, *What a hack! There must be a better way.* Don't ignore those voices. Cultivate them. The recipe for great work is: very exacting taste, plus the ability to gratify it.

Chapter 10

Programming Languages Explained

ANY MACHINE HAS A LIST OF THINGS YOU CAN TELL IT TO DO. Sometimes the list is short. There are only two things I can do to my electronic kettle: turn it on and turn it off. My CD player is more complicated. As well as turning it on and off, I can turn the volume up and down, tell it to play or pause, move back or forward one song, and ask it to play songs in random order.

Like any other kind of machine, a computer has a list of things it can do. For example, every computer can be told to add two numbers. The complete list of things a computer can do is its *machine language*.

Machine Language

When computers were first invented, all programs had to be written as sequences of machine language instructions. Soon after, they started to be written in a slightly more convenient form called *assembly language*. In assembly language the list of commands is the same, but you get to use more programmer-friendly names. Instead of referring to the add instruction as 11001101, which is what the machine might call it, you get to say add.

The problem with machine/assembly language is that most computers can only do very simple things. For example, suppose you want to tell a computer to beep 10 times. There's not likely to be a machine instruction to do something *n* times. So if you wanted to tell a computer to do something 10 times using actual machine instructions, you'd have to say something equivalent to:

```
      put the number 10 in memory location 0
a     if location 0 is negative, go to line b
      beep
      subtract 1 from the number in location 0
      go to line a
b     ...rest of program...
```

If you have to do this much work to make the machine beep 10 times, imagine the labor of writing something like a word processor or a spreadsheet.

And by the way, take another look at the program. Will it actually beep ten times? Nope, eleven. In the first line I should have said 9 instead of 10. I deliberately put a bug in our example to illustrate an important point about languages. The more you have to say to get something done, the harder it is to see bugs.

High-Level Languages

Imagine you had to produce assembly language programs, but you had an assistant to do all the dirty work for you. So you could just write something like

```
dotimes 10 beep
```

and your assistant would write the assembly language for you (but without bugs).

In fact, this is how most programmers do work. Except the assistant isn't a person, but a *compiler*. A compiler is a program that translates programs written in a convenient form, like the one-liner above, into the simple-minded language that the hardware understands.

The more convenient language that you feed to the compiler is called a *high-level language*. It lets you build your programs out of powerful commands, like "do something *n* times" instead of wimpy ones like "add two numbers."

When you get to build your programs out of bigger concepts, you don't need to use as many of them. Written in our imaginary high-level language, our program is only a fifth as long. And if there were a mistake in it, it would be easy to see.

Another advantage of high-level languages is that they make your programs more *portable*. Different computers all have slightly different machine languages. You cannot, as a rule, take a machine language program written for one computer and run it on another. If you wrote your programs in machine language, you'd have to rewrite them all to run them on a new computer. If you use a high-level language, all you have to rewrite is the compiler.

Compilers aren't the only way to implement high-level languages. You could also use an *interpreter*, which examines your program one piece at a time and executes the corresponding machine language commands, instead of translating the whole thing into machine language and running that.

Open Source

The high-level language that you feed to the compiler is also known as *source code*, and the machine language translation it generates is called *object code*. When you buy commercial software, you usually only get the object code. (Object code is so hard to read that it is effectively encrypted, thus protecting the company's trade secrets.) But lately there is an alternative approach: *open source* software, where you get the source code as well, and are free to modify it if you want.

There is a real difference between the two models. Open source gives you a lot more control. When you're using open source software and you want to understand what it's doing, you can read the source code and find out. If you want, you can even change the software and recompile it.

One reason you might want to do that is to fix a bug. You can't fix bugs in Microsoft Windows, for example, because you don't have the source code. (In theory you could hack the object code, but in practice this is very hard. It's also probably forbidden by the license agreement.) This can be a real problem. When a new security hole is discovered in Windows, you have to wait for

Microsoft to release a fix. And security holes at least get fixed fast. If the bug merely paralyzes your computer occasionally, you may have to wait till the next full release for it to be fixed.

But the advantage of open source isn't just that you can fix it when you need to. It's that everyone can. Open source software is like a paper that has been subject to peer review. Lots of smart people have examined the source code of open source operating systems like Linux and FreeBSD and have already found most of the bugs. Whereas Windows is only as reliable as big-company QA can make it.

Open source advocates are sometimes seen as wackos who are against the idea of property in general. A few are. But I'm certainly not against the idea of property, and yet I would be very reluctant to install software I didn't have the source code for. The average end user may not need the source code of their word processor, but when you really need reliability, there are solid engineering reasons for insisting on open source.

Language Wars

Most programmers, most of the time, program in high-level languages. Few use assembly language now. Computer time has become much cheaper, while programmer time is as expensive as ever, so it's rarely worth the trouble of writing programs in assembly language. You might do it in a few critical parts of, say, a computer game, where you wanted to micromanage the hardware to squeeze out that last increment of speed.

Fortran, Lisp, Cobol, Basic, C, Pascal, Smalltalk, C++, Java, Perl, and Python are all high-level languages. Those are just some of the better known ones. There are literally hundreds of different high-level languages. And unlike machine languages, which all offer similar instruction sets, these high-level languages give you quite different concepts to build programs out of.

So which one do you use? Ah, well, there is a great deal of disagreement about that. Part of the problem is that if you use a language for long enough, you start to think in it. So any language that's substantially different feels terribly awkward, even if there's nothing intrinsically wrong with it. Inexperienced programmers' judgements about the relative merits of programming languages are often skewed by this effect.

Other hackers, perhaps from a desire to seem sophisticated, will tell you that all languages are basically the same. I've programmed in all kinds of languages, said the tough old hacker as he eased up to the bar, and it don't matter which you use. What matters is whether you have the right stuff. Or something along those lines.

This is nonsense, of course. There is a world of difference between, say, Fortran I and the latest version of Perl—or for that matter between early versions of Perl and the latest version of Perl. But the tough old hacker may himself believe what he's saying. It's possible to write the same primitive Pascal-like programs in almost every language. If you only ever eat at McDonald's, it will seem that food is much the same in every country.

Some hackers prefer the language they're used to, and dislike anything else. Others say that all languages are the same. The truth is somewhere between these two extremes. Languages do differ, but it's hard to say for certain which are best. The field is still evolving.

Abstractness

Just as high-level languages are more abstract than assembly language, some high-level languages are more abstract than others. For example, C is quite low-level, almost a portable assembly language, whereas Lisp is very high-level.

If high-level languages are better to program in than assembly language, then you might expect that the higher-level the language, the better. Ordinarily, yes, but not always. A language can be very abstract, but offer the wrong abstractions. I think this happens in Prolog, for example. It has fabulously powerful abstractions for solving about 2% of problems, and the rest of the time you're bending over backward to misuse these abstractions to write de facto Pascal programs.

Another reason you might want to use a lower-level language is efficiency. If you need code to be super fast, it's better to stay close to the machine. Most operating systems are written in C, and it is not a coincidence. As hardware gets faster, there is less pressure to write applications in languages as low-level as C, but everyone still seems to want operating systems to be as fast as possible. (Or maybe they want the prospect of buffer-overflow attacks to keep them on their toes.[1])

Seat Belts or Handcuffs?

The biggest debate in language design is probably the one between those who think that a language should prevent programmers from doing stupid things, and those who think programmers should be allowed to do whatever they want. Java is in the former camp, and Perl in the latter. (Not surprisingly, the DoD is big on Java.)

Partisans of permissive languages ridicule the other sort as "B&D" (bondage and discipline) languages, with the rather impudent implication that those who like to program in them are bottoms. I don't know what the other side call languages like Perl. Perhaps they are not the sort of people to make up amusing names for the opposition.

The debate resolves into several smaller ones, because there are several ways to prevent programmers from doing stupid things. One of the more active questions at the moment is *static* versus *dynamic typing*. In a statically-typed language, you have to know the kind of values each variable can have at the time you write the program. With dynamic typing, you can set any variable to any value, whenever you want.

Advocates of static typing argue that it helps to prevent bugs and helps compilers to generate fast code (both true). Advocates of dynamic typing argue that static typing restricts what programs you can write (also true). I prefer dynamic typing. I hate a language that tells me what to do. But some smart people seem to like static typing, so the question must still be an open one.

OO

Another big topic at the moment is *object-oriented* programming. It means a different way of organizing programs. Suppose you want to write a program to find the areas of two-dimensional figures. At first it only has to know about circles and squares. One way to do it would be to write a single piece of code, within which you test whether you're being asked about a circle or a square, and then use the corresponding formula to find the area. The object-oriented way to write this program would be to create two *classes*, circle and square, and then attach to each class a snippet of code (called a *method*) for finding the area of that type of figure. When you need to find the area of something, you ask what its class is, retrieve the corresponding method, and run that to get the answer.

These two cases may sound very similar, and indeed what actually *happens* when you run the code is much the same. (Not surprisingly, since you're solving the same problem.) But the code can end up looking quite different. In the object-oriented version, the code for finding the areas of squares and circles may even end up in different files, one part in the file containing all the stuff to do with circles, and the other in the file containing the stuff to do with squares.

The advantage of the object-oriented approach is that if you want to change the program to find the area of, say, triangles, you just add another chunk of code for them, and you don't even have to look at the rest. The disadvantage, critics would counter, is that adding things without looking at what was already there tends to produce the same results in programs that it does in buildings.

The debate about object-oriented programming is not as clear-cut as the one about static versus dynamic typing. With typing you have to choose one or the other. But the object-orientedness of a language is a matter of degree. Indeed, there are two senses of object-oriented: some languages are object-oriented in the sense that they let you program in that style, and others in the sense that they force you to.

I see little advantage in the latter. Surely a language that lets you do x is at least as good as one that forces you to. So as regards *languages*, at least, we can finesse this question. Sure, use a language that lets you write object-oriented programs. Whether you ever actually want to then becomes a separate question.

Renaissance

One thing I think everyone in the language business will agree on is that there are a lot of new programming languages lately. Until the 1980s, only institutions could afford the hardware needed to develop programming languages, and so most were designed by professors or researchers at large companies. Now a high school kid can afford all the hardware necessary.

Inspired largely by the example of Larry Wall, the designer of Perl, lots of hackers are thinking, why can't I design my own language? Those who manage to harness the power of the open source community can get a lot of code written for them very quickly.

The result is a kind of language you might call *top-heavy:* a language whose inner core is not very well designed, but which has enormously powerful libraries of code for solving specific problems. (Imagine a Yugo with a jet engine bolted to the roof.) For the little, everyday problems that programmers spend so much of their time solving, libraries are probably more important than the core language. And so these odd hybrids are quite useful, and become correspondingly popular. A Yugo with a jet engine bolted to the roof might actually work, as long as you didn't try to take a corner in it.[2]

Another result is a great deal of variety. There has always been a lot of variety in programming languages. Fortran, Lisp, and APL differ from one another as much as starfish, bears, and dragonflies, and all were designed before 1970. But the new open source languages have certainly continued this tradition.

I seem to hear about a new language every couple days. Jonathan Erickson has called it "the programming language renaissance." Another phrase people sometimes use is "the language wars." But there is no contradiction here. The Renaissance was full of wars.

Indeed, many historians believe that the wars were a byproduct of the forces that created the Renaissance.[3] The key to Europe's vigor may have been the fact that it was divided up into a number of small, competing states. These were close enough that ideas could travel from one to the other, but independent enough that no one ruler could put a lid on innovation—as the Chinese court disastrously did when they forbade the development of large ocean-going ships.

So it is probably all to the good that programmers live in a post-Babel world. If we were all using the same language, it would probably be the wrong one.

Chapter 11

The Hundred-Year Language

IT'S HARD TO PREDICT WHAT LIFE WILL BE LIKE IN A HUNDRED years. There are only a few things we can say with certainty. We know that everyone will drive flying cars, that zoning laws will be relaxed to allow buildings hundreds of stories tall, that it will be dark most of the time, and that women will all be trained in the martial arts. Here I want to zoom in on one detail of this picture. What kind of programming language will they use to write the software controlling those flying cars?

This is worth thinking about not so much because we'll actually get to use these languages as because, if we're lucky, we'll use languages on the path from this point to that.

I think that, like species, languages will form evolutionary trees, with dead-ends branching off all over. We can see this happening already. Cobol, for all its sometime popularity, does not seem to have any intellectual descendants. It is an evolutionary dead-end—a Neanderthal language.

I predict a similar fate for Java. People sometimes send me mail saying, "How can you say that Java won't turn out to be a successful language? It's already a successful language." And I admit that it is, if you measure success by shelf space taken up by books on it, or by the number of undergrads who believe they have to learn it to get a job. When I say Java won't turn out to be a successful language, I mean something more specific: that Java will turn out to be an evolutionary dead-end, like Cobol.

This is just a guess. I may be wrong. My point here is not to diss Java, but to raise the issue of evolutionary trees and get people asking, where on the tree is language x? The reason to ask this question isn't just so that in a hundred years our ghosts can say, I told you so. It's because staying close to the main branches is a useful heuristic for finding languages that will be good to program in now.

At any given time, you'll probably be happiest on the main branches of an evolutionary tree. Even when there were still plenty of Neanderthals, it must have sucked to be one. The Cro-Magnons would have been constantly coming over and beating you up and stealing your food.

The reason I want to know what languages will be like in a hundred years is so that I know which branch of the tree to bet on now.

The evolution of languages differs from the evolution of species because branches can converge. The Fortran branch, for example, seems to be merging with the descendants of Algol. In theory this is possible for species too, but it's so unlikely that it has probably never happened.

Convergence is more likely for languages partly because the space of possibilities is smaller, and partly because mutations are not random. Language designers deliberately incorporate ideas from other languages.

It's especially useful for language designers to think about where the evolution of programming languages is likely to lead, because they can steer accordingly. In that case, "stay on a main branch" becomes more than a way to choose a good language. It becomes a heuristic for making the right decisions about language design.

Any programming language can be divided into two parts: some set of fundamental operators that play the role of axioms, and the rest of the language, which could in principle be written in terms of these fundamental operators.

I think the fundamental operators are the most important factor in a language's long term survival. The rest you can change. It's like the rule that in buying a house you should consider location first of all. Everything else you can fix later, but you can't fix the location.

It's important not just that the axioms be well chosen, but that there be few of them. Mathematicians have always felt this way about axioms—the fewer, the better—and I think they're onto something.

At the very least, it has to be a useful exercise to look closely at the core of a language to see if there are any axioms that could be weeded out. I've found in my long career as a slob that cruft breeds cruft, and I've seen this happen in software as well as under beds and in the corners of rooms.

I have a hunch that the main branches of the evolutionary tree pass through the languages that have the smallest, cleanest cores. The more of a language you can write in itself, the better.

Of course, I'm making a big assumption in even asking what programming languages will be like in a hundred years. Will we even be writing programs in a hundred years? Won't we just tell computers what we want them to do?

There hasn't been a lot of progress in that department so far. My guess is that a hundred years from now people will still tell computers what to do using programs we would recognize as such. There may be tasks that we solve now by writing programs and that in a hundred years you won't have to write programs to solve, but I think there will still be a good deal of programming of the type we do today.

It may seem presumptuous to think that anyone can predict what any technology will look like in a hundred years. But remember that we already have almost fifty years of history behind us. Looking forward a hundred years is a graspable idea when we consider how slowly languages have evolved in the past fifty.

Languages evolve slowly because they're not really technologies. Languages are notation. A program is a formal description of the problem you want a computer to solve for you. So the rate of evolution in programming languages is more like the rate of evolution in mathematical notation than, say, transportation or communications. Mathematical notation does evolve, but not with the giant leaps you see in technology.

Whatever computers are made of in a hundred years, it seems safe to predict they will be much faster. If Moore's Law continues to put out, they will be 74 quintillion (73,786,976,294,838,206,464) times faster. That's kind of hard to imagine. And indeed, the most likely prediction in the speed department may be that Moore's Law will stop working. Anything that's supposed to double every eighteen months seems likely to run up against some kind of fundamental limit eventually. But I have no trouble believing that computers will be very much faster. Even if they only end up being a paltry million times faster, that should change the ground rules for programming languages substantially. Among other things, there will be more room for what would now be considered slow languages, meaning languages that don't yield very efficient code.

And yet some applications will still demand speed. Some of the problems we want to solve with computers are created by computers; for example, the rate at which you have to process video images depends on the rate at which another computer can generate them. And there is another class of problems that inherently have an unlimited capacity to soak up cycles: image rendering, cryptography, simulations.

If some applications can be increasingly inefficient while others continue to demand all the speed the hardware can deliver, faster computers will mean that languages have to cover an ever wider range of efficiencies. We've seen this happening already. Current implementations of some popular new languages are shockingly wasteful by the standards of previous decades.

This isn't just something that happens with programming languages. It's a general historical trend. As technologies improve, each generation can do things that the previous generation would have considered wasteful. People thirty years ago would be astonished at how casually we make long distance phone calls. People a hundred years ago would be even more astonished that a package would one day travel from Boston to New York via Memphis.

I can already tell you what's going to happen to all those extra cycles that faster hardware is going to give us in the next hundred years. They're nearly all going to be wasted.

I learned to program when computer power was scarce. I can remember taking all the spaces out of my Basic programs so they would fit into the memory of a 4K TRS-80. The thought of all this stupendously inefficient software burning up cycles doing the same thing over and over seems kind of gross to me. But I think my intuitions here are wrong. I'm like someone who grew up poor and can't bear to spend money even for something important, like going to the doctor.

Some kinds of waste really are disgusting. SUVs, for example, would arguably be gross even if they ran on a fuel that would never run out and generated no pollution. SUVs are gross because they're the solution to a gross problem. (How to make minivans look more masculine.) But not all waste is bad. Now that we have the infrastructure to support it, counting the minutes of your long-distance calls starts to seem niggling. If you have the resources, it's more elegant to think of all phone calls as one kind of thing, no matter where the other person is.

There's good waste, and bad waste. I'm interested in good waste—the kind where, by spending more, we can get simpler designs. How will we take advantage of the opportunities to waste cycles that we'll get from new, faster hardware?

The desire for speed is so deeply ingrained in us, with our puny computers, that it will take a conscious effort to overcome it. In language design, we should be consciously seeking out situations where we can trade efficiency for even the smallest increase in convenience.

Most data structures exist because of speed. For example, many languages today have both strings and lists. Semantically, strings are more or less a subset of lists in which the elements are characters. So why do you need a separate data type? You don't, really. Strings only exist for efficiency. But it's lame to clutter up the semantics of a language with hacks to make programs run faster. Having strings in a language seems to be a case of premature optimization.

If we think of the core of a language as a set of axioms, surely it's gross to have additional axioms that add no expressive power, simply for the sake of efficiency. Efficiency is important, but I don't think that's the right way to get it.

The right way to solve that problem is to separate the meaning of a program from the implementation details. Instead of having both lists and strings, have just lists, with some way to give the compiler optimization advice that will allow it to lay out strings as contiguous bytes if necessary.[1]

Since speed doesn't matter in most of a program, you won't ordinarily need to bother with this sort of micromanagement. This will be more and more true as computers get faster.

Saying less about implementation should also make programs more flexible. Specifications change while a program is being written, and this is not only inevitable, but desirable.

The word "essay" comes from the French verb "essayer," which means "to try." An essay, in the original sense, is something you write to try to figure something out. This happens in software too. I think some of the best programs were essays, in the sense that the authors didn't know when they started exactly what they were trying to write.

Lisp hackers already know about the value of being flexible with data structures. We tend to write the first version of a program so that it does everything with lists. These initial versions can be so shockingly inefficient that it takes a conscious effort not to think about what they're doing, just as, for me at least, eating a steak requires a conscious effort not to think where it came from.

What programmers in a hundred years will be looking for, most of all, is a language where you can throw together an unbelievably inefficient version 1 of a program with the least possible effort. At least, that's how we'd describe it in present-day terms. What they'll say is that they want a language that's easy to program in.

Inefficient software isn't gross. What's gross is a language that makes programmers do needless work. Wasting programmer time is the true inefficiency, not wasting machine time. This will become ever more clear as computers get faster.

I think getting rid of strings is already something we could bear to think about. We did it in Arc, and it seems to be a win; some operations that would be awkward to describe as regular expressions can be described easily as recursive functions.

How far will this flattening of data structures go? I can think of possibilities that shock even me, with my conscientiously broadened mind. Will we get rid of arrays, for example? After all, they're just a subset of hash tables where the keys are vectors of integers. Will we replace hash tables themselves with lists?

There are more shocking prospects even than that. Logically, you don't need to have a separate notion of numbers, because you can represent them as lists: the integer n could be represented as a list of n elements. You can do math this way. It's just unbearably inefficient.

Could a programming language go so far as to get rid of numbers as a fundamental data type? I ask this less as a serious question than as a way to play chicken with the future. It's like the hypothetical case of an irresistible force meeting an immovable object—here, an unimaginably inefficient implementation meeting unimaginably great resources. I don't see why not. The future is pretty long. If there's something we can do to decrease the number of axioms in the core language, that would seem the side to bet on as t approaches infinity. If the idea still seems unbearable in a hundred years, maybe it won't in a thousand.

Just to be clear about this, I'm not proposing that all numerical calculations would actually be carried out using lists. I'm proposing that the core language, prior to any additional notations about implementation, be defined this way. In practice any program that wanted to do any amount of math would probably represent numbers in binary, but this would be an optimization, not part of the core language semantics.

Another way to burn up cycles is to have many layers of software between the application and the hardware. This too is a trend we see happening already: many recent languages are compiled into byte code. Bill Woods once told me that, as a rule of thumb, each layer of interpretation costs a factor of ten in speed. This extra cost buys you flexibility.

The very first version of Arc was an extreme case of this sort of multi-level slowness, with corresponding benefits. It was a classic "metacircular" interpreter written on top of Common Lisp, with a definite family resemblance to the *eval* function defined in McCarthy's original Lisp paper. The whole thing was only a couple hundred lines of code, so it was easy to understand and change. The Common Lisp we used, CLisp, itself runs on top of a byte code interpreter. So here we had two levels of interpretation, one of them (the top one) shockingly inefficient, and the language was usable. Barely usable, I admit, but usable.

Writing software as multiple layers is a powerful technique even within applications. Bottom-up programming means writing a program as a series of layers, each of which serves as a language for the one above. This approach tends to yield smaller, more flexible programs. It's also the best route to that holy grail, reusability. A language is by definition reusable. The more of your application you can push down into a language for writing that type of application, the more of your software will be reusable.

Somehow the idea of reusability got attached to object-oriented programming in the 1980s, and no amount of evidence to the contrary seems to be able to shake it free. But although some object-oriented software is reusable, what makes it reusable is its bottom-upness, not its object-orientedness. Consider libraries: they're reusable because they're language, whether they're written in an object-oriented style or not.

I don't predict the demise of object-oriented programming, by the way. Though I don't think it has much to offer good programmers, except in certain specialized domains, it is irresistible to large organizations. Object-oriented programming offers a sustainable way to write spaghetti code. It lets you accrete programs as a series of patches. Large organizations always tend to develop software this way, and I expect this to be as true in a hundred years as it is today.

As long as we're talking about the future, we had better talk about parallel computation, because that's where this idea seems to live. At any given time, it always seems to be something that's going to happen in the future.

Will the future ever catch up with it? People have been talking about parallel computation as something imminent for at least twenty years, and it hasn't affected programming practice much so far. Or hasn't it? Already chip designers have to think about it, and so must people trying to write systems software on multi-CPU computers.

The real question is, how far up the ladder of abstraction will parallelism go? In a hundred years will it affect even application programmers? Or will it be something that compiler writers think about, but which is usually invisible in the source code of applications?

One thing that does seem likely is that most opportunities for parallelism will be wasted. This is a special case of my more general prediction that most of the extra computer power we're given will go to waste. I expect that, as with the stupendous speed of the underlying hardware, parallelism will be something that is available if you ask for it explicitly, but ordinarily not used. This implies that the kind of parallelism we have in a hundred years will not, except in special applications, be massive parallelism. I expect for ordinary programmers it will be more like being able to fork off processes that all end up running in parallel.

And this will, like asking for specific implementations of data structures, be something that you do fairly late in the life of a program, when you try to optimize it. Version 1s will ordinarily ignore any advantages to be got from parallel computation, just as they will ignore advantages to be got from specific representations of data.

Except in special kinds of applications, parallelism won't pervade the programs that are written in a hundred years. It would be premature optimization if it did.

How many programming languages will there be in a hundred years? There seem to be a huge number of new programming languages lately. Part of the reason is that faster hardware has allowed programmers to make different tradeoffs between speed and convenience, depending on the application. If this is a real trend, the hardware we'll have in a hundred years should only increase it.

And yet there may be only a few widely used languages in a hundred years. Part of the reason I say this is optimism: it seems that, if you did a really good job, you could make a language that was ideal for writing a slow version 1, and yet with the right optimization advice to the compiler would also yield fast code when necessary. So, since I'm optimistic, I'm going to predict that despite the huge gap they'll have between acceptable and maximal efficiency, programmers in a hundred years will have languages that can span most of it.

As this gap widens, profilers will become increasingly important. Little attention is paid to profiling now. Many people still seem to believe that the way to get fast applications is to write compilers that generate fast code. As the gap between acceptable and maximal performance widens, it will become increasingly clear that the way to get fast applications is to have a good guide from one to the other.

When I say there may only be a few languages, I'm not including domain-specific "little languages." I think such embedded languages are a great idea, and I expect them to proliferate. But I expect them to be written as thin enough skins that users can see the general-purpose language underneath.

Who will design the languages of the future? One of the most exciting trends in the last ten years has been the rise of open source languages like Perl, Python, and Ruby. Language design is being taken over by hackers. The results so far are messy, but encouraging. There are some stunningly novel ideas in Perl, for example. Many are stunningly bad, but that's always true of ambitious efforts. At its current rate of mutation, God knows what Perl might evolve into in a hundred years.

It's not true that those who can't do, teach (some of the best hackers I know are professors), but it is true that there are a lot of things that those who teach can't do. Research imposes constraining caste restrictions. In any academic field, there are topics that are ok to work on and others that aren't. Unfortunately the distinction between acceptable and forbidden topics is usually based on how intellectual the work sounds when described in research papers, rather than how important it is for getting good results. The extreme case is probably literature; people studying literature rarely say anything that would be of the slightest use to those producing it.

Though the situation is better in the sciences, the overlap between the kind of work you're allowed to do and the kind of work that yields good languages is distressingly small. (Olin Shivers has grumbled eloquently about this.) For example, types seem to be an inexhaustible source of research papers, despite the fact that static typing seems to preclude true macros—without which, in my opinion, no language is worth using.

The trend is not merely toward languages being developed as open source projects rather than "research," but toward languages being designed by the application programmers who need to use them, rather than by compiler writers. This seems a good trend and I expect it to continue.

Unlike physics in a hundred years, which is almost necessarily impossible to predict, it may be possible in principle to design a language now that would appeal to users in a hundred years.

One way to design a language is to just write down the program you'd like to be able to write, regardless of whether there is a compiler that can translate it or hardware that can run it. When you do this you can assume unlimited resources. It seems like we ought to be able to imagine unlimited resources as well today as in a hundred years.

What program would one like to write? Whatever is least work. Except not quite: whatever *would* be least work if your ideas about programming weren't already influenced by the languages you're currently used to. Such influence can be so pervasive that it takes a great effort to overcome it. You'd think it would be obvious to creatures as lazy as us how to express a program with the least effort. In fact, our ideas about what's possible tend to be so limited by whatever language we think in that easier formulations of programs seem very surprising. They're something you have to discover, not something you naturally sink into.

One helpful trick here is to use the length of the program as an approximation for how much work it is to write. Not the length in characters, of course, but the length in distinct syntactic elements—basically, the size of the parse tree. It may not be quite true that the shortest program is the least work to write, but it's close enough that you're better off aiming for the solid target of brevity than the fuzzy, nearby one of least work. Then the algorithm for language design becomes: look at a program and ask, is there a shorter way to write this?

In practice, writing programs in an imaginary hundred-year language will work to varying degrees depending on how close you are to the core. Sort routines you can write now. But it would be hard to predict now what kinds of libraries might be needed in a hundred years. Presumably many libraries will be for domains that don't even exist yet. If SETI@home works, for example, we'll need libraries for communicating with aliens. Unless of course they are sufficiently advanced that they already communicate in XML.

At the other extreme, I think you might be able to design the core language today. In fact, some might argue that it was already mostly designed in 1958.

If the hundred-year language were available today, would we want to program in it? One way to answer this question is to look back. If present-day programming languages had been available in 1960, would anyone have wanted to use them?

In some ways, the answer is no. Languages today assume infrastructure that didn't exist in 1960. For example, a language in which indentation is significant, like Python, would not work very well on printer terminals. But putting such problems aside—assuming, for example, that programs were all just written on paper—would programmers of the 1960s have liked writing programs in the languages we use now?

I think so. Some of the less imaginative ones, who had artifacts of early languages built into their ideas of what a program was, might have had trouble. (How can you manipulate data without doing pointer arithmetic? How can you implement flowcharts without gotos?) But I think the smartest programmers would have had no trouble making the most of present-day languages, if they'd had them.

If we had the hundred-year language now, it would at least make a great pseudocode. What about using it to write software? Since the hundred-year language will need to generate fast code for some applications, presumably it could generate code efficient enough to run acceptably well on our hardware. We might have to give more optimization advice than users in a hundred years, but it still might be a net win.

Now we have two ideas that, if you combine them, suggest interesting possibilities: (1) the hundred-year language could, in principle, be designed today, and (2) such a language, if it existed, might be good to program in today. When you see these ideas laid out like that, it's hard not to think, why not try writing the hundred-year language now?

When you're working on language design, I think it's good to have such a target and to keep it consciously in mind. When you learn to drive, one of the principles they teach you is to align the car not by lining up the hood with the stripes painted on the road, but by aiming at some point in the distance. Even if all you care about is what happens in the next ten feet, this is the right answer. I think we should do the same thing with programming languages.

Chapter 12

Beating the Averages

IN 1995 ROBERT MORRIS AND I STARTED A STARTUP CALLED Viaweb. Our plan was to write software that would let end users build online stores. What was novel about this software, at the time, was that it ran on our server, using ordinary Web pages as the interface.

A lot of people could have been having this idea at the same time, of course, but as far as I know, Viaweb was the first Web-based application. It seemed such a novel idea to us that we named the company after it: Viaweb, because our software worked via the Web, instead of running on your desktop computer.

Another unusual thing about this software was that it was written primarily in a programming language called Lisp.[1] It was one of the first big end-user applications to be written in Lisp, which up till then had been used mostly in universities and research labs.

The Secret Weapon

Eric Raymond has written an essay called "How to Become a Hacker," and in it, among other things, he tells would-be hackers what languages they should learn. He suggests starting with Python and Java, because they are easy to learn. The serious hacker will also want to learn C, in order to hack Unix, and Perl for system administration and CGI scripts. Finally, the truly serious hacker should consider learning Lisp:

> Lisp is worth learning for the profound enlightenment experience you will have when you finally get it; that experience will make you a better programmer for the rest of your days, even if you never actually use Lisp itself a lot.

This is the same argument you tend to hear for learning Latin. It won't get you a job, except perhaps as a classics professor, but it will improve your mind, and make you a better writer in languages you do want to use, like English.

But wait a minute. This metaphor doesn't stretch that far. The reason Latin won't get you a job is that no one speaks it. If you write in Latin, no one can understand you. But Lisp is a computer language, and computers speak whatever language you, the programmer, tell them to.

So if Lisp makes you a better programmer, like he says, why wouldn't you want to use it? If a painter were offered a brush that would make him a better painter, it seems to me that he would want to use it in all his paintings, wouldn't he? I'm not trying to make fun of Eric Raymond here. On the whole, his advice is good. What he says about Lisp is pretty much the conventional wisdom. But there is a contradiction in the conventional wisdom: Lisp will make you a better programmer, and yet you won't use it.

Why not? Programming languages are just tools, after all. If Lisp really does yield better programs, you should use it. And if it doesn't, then who needs it?

This is not just a theoretical question. Software is a very competitive business, prone to natural monopolies. A company that gets software written faster and better will, all other things being equal, put its competitors out of business. And when you're starting a startup, you feel this keenly. Startups tend to be an all-or-nothing proposition. You either get rich, or you get nothing. In a startup, if you bet on the wrong technology, your competitors will crush you.

Robert and I both knew Lisp well, and we couldn't see any reason not to trust our instincts and use it. We knew that everyone else was writing their software in C++ or Perl. But we also knew that that didn't mean anything. If you chose technology that way, you'd be running Windows. When you choose technology, you have to ignore what other people are doing, and consider only what will work best.

With Robert Morris, Viaweb, early 1996.

This is especially true in a startup. In a big company, you can do what all the other big companies are doing. But a startup can't do what all the other startups do. I don't think a lot of people realize this, even in startups.

The average big company grows at about ten percent a year. So if you're running a big company and you do everything the way the average big company does it, you can expect to do as well as the average big company—that is, to grow about ten percent a year.

The same thing will happen if you're running a startup, of course. If you do everything the way the average startup does it, you should expect average performance. The problem here is, average performance means you'll go out of business. The survival rate for startups is way less than fifty percent. So if you're running a startup, you had better be doing something odd. If not, you're in trouble.

Back in 1995, we knew something that I don't think our competitors understood, and few understand even now: when you're writing software that only has to run on your own servers, you can use any language you want. When you're writing desktop software, there's a strong bias toward writing applications in the same language as the operating system. Ten years ago, writing applications meant writing applications in C. But with Web-based software, especially when you have the source code of both the language and the operating system, you can use whatever language you want.

This new freedom is a double-edged sword, however. Now that you can use any language, you have to think about which one to use. Companies that try to pretend nothing has changed risk finding that their competitors do not.

If you can use any language, which do you use? We chose Lisp. For one thing, it was obvious that rapid development would be important in this market. We were all starting from scratch, so a company that could get new features done before its competitors would have a big advantage. We knew Lisp was a really good language for writing software quickly, and server-based applications magnify the effect of rapid development, because you can release software the minute it's done.

If other companies didn't want to use Lisp, so much the better. It might give us a technological edge, and we needed all the help we could get. When we started Viaweb, we had no experience in business. We didn't know anything about marketing, or hiring people, or raising money, or getting customers. Neither of us had ever even had what you would call a real job. The only thing we were good at was writing software. We hoped that would save us. Any advantage we could get in the software department, we would take.

So you could say that using Lisp was an experiment. Our hypothesis was that if we wrote our software in Lisp, we'd be able to get features done faster than our competitors, and also to do things in our software that they couldn't do. And because Lisp was so high-level, we wouldn't need a big development team, so our costs would be lower. If this were so, we could offer a better product for less money, and still make a profit. We would end up getting all the users, and our competitors would get none, and eventually go out of business. That was what we hoped would happen, anyway.

What were the results of this experiment? Somewhat surprisingly, it worked. We eventually had many competitors, about twenty to thirty of them, but none of their software could compete with ours. We had a wysiwyg online store builder that ran on the server and yet felt like a desktop application. Our competitors had CGI scripts. And we were always far ahead of them in features. Sometimes, in desperation, competitors would try to introduce features that we didn't have. But with Lisp our development cycle was so fast that we could sometimes duplicate a new feature within a day or two of a competitor announcing it in a press release. By the time journalists covering the press release got round to calling us, we would have the new feature too.

It must have seemed to our competitors that we had some kind of secret weapon—that we were decoding their Enigma traffic or something. In fact we did have a secret weapon, but it was simpler than they realized. No one was leaking news of their features to us. We were just able to develop software faster than anyone thought possible.

When I was about nine I happened to get hold of a copy of *The Day of the Jackal*, by Frederick Forsyth. The main character is an assassin who is hired to kill the president of France. The assassin has to get past the police to get up to an apartment that overlooks the president's route. He walks right by them, dressed up as an old man on crutches, and they never suspect him.

Our secret weapon was similar. We wrote our software in a weird AI language, with a bizarre syntax full of parentheses. For years it had annoyed me to hear Lisp described that way. But now it worked to our advantage. In business, there is nothing more valuable than a technical advantage your competitors don't understand. In business, as in war, surprise is worth as much as force.

And so, I'm a little embarrassed to say, I never said anything publicly about Lisp while we were working on Viaweb. We never mentioned it to the press, and if you searched for Lisp on our web site, all you'd find were the titles of two books in my bio. This was no accident. A startup should give its competitors as little information as possible. If they didn't know what language our software was written in, or didn't care, I wanted to keep it that way.[2]

The people who understood our technology best were the customers. They didn't care what language Viaweb was written in either, but they noticed that it worked really well. It let them build great looking online stores literally in minutes. And so, by word of mouth mostly, we got more and more users. By the end of 1996 we had about 70 stores online. At the end of 1997 we had 500. Six months later, when Yahoo bought us, we had 1070 users. Today, as Yahoo Store, this software continues to dominate its market. It's one of the more profitable pieces of Yahoo, and the stores built with it are the foundation of Yahoo Shopping. I left Yahoo in 1999, so I don't know exactly how many users they have now, but the last I heard there were over 20,000.

The Blub Paradox

What's so great about Lisp? And if Lisp is so great, why doesn't everyone use it? These sound like rhetorical questions, but actually they have straightforward answers. Lisp is so great not because of some magic quality visible only to devotees, but because it is simply the most powerful language available. And the reason everyone doesn't use it is that programming languages are not merely technologies, but habits of mind as well, and nothing changes slower. Of course, both these answers need explaining.

I'll begin with a shockingly controversial statement: programming languages vary in power.

Few would dispute, at least, that high-level languages are more powerful than machine language. Most programmers today would agree that you do not, ordinarily, want to program in machine language. Instead, you should program in a high-level language, and have a compiler translate it into machine language for you. This idea is even built into the hardware now: since the 1980s, instruction sets have been designed for compilers rather than human programmers.

Everyone knows it's a mistake to write your whole program by hand in machine language. What's less often understood is that there is a more general principle here: that if you have a choice of several languages, it is, all other things being equal, a mistake to program in anything but the most powerful one.[3]

There are many exceptions to this rule. If you're writing a program that has to work closely with a program written in a certain language, it might be a good idea to write the new program in the same language. If you're writing a program that only has to do something simple, like number crunching or bit manipulation, you may as well use a less abstract language, especially since it may be slightly faster. And if you're writing a short, throwaway program, you may be better off just using whatever language has the best libraries for the task. But in general, for application software, you want to be using the most powerful (reasonably efficient) language you can get, and using anything else is a mistake, of exactly the same kind, though possibly in a lesser degree, as programming in machine language.

You can *see* that machine language is very low-level. But, at least as a kind of social convention, high-level languages are often all treated as equivalent. They're not. Technically the term "high-level language" doesn't mean anything very definite. There's no dividing line with machine languages on one side and all the high-level languages on the other. Languages fall along a continuum of abstractness,[4] from the most powerful all the way down to machine languages, which themselves vary in power.

Consider Cobol. Cobol is a high-level language, in the sense that it gets compiled into machine language. Would anyone seriously argue that Cobol is equivalent in power to, say, Python? It's probably closer to machine language than Python.

Or how about Perl 4? Between Perl 4 and Perl 5, lexical closures got added to the language. Most Perl hackers would agree that Perl 5 is more powerful than Perl 4. But once you've admitted that, you've admitted that one high-level language can be more powerful than another. And it follows inexorably that, except in special cases, you ought to use the most powerful you can get.

This idea is rarely followed to its conclusion, though. After a certain age, programmers rarely switch languages voluntarily. Whatever language people happen to be used to, they tend to consider just good enough.

Programmers get very attached to their favorite languages, and I don't want to hurt anyone's feelings, so to explain this point I'm going to use a hypothetical language called Blub. Blub falls right in the middle of the abstractness continuum. It is not the most powerful language, but it is more powerful than Cobol or machine language.

And in fact, our hypothetical Blub programmer wouldn't use either of them. Of course he wouldn't program in machine language. That's what compilers are for. And as for Cobol, he doesn't know how anyone can get anything done with it. It doesn't even have x (Blub feature of your choice).

As long as our hypothetical Blub programmer is looking down the power continuum, he knows he's looking down. Languages less powerful than Blub are obviously less powerful, because they are missing some feature he's used to. But when our hypothetical Blub programmer looks in the other direction, up the power continuum, he doesn't realize he's looking up. What he sees are merely *weird* languages. He probably considers them about equivalent in power to Blub, but with all this other hairy stuff thrown in as well. Blub is good enough for him, because he thinks in Blub.

When we switch to the point of view of a programmer using any of the languages higher up the power continuum, however, we find that he in turn looks down upon Blub. How can you get anything done in Blub? It doesn't even have y.

By induction, the only programmers in a position to see all the differences in power between the various languages are those who understand the most powerful one. (This is probably what Eric Raymond meant about Lisp making you a better programmer.) You can't trust the opinions of the others, because of the Blub paradox: they're satisfied with whatever language they happen to use, because it dictates the way they think about programs.

I know this from my own experience, as a high school kid writing programs in Basic. That language didn't even support recursion. It's hard to imagine writing programs without using recursion, but I didn't miss it at the time. I thought in Basic. And I was a whiz at it. Master of all I surveyed.

The five languages that Eric Raymond recommends to hackers fall at various points on the power continuum. Where they fall relative to one another is a sensitive topic. What I will say is that I think Lisp is at the top. And to support this claim I'll tell you about one of the things I find missing when I look at the other four languages. How can you get anything done in them, I think, without macros?[5]

Many languages have something called a macro. But Lisp macros are unique. And believe it or not, what they do is related to the parentheses. The designers of Lisp didn't put all those parentheses in the language just to be different. To the Blub programmer, Lisp code looks weird. But those parentheses are there for a reason. They are the outward evidence of a fundamental difference between Lisp and other languages.

Lisp code is made out of Lisp data objects. And not in the trivial sense that the source files contain characters, and strings are one of the data types supported by the language. Lisp code, after it's read by the parser, is made of data structures that you can traverse.

If you understand how compilers work, what's really going on is not so much that Lisp has a strange syntax as that Lisp has no syntax. You write programs in the parse trees that get generated within the compiler when other languages are parsed. But these parse trees are fully accessible to your programs. You can write programs that manipulate them. In Lisp, these programs are called macros. They are programs that write programs.

Programs that write programs? When would you ever want to do that? Not very often, if you think in Cobol. All the time, if you think in Lisp. It would be convenient here if I could give an example of a powerful macro, and say, there! how about that? But if I did, it would just look like gibberish to someone who didn't know Lisp; there isn't room here to explain everything you'd need to know to understand what it meant. In *Ansi Common Lisp* I tried to move things along as fast as I could, and even so I didn't get to macros until page 160.

But I think I can give a kind of argument that might be convincing. The source code of the Viaweb editor was probably about 20-25% macros. Macros are harder to write than ordinary Lisp functions, and it's bad style to use them when they're not necessary. So every macro in that code is there because it has to be. What that means is that at least 20-25% of the code in this program is doing things that you can't easily do in any other language. However skeptical the Blub programmer might be about my claims for the mysterious powers of Lisp, this ought to make him curious. We weren't writing this code for our own amusement. We were a tiny startup, programming as hard as we could in order to put technical barriers between us and our competitors.

A suspicious person might begin to wonder if there was some correlation here. A big chunk of our code was doing things that are hard to do in other languages. The resulting software did things our competitors' software couldn't do. Maybe there was some kind of connection. I encourage you to follow that thread. There may be more to that old man hobbling along on his crutches than meets the eye.

Aikido for Startups

But I don't expect to convince anyone (over 25) to go out and learn Lisp. My purpose here is not to change anyone's mind, but to reassure people already interested in using Lisp—people who know that Lisp is a powerful language, but worry because it isn't widely used. In a competitive situation, that's an advantage. Lisp's power is multiplied by the fact that your competitors don't get it.

If you think of using Lisp in a startup, you shouldn't worry that it isn't widely understood. You should hope that it stays that way. And it's likely to. It's the nature of programming languages to make most people satisfied with whatever they currently use.

Computer hardware changes so much faster than personal habits that programming practice is usually ten to twenty years behind the processor. At places like MIT they were writing programs in high-level languages in the early 1960s, but many companies continued to write code in machine language well into the 1980s. I bet a lot of people continued to write machine language until the processor, like a bartender eager to close up and go home, finally kicked them out by switching to a RISC instruction set.

Ordinarily technology changes fast. But programming languages are different: programming languages are not just technology, but what programmers think in. They're half technology and half religion.[6] And so the median language, meaning whatever language the median programmer uses, moves as slow as an iceberg. Garbage collection, introduced by Lisp in about 1960, is now widely considered to be a good thing. Dynamic typing, ditto, is growing in popularity. Lexical closures, introduced by Lisp in the early 1960s, are now, just barely, on the radar screen. Macros, introduced by Lisp in the mid 1960s, are still terra incognita.

Obviously, the median language has enormous momentum. I'm not proposing that you can fight this powerful force. What I'm proposing is exactly the opposite: that, like a practitioner of Aikido, you can use it against your opponents.

If you work for a big company, this may not be easy. You will have a hard time convincing the pointy-haired boss to let you build things in Lisp, when he has just read in the paper that some other language is poised, like Ada was twenty years ago, to take over the world. But if you work for a startup that doesn't have pointy-haired bosses yet, you can, like we did, turn the Blub paradox to your advantage: you can use technology that your competitors, glued immovably to the median language, will never be able to match.

If you ever do find yourself working for a startup, here's a handy tip for evaluating competitors. Read their job listings. Everything else on their site may be stock photos or the prose equivalent, but the job listings have to be specific about what they want, or they'll get the wrong candidates.

During the years we worked on Viaweb I read a lot of job descriptions. A new competitor seemed to emerge out of the woodwork every month or so. The first thing I would do, after checking to see if they had a live online demo, was look at their job listings. After a couple years of this I could tell which companies to worry about and which not to. The more of an IT flavor the job descriptions had, the less dangerous the company was. The safest kind were the ones that wanted Oracle experience. You never had to worry about those. You were also safe if they said they wanted C++ or Java developers. If they wanted Perl or Python programmers, that would be a bit frightening—that's starting to sound like a company where the technical side, at least, is run by real hackers. If I had ever seen a job posting looking for Lisp hackers, I would have been really worried.

Chapter 13

Revenge of the Nerds

IN THE SOFTWARE BUSINESS THERE IS AN ONGOING STRUGGLE between the pointy-headed academics, and another equally formidable force, the pointy-haired bosses. I believe everyone knows who the pointy-haired boss is.[1] I think most people in the technology world not only recognize this cartoon character, but know the actual person in their company that he is modelled upon.

The pointy-haired boss miraculously combines two qualities that are common by themselves, but rarely seen together: (a) he knows nothing whatsoever about technology, and (b) he has very strong opinions about it.

Suppose, for example, you need to write a piece of software. The pointy-haired boss has no idea how this software has to work and can't tell one programming language from another, and yet he knows what language you should write it in. Exactly. He thinks you should write it in Java.

Why does he think this? Let's take a look inside the brain of the pointy-haired boss. What he's thinking is something like this. Java is a standard. I know it must be, because I read about it in the press all the time. Since it is a standard, I won't get in trouble for using it. And that also means there will always be lots of Java programmers, so if those working for me now quit, as programmers working for me mysteriously always do, I can easily replace them.

Well, this doesn't sound that unreasonable. But it's all based on one unspoken assumption, and that assumption turns out to be false. The pointy-haired boss believes that all programming languages are pretty much equivalent. If that were true, he would be right on target. If languages are all equivalent, sure, use whatever language everyone else is using.

But all languages are not equivalent, and I think I can prove this to you without even getting into the differences between them. If you asked the pointy-haired boss in 1992 what language software should be written in, he would have answered with as little hesitation as he does today. Software should be written in C++. But if languages are all equivalent, why should the pointy-haired boss's opinion ever change? In fact, why should the developers of Java have even bothered to create a new language?

Presumably, if you create a new language, it's because you think it's better in some way than what people already had. And in fact, Gosling makes it clear in the first Java white paper that Java was designed to fix some problems with C++. So there you have it: languages are not all equivalent. If you follow the trail through the pointy-haired boss's brain to Java and then back through Java's history to its origins, you end up holding an idea that contradicts the assumption you started with.

So, who's right? James Gosling, or the pointy-haired boss? Not surprisingly, Gosling is right. Some languages *are* better, for certain problems, than others. And you know, that raises some interesting questions. Java was designed to be better, for certain problems, than C++. What problems? When is Java better and when is C++? Are there situations where other languages are better than either of them?

Once you start considering this question, you've opened a real can of worms. If the pointy-haired boss had to think about the problem in its full complexity, it would make his head explode. As long as he considers all languages equivalent, all he has to do is choose the one that seems to have the most momentum, and since that's more a question of fashion than technology, even he can probably get the right answer. But if languages vary, he suddenly has to solve two simultaneous equations, trying to find an optimal balance between two things he knows nothing about: the relative suitability of the twenty or so leading languages for the problem he needs to solve, and the odds of finding programmers, libraries, etc. for each. If that's what's on the other side of the door, it is no surprise that the pointy-haired boss doesn't want to open it.

The disadvantage of believing that all programming languages are equivalent is that it's not true. But the advantage is that it makes your life a lot simpler. And I think that's the main reason the idea is so widespread. It is a *comfortable* idea.

We know that Java must be pretty good, because it is the cool, new programming language. Or is it? If you look at the world of programming languages from a distance, it looks like Java is the latest thing. (From far enough away, all you can see is the large, flashing billboard paid for by Sun.) But if you look at this world up close, you find there are degrees of coolness. Within the hacker subculture, there is another language called Perl that is considered a lot cooler than Java. Slashdot, for example, is generated by Perl. I don't think you would find those guys using Java Server Pages. But there is another, newer language, called Python, whose users tend to look down on Perl, and another called Ruby that some see as the heir apparent of Python.

If you look at these languages in order, Java, Perl, Python, Ruby, you notice an interesting pattern. At least, you notice this pattern if you are a Lisp hacker. Each one is progressively more like Lisp. Python copies even features that many Lisp hackers consider to be mistakes. And if you'd shown people Ruby in 1975 and described it as a dialect of Lisp with syntax, no one would have argued with you. Programming languages have almost caught up with 1958.

Catching Up with Math

What I mean is that Lisp was first discovered by John McCarthy in 1958, and popular programming languages are only now catching up with the ideas he developed then.

Now, how could that be true? Isn't computer technology something that changes very rapidly? In 1958, computers were refrigerator-sized behemoths with the processing power of a wristwatch.[2] How could any technology that old even be relevant, let alone superior to the latest developments?

IBM 704, Lawrence Livermore, 1956.

I'll tell you how. It's because Lisp was not really designed to be a programming language, at least not in the sense we mean today. What we mean by a programming language is something we use to tell a computer what to do. McCarthy did eventually intend to develop a programming language in this sense, but the Lisp we actually ended up with was based on something separate that he did as a theoretical exercise—an effort to define a more convenient alternative to the Turing machine. As McCarthy said later,

> Another way to show that Lisp was neater than Turing machines was to write a universal Lisp function and show that it is briefer and more comprehensible than the description of a universal Turing machine. This was the Lisp function *eval*..., which computes the value of a Lisp expression.... Writing *eval* required inventing a notation representing Lisp functions as Lisp data, and such a notation was devised for the purposes of the paper with no thought that it would be used to express Lisp programs in practice.

Alpha nerd: John McCarthy.

But in late 1958, Steve Russell,[3] one of McCarthy's grad students, looked at this definition of *eval* and realized that if he translated it into machine language, the result would be a Lisp interpreter.

This was a big surprise at the time. Here is what McCarthy said about it later:

Steve Russell said, look, why don't I program this *eval*..., and I said to him, ho, ho, you're confusing theory with practice, this *eval* is intended for reading, not for computing. But he went ahead and did it. That is, he compiled the *eval* in my paper into [IBM] 704 machine code, fixing bugs, and then advertised this as a Lisp interpreter, which it certainly was. So at that point Lisp had essentially the form that it has today. . . .

Suddenly, in a matter of weeks, McCarthy found his theoretical exercise transformed into an actual programming language—and a more powerful one than he had intended.

So the short explanation of why this 1950s language is not obsolete is that it was not technology but math, and math doesn't get stale. The right thing to compare Lisp to is not 1950s hardware but the Quicksort algorithm, which was discovered in 1960 and is still the fastest general-purpose sort.

There is one other language still surviving from the 1950s, Fortran, and it represents the opposite approach to language design. Lisp was a piece of theory that unexpectedly got turned into a programming language. Fortran was developed intentionally as a programming language, but what we would now consider a very low-level one.

Fortran I, the language that was developed in 1956, was a very different animal from present-day Fortran. Fortran I was pretty much assembly language with math. In some ways it was less powerful than more recent assembly languages; there were no subroutines, for example, only branches. Present-day Fortran is now arguably closer to Lisp than to Fortran I.

Lisp and Fortran were the trunks of two separate evolutionary trees, one rooted in math and one rooted in machine architecture. These two trees have been converging ever since. Lisp started out powerful, and over the next twenty years got fast. So-called mainstream languages started out fast, and over the next forty years gradually got more powerful, until now the most advanced of them are fairly close to Lisp. Close, but they are still missing a few things.

What Made Lisp Different

When it was first developed, Lisp embodied nine new ideas. Some of these we now take for granted, others are only seen in more advanced languages, and two are still unique to Lisp. The nine ideas are, in order of their adoption by the mainstream,

1. Conditionals. A conditional is an if-then-else construct. We take these for granted now, but Fortran I didn't have them. It had only a conditional goto closely based on the underlying machine instruction.

2. A function type. In Lisp, functions are a data type just like integers or strings. They have a literal representation, can be stored in variables, can be passed as arguments, and so on.

3. Recursion. Lisp was the first high-level language to support recursive functions.[4]

4. Dynamic typing. In Lisp, all variables are effectively pointers. Values are what have types, not variables, and assigning values to variables means copying pointers, not what they point to.

5. Garbage-collection.

6. Programs composed of expressions. Lisp programs are trees of expressions, each of which returns a value. This is in contrast to Fortran and most succeeding languages, which distinguish between expressions and statements.

   This distinction was natural in Fortran I because you could not nest statements. So while you needed expressions for math to work, there was no point in making anything else return a value, because there could not be anything waiting for it.

   This limitation went away with the arrival of block-structured languages, but by then it was too late. The distinction between expressions and statements was entrenched. It spread from Fortran into Algol and then to both their descendants.

7. A symbol type. Symbols are effectively pointers to strings stored in a hash table. So you can test equality by comparing a pointer, instead of comparing each character.

8. A notation for code using trees of symbols and constants.

9. The whole language there all the time. There is no real distinction between read-time, compile-time, and runtime. You can compile or run code while reading, read or run code while compiling, and read or compile code at runtime.

Running code at read-time lets users reprogram Lisp's syntax; running code at compile-time is the basis of macros; compiling at runtime is the basis of Lisp's use as an extension language in programs like Emacs; and reading at runtime enables programs to communicate using s-expressions, an idea recently reinvented as XML.[5]

When Lisp first appeared, these ideas were far removed from ordinary programming practice, which was dictated largely by the hardware available in the late 1950s. Over time, the default language, embodied in a succession of popular languages, has gradually evolved toward Lisp. Ideas 1-5 are now widespread. Number 6 is starting to appear in the mainstream. Python has a form of 7, though there doesn't seem to be any syntax for it.

As for number 8, this may be the most interesting of the lot. Ideas 8 and 9 only became part of Lisp by accident, because Steve Russell implemented something McCarthy had never intended to be implemented. And yet these ideas turn out to be responsible for both Lisp's strange appearance and its most distinctive features. Lisp looks strange not so much because it has a strange syntax as because it has no syntax; you express programs directly in the parse trees that get built behind the scenes when other languages are parsed, and these trees are made of lists, which are Lisp data structures.

Expressing the language in its own data structures turns out to be a very powerful feature. Ideas 8 and 9 together mean that you can write programs that write programs. That may sound like a bizarre idea, but it's an everyday thing in Lisp. The most common way to do it is with something called a *macro*.

The term "macro" does not mean in Lisp what it means in other languages. A Lisp macro can be anything from an abbreviation to a compiler for a new language. If you really want to understand

Lisp, or just expand your programming horizons, I would learn more about macros.

Macros (in the Lisp sense) are still, as far as I know, unique to Lisp. This is partly because in order to have macros you probably have to make your language look as strange as Lisp. It may also be because if you do add that final increment of power, you can no longer claim to have invented a new language, but only a new dialect of Lisp.

I mention this mostly as a joke, but it is quite true. If you define a language that has car, cdr, cons, quote, cond, atom, eq, and a notation for functions expressed as lists, then you can build all the rest of Lisp out of it. That is in fact the defining quality of Lisp: it was in order to make this so that McCarthy gave Lisp the shape it has.

Where Languages Matter

Even if Lisp does represent a kind of limit that mainstream languages are approaching asymptotically, does that mean you should actually use it to write software? How much do you lose by using a less powerful language? Isn't it wiser, sometimes, not to be at the very edge of innovation? And isn't popularity to some extent its own justification? Isn't the pointy-haired boss right, for example, to want to use a language for which he can easily hire programmers?

There are, of course, projects where the choice of programming language doesn't matter much. As a rule, the more demanding the application, the more leverage you get from using a powerful language. But plenty of projects are not demanding at all. Most programming probably consists of writing little glue programs, and for little glue programs you can use any language that you're already familiar with and that has good libraries for whatever you need to do. If you just need to feed data from one Windows app to another, sure, use Visual Basic.

You can write little glue programs in Lisp too (I use it as a desktop calculator), but the biggest win for languages like Lisp is at the other end of the spectrum, where you need to write sophisticated programs to solve hard problems in the face of fierce competition. A good example is the airline fare search program that ITA Software licenses to Orbitz. These guys entered a market already dominated by two big, entrenched competitors, Travelocity and Expedia, and seem to have just humiliated them technologically.

The core of ITA's application is a 200,000-line Common Lisp program that searches many orders of magnitude more possibilities than their competitors, who apparently are still using mainframe-era programming techniques. I have never seen any of ITA's code, but according to one of their top hackers they use a lot of macros, and I am not surprised to hear it.

Centripetal Forces

I'm not saying there is no cost to using uncommon technologies. The pointy-haired boss is not completely mistaken to worry about this. But because he doesn't understand the risks, he tends to magnify them.

I can think of three problems that could arise from using less common languages. Your programs might not work well with programs written in other languages. You might have fewer libraries at your disposal. And you might have trouble hiring programmers.

How big a problem is each of these? The importance of the first varies depending on whether you have control over the whole system. If you're writing software that has to run on a remote user's machine on top of a buggy, proprietary operating system (I mention no names), there may be advantages to writing your application in the same language as the OS. But if you control the whole system and have the source code of all the parts, as ITA presumably does, you can use whatever languages you want. If any incompatibility arises, you can fix it yourself.

In server-based applications you can get away with using the most advanced technologies, and I think this is the main cause of what Jonathan Erickson calls the "programming language renaissance." This is why we even hear about new languages like

Perl and Python. We're not hearing about these languages be-cause people are using them to write Windows apps, but because people are using them on servers. And as software shifts off the desktop and onto servers (a future even Microsoft seems resigned to), there will be less and less pressure to use middle-of-the-road technologies.

As for libraries, their importance also depends on the appli-cation. For less demanding problems, the availability of libraries can outweigh the intrinsic power of the language. Where is the breakeven point? Hard to say exactly, but wherever it is, it is short of anything you'd be likely to call an application. If a company considers itself to be in the software business, and they're writ-ing an application that will be one of their products, then it will probably involve several hackers and take at least six months to write. In a project of that size, powerful languages probably start to outweigh the convenience of pre-existing libraries.

The third worry of the pointy-haired boss, the difficulty of hir-ing programmers, I think is a red herring. How many hackers do you need to hire, after all? Surely by now we all know that soft-ware is best developed by teams of less than ten people. And you shouldn't have trouble hiring hackers on that scale for any language anyone has ever heard of. If you can't find ten Lisp hackers, then your company is probably based in the wrong city for developing software.

In fact, choosing a more powerful language probably decreases the size of the team you need, because (a) if you use a more pow-erful language, you probably won't need as many hackers, and (b) hackers who work in more advanced languages are likely to be smarter.

I'm not saying that you won't get a lot of pressure to use what are perceived as "standard" technologies. At Viaweb we raised some eyebrows among VCs and potential acquirers by using Lisp. But we also raised eyebrows by using generic Intel boxes as servers instead of "industrial strength" servers like Suns, for using a then-obscure open source Unix called FreeBSD instead of a real com-mercial OS like Windows NT, for ignoring a supposed e-commerce standard called SET that no one now even remembers, and so on.

You can't let the suits make technical decisions for you. Did it alarm potential acquirers that we used Lisp? Some, slightly, but if we hadn't used Lisp, we wouldn't have been able to write the software that made them want to buy us. What seemed like an anomaly to them was in fact cause and effect.

If you start a startup, don't design your product to please VCs or potential acquirers. *Design your product to please the users.* If you win the users, everything else will follow. And if you don't, no one will care how comfortably orthodox your technology choices were.

The Cost of Being Average

How much do you lose by using a less powerful language? There is actually some data out there about that.

The most convenient measure of power is probably code size. The point of high-level languages is to give you bigger abstractions—bigger bricks, as it were, so you don't need as many to build a wall of a given size. So the more powerful the language, the shorter the program (not simply in characters, of course, but in distinct elements).

How does a more powerful language enable you to write shorter programs? One technique you can use, if the language will let you, is something called bottom-up programming. Instead of simply writing your application in the base language, you build on top of the base language a language for writing programs like yours, then write your program in it. The combined code can be much shorter than if you had written your whole program in the base language—indeed, this is how most compression algorithms work. A bottom-up program should be easier to modify as well, because in many cases the language layer won't have to change at all.

Code size is important, because the time it takes to write a program depends mostly on its length. If your program would be three times as long in another language, it will take three times as long to write—and you can't get around this by hiring more people, because beyond a certain size new hires are actually a net lose. Fred Brooks described this phenomenon in his famous book *The Mythical Man-Month*, and everything I've seen has tended to confirm what he said.

So how much shorter are your programs if you write them in Lisp? Most of the numbers I've heard for Lisp versus C, for example, have been around 7-10x. But a recent article about ITA in *New Architect* magazine said that "one line of Lisp can replace 20 lines of C," and since this article was full of quotes from ITA's president, I assume they got this number from ITA.[6] If so then we can put some faith in it; ITA's software includes a lot of C and C++ as well as Lisp, so they are speaking from experience.

My guess is that these multiples aren't even constant. I think they increase when you face harder problems and also when you have smarter programmers. A really good hacker can squeeze more out of better tools.

As one data point on the curve, at any rate, if you were to compete with ITA and chose to write your software in C, they would be able to develop software twenty times faster than you. If you spent a year on a new feature, they'd be able to duplicate it in less than three weeks. Whereas if they spent just three months developing something new, it would be *five years* before you had it too.

And you know what? That's the best-case scenario. When you talk about code-size ratios, you're implicitly assuming that you can actually write the program in the weaker language. But in fact there are limits on what programmers can do. If you're trying to solve a hard problem with a language that's too low-level, you reach a point where there is just too much to keep in your head at once.

So when I say it would take ITA's imaginary competitor five years to duplicate something ITA could write in Lisp in three months, I mean five years if nothing goes wrong. In fact, the way things work in most companies, any development project that would take five years is likely never to get finished at all.

I admit this is an extreme case. ITA's hackers seem to be unusually smart, and C is a pretty low-level language. But in a competitive market, even a differential of two or three to one would be enough to guarantee that you'd always be behind.

A Recipe

This is the kind of possibility that the pointy-haired boss doesn't even want to think about. And so most of them don't. Because, you know, when it comes down to it, the pointy-haired boss doesn't mind if his company gets their ass kicked, so long as no one can prove it's his fault. The safest plan for him personally is to stick close to the center of the herd.

Within large organizations, the phrase used to describe this approach is "industry best practice." Its purpose is to shield the pointy-haired boss from responsibility: if he chooses something that is "industry best practice," and the company loses, he can't be blamed. He didn't choose, the industry did.

I believe this term was originally used to describe accounting methods and so on. What it means, roughly, is *don't do anything weird*. And in accounting that's probably a good idea. The terms "cutting-edge" and "accounting" do not sound good together. But when you import this criterion into decisions about technology, you start to get the wrong answers.

Technology often *should* be cutting-edge. In programming languages, as Erann Gat has pointed out, what "industry best practice" actually gets you is not the best, but merely the average. When a decision causes you to develop software at a fraction of the rate of more aggressive competitors, "best practice" does not really seem the right name for it.

So here we have two pieces of information that I think are very valuable. In fact, I know it from my own experience. Number 1, languages vary in power. Number 2, most managers deliberately ignore this. Between them, these two facts are literally a recipe for making money. ITA is an example of this recipe in action. If you want to win in a software business, just take on the hardest problem you can find, use the most powerful language you can get, and wait for your competitors' pointy-haired bosses to revert to the mean.

———

Appendix: Power

As an illustration of what I mean about the relative power of programming languages, consider the following problem. We want to write a function that generates accumulators—a function that takes a number *n*, and returns a function that takes another number *i* and returns *n* incremented by *i*. (That's *incremented by*, not plus. An accumulator has to accumulate.)

In Common Lisp[7] this would be:

```
(defun foo (n)
  (lambda (i) (incf n i)))
```

In Ruby it's almost identical:

```
def foo (n)
  lambda {|i| n += i } end
```

Whereas in Perl 5 it's

```
sub foo {
  my ($n) = @_;
  sub {$n += shift}
}
```

which has more elements than the Lisp/Ruby version because you have to extract parameters manually in Perl.

In Smalltalk the code is also slightly longer than in Lisp and Ruby:

```
foo: n
 |s|
 s := n.
 ^[:i| s := s+i. ]
```

because although in general lexical variables work, you can't do an assignment to a parameter, so you have to create a new variable s to hold the accumulated value.

In Javascript the example is, again, slightly longer, because Javascript retains the distinction between statements and expressions, so you need explicit return statements to return values:

```
function foo(n) {
  return function (i) {
          return n += i } }
```

(To be fair, Perl also retains this distinction, but deals with it in typical Perl fashion by letting you omit returns.)

If you try to translate the Lisp/Ruby/Perl/Smalltalk/Javascript code into Python you run into some limitations. Because Python doesn't fully support lexical variables, you have to create a data structure to hold the value of *n*. And although Python does have a function data type, there is no literal representation for one (unless the body is only a single expression) so you need to create a named function to return. This is what you end up with:

```
def foo(n):
  s = [n]
  def bar(i):
    s[0] += i
    return s[0]
  return bar
```

Python users might legitimately ask why they can't just write

```
def foo(n):
  return lambda i: return n += i
```

or even

```
def foo(n):
   lambda i: n += i
```

and my guess is that they probably will, one day. (But if they don't want to wait for Python to evolve the rest of the way into Lisp, they could always just. . .)

In OO languages, you can, to a limited extent, simulate a closure (a function that refers to variables defined in surrounding code) by defining a class with one method and a field to replace each variable from an enclosing scope. This makes the programmer do the kind of code analysis that would be done by the compiler in a language with full support for lexical scope, and it won't work if more than one function refers to the same variable, but it is enough in simple cases like this.

Python experts seem to agree that this is the preferred way to solve the problem in Python, writing either

```
def foo(n):
   class acc:
     def __init__(self, s):
         self.s = s
     def inc(self, i):
         self.s += i
         return self.s
   return acc(n).inc
```

or

```
class foo:
   def __init__(self, n):
       self.n = n
   def __call__(self, i):
       self.n += i
       return self.n
```

I include these because I wouldn't want Python advocates to say I was misrepresenting the language, but both seem to me more complex than the first version. You're doing the same thing, setting up a separate place to hold the accumulator; it's just a field in an object instead of the head of a list. And the use of these special, reserved field names, especially __call__, seems a bit of a hack.

In the rivalry between Perl and Python, the claim of the Python hackers seems to be that Python is a more elegant alternative to Perl, but what this case shows is that power is the ultimate elegance: the Perl program is simpler (has fewer elements), even if the syntax is a bit uglier.

How about other languages? In the other languages mentioned here—Fortran, C, C++, Java, and Visual Basic—it does not appear that you can solve this problem at all. Ken Anderson says this is about as close as you can get in Java:

```
public interface Inttoint {
  public int call(int i);
}

public static Inttoint foo(final int n) {
  return new Inttoint() {
    int s = n;
    public int call(int i) {
    s = s + i;
    return s;
    }};
}
```

which falls short of the spec because it only works for integers.

It's not literally true that you can't solve this problem in other languages, of course. The fact that all these languages are Turing-equivalent means that, strictly speaking, you can write any program in any of them. So how would you do it? In the limit case, by writing a Lisp interpreter in the less powerful language.

That sounds like a joke, but it happens so often to varying degrees in large programming projects that there is a name for the phenomenon, Greenspun's Tenth Rule:

> Any sufficiently complicated C or Fortran program contains an ad hoc informally-specified bug-ridden slow implementation of half of Common Lisp.

If you try to solve a hard problem, the question is not whether you will use a powerful enough language, but whether you will (a) use a powerful language, (b) write a de facto interpreter for one, or (c) yourself become a human compiler for one. We see this already beginning to happen in the Python example, where we are in effect simulating the code that a compiler would generate to implement a lexical variable.

This practice is not only common, but institutionalized. For example, in the OO world you hear a good deal about "patterns." I wonder if these patterns are not sometimes evidence of case (c), the human compiler, at work.[8] When I see patterns in my programs, I consider it a sign of trouble. The shape of a program should reflect only the problem it needs to solve. Any other regularity in the code is a sign, to me at least, that I'm using abstractions that aren't powerful enough—often that I'm generating by hand the expansions of some macro that I need to write.

Chapter 14

The Dream Language

Of all tyrannies, a tyranny exercised for the good of its
victims may be the most oppressive.

C. S. Lewis

A FRIEND OF MINE ONCE TOLD AN EMINENT OPERATING SYS-
tems expert that he wanted to design a really good programming
language. The expert said that it would be a waste of time, that programming languages don't become popular or unpopular based
on their merits, and so no matter how good his language was, no
one would use it. At least, that was what had happened to the
language *he* had designed.

What does make a language popular? Do popular languages
deserve their popularity? Is it worth trying to define a good programming language? How would you do it?

I think the answers to these questions can be found by looking
at hackers, and learning what they want. Programming languages
are for hackers, and a programming language is good as a programming language (rather than, say, an exercise in denotational
semantics or compiler design) if and only if hackers like it.

The Mechanics of Popularity

It's true, certainly, that most people don't choose programming
languages simply based on their merits. Most programmers are
told what language to use by someone else. And yet I think the
effect of such external factors on the popularity of programming
languages is not as great as it's sometimes thought to be. I think

a bigger problem is that a hacker's idea of a good programming language is not the same as most language designers'.

Between the two, the hacker's opinion is the one that matters. Programming languages are not theorems. They're tools, designed for people, and they have to be designed to suit human strengths and weaknesses as much as shoes have to be designed for human feet. If a shoe pinches when you put it on, it's a bad shoe, however elegant it may be as a piece of sculpture.

It may be that the majority of programmers can't tell a good language from a bad one. But that's no different with any other tool. It doesn't mean that it's a waste of time to try designing a good language. Expert hackers can tell a good language when they see one, and they'll use it. Expert hackers are a tiny minority, admittedly, but that tiny minority write all the good software, and their influence is such that the rest of the programmers will tend to use whatever language they use. Often, indeed, it is not merely influence but command: often the expert hackers are the very people who, as their bosses or faculty advisors, tell the other programmers what language to use.

The opinion of expert hackers is not the only force that determines the relative popularity of programming languages—legacy software (Fortran, Cobol) and hype (Ada, Java) also play a role—but I think it is the most powerful force over the long term. Given an initial critical mass and enough time, a programming language probably becomes about as popular as it deserves to be. And popularity further separates good languages from bad ones, because feedback from real live users always leads to improvements. Look at how much any popular language has changed during its life. Perl and Fortran are extreme cases, but even Lisp has changed a lot.

So whether or not a language has to be good to be popular, I think a language has to be popular to be good. And it has to stay popular to stay good. The state of the art in programming languages doesn't stand still. Though there is little change in the depths of the sea, in core language features, there is quite a lot up on the surface, in things like libraries and environments.

Of course, hackers have to know about a language before they can use it. How are they to hear? From other hackers. But there has to be some initial group of hackers using the language for others even to hear about it. I wonder how large this group has to be; how many users make a critical mass? Off the top of my head, I'd say twenty. If a language had twenty separate users, meaning twenty users who decided on their own to use it, I'd consider it to be real.

Getting there can't be easy. I would not be surprised if it is harder to get from zero to twenty than from twenty to a thousand. The best way to get those initial twenty users is probably a trojan horse: give people an application they want, which happens to be written in the new language.

External Factors

Let's start by acknowledging one external factor that does affect the popularity of a programming language. To become popular, a programming language has to be the scripting language of a popular system. Fortran and Cobol were the scripting languages of early IBM mainframes. C was the scripting language of Unix, and so, later, were Perl and Python. Tcl is the scripting language of Tk, Visual Basic of Windows, (a form of) Lisp of Emacs, PHP of web servers, and Java and Javascript of web browsers.

Programming languages don't exist in isolation. To hack is a transitive verb—hackers are usually hacking something—and in practice languages are judged relative to whatever they're used to hack. So if you want to design a popular language, you either have to supply more than a language, or you have to design your language to replace the scripting language of some existing system.

One way to describe this situation is to say that a language isn't judged on its own merits. Another view is that a programming language really isn't a programming language unless it's also the scripting language of something. This only seems unfair if it comes as a surprise. I think it's no more unfair than expecting a programming language to have, say, an implementation. It's just part of what a programming language is.

A programming language does need a good implementation, of course, and this must be free. Companies will pay for software, but individual hackers won't, and it's the hackers you need to attract.

A language also needs to have a book about it. The book should be thin, well-written, and full of good examples. Kernighan and Ritchie's *C Programming Language* is the ideal here. At the moment I'd almost say that a language has to have a book published by O'Reilly. That's becoming the test of mattering to hackers.

There should be online documentation as well. In fact, the book can start as online documentation. But physical books aren't obsolete yet. Their format is convenient, and the de facto censorship imposed by publishers is a useful if imperfect filter. Bookstores are one of the most important places for learning about new languages.

Succinctness

Given that you can supply the three things any language needs— a free implementation, a book, and something to hack—how do you make a language that hackers will like?

One thing hackers like is succinctness. Hackers are lazy, in the same way that mathematicians and modernist architects are lazy: they hate anything extraneous. It would not be far from the truth to say that a hacker about to write a program decides what language to use, at least subconsciously, based on the total number of characters he'll have to type. If this isn't precisely how hackers think, a language designer would do well to act as if it were.

The most important kind of succinctness comes from making the language more abstract. It is to get this that we use high-level languages in the first place. So it would seem that the more of it you can get, the better. A language designer should always be looking at programs and asking, is there some way to express this in fewer tokens? If you can do something that makes many different programs shorter, it's probably not a coincidence: you've probably discovered a useful new abstraction.

It's a mistake to try to baby the user with long-winded expressions meant to resemble English. Cobol is notorious for this flaw. A hacker would consider being asked to write

```
add x to y giving z
```

instead of

```
z = x + y
```

as something between an insult to his intelligence and a sin against God.

Succinctness is one place where statically typed languages lose. All other things being equal, no one wants to begin a program with a bunch of declarations. Anything that can be implicit, should be. The amount of boilerplate in a Java hello-world program is almost enough evidence, by itself, to convict.[1]

Individual tokens should be short as well. Perl and Common Lisp occupy opposite poles on this question. Perl programs can be cryptically dense, while the names of built-in Common Lisp operators are comically long. The designers of Common Lisp probably expected users to have text editors that would type these long names for them. But the cost of a long name is not just the cost of typing it. There is also the cost of reading it, and the cost of the space it takes up on your screen.

Hackability

There is one thing more important than succinctness to a hacker: being able to do what you want. In the history of programming languages, a surprising amount of effort has gone into preventing programmers from doing things considered to be improper. This is a dangerously presumptuous plan. How can the language designer know what the programmer will need to do? I think language designers would do better to consider their target user to be a genius who will need to do things they never anticipated, rather than a bumbler who needs to be protected from himself. The bumbler will shoot himself in the foot anyway. You may save him from referring to variables in another module, but you can't save him from writing a badly designed program to solve the wrong problem, and taking forever to do it.

Good programmers often want to do dangerous and unsavory things. By unsavory I mean things that go behind whatever semantic facade the language is trying to present: getting hold of the internal representation of some high-level abstraction, for example. Hackers like to hack, and hacking means getting inside things and second-guessing the original designer.

Let yourself be second-guessed. When you make any tool, people use it in ways you didn't intend, and this is especially true of a highly articulated tool like a programming language. Many a hacker will want to tweak your semantic model in a way that you never imagined. I say, let them. Give the programmer access to as much internal stuff as you can.

A hacker may only want to subvert the intended model of things once or twice in a big program. But what a difference it makes to be able to. And it may be more than a question of just solving a problem. There is a kind of pleasure here too. Hackers share the surgeon's secret pleasure in poking about in gross innards, the teenager's secret pleasure in popping zits.[2] For boys, at least, certain kinds of horrors are fascinating. *Maxim* magazine publishes an annual volume of photographs, containing a mix of pin-ups and grisly accidents. They know their audience.

A really good language should be both clean and dirty: cleanly designed, with a small core of well understood and highly orthogonal operators, but dirty in the sense that it lets hackers have their way with it. C is like this. So were the early Lisps. A real hacker's language will always have a slightly raffish character.

A good programming language should have features that make the kind of people who use the phrase "software engineering" shake their heads disapprovingly. At the other end of the continuum are languages like Pascal, models of propriety that are good for teaching and not much else.

Throwaway Programs

To be attractive to hackers, a language must be good for writing the kinds of programs they want to write. And that means, perhaps surprisingly, that it has to be good for writing throwaway programs.

A throwaway program is a program you write quickly for some limited task: a program to automate some system administration task, or generate test data for a simulation, or convert data from one format to another. The surprising thing about throwaway programs is that, like the "temporary" buildings built at so many American universities during World War II, they often don't get thrown away. Many evolve into real programs, with real features and real users.

I have a hunch that the best big programs begin life this way, rather than being designed big from the start, like the Hoover Dam. It's terrifying to build something big from scratch. When people take on a project that's too big, they become overwhelmed. The project either gets bogged down, or the result is sterile and wooden: a shopping mall rather than a real downtown, Brasilia rather than Rome, Ada rather than C.

Another way to get a big program is to start with a throwaway program and keep improving it. This approach is less daunting, and the design of the program benefits from evolution. Programs that did evolve this way are probably still written in whatever language they were first written in, because it's rare for a program to be ported, except for political reasons. And so, paradoxically, if you want to make a language that is used for big systems, you have to make it good for writing throwaway programs, because that's where big systems come from.

Perl is a striking example of this idea. It was not only designed for writing throwaway programs, but was pretty much a throwaway program itself. Perl began life as a collection of utilities for generating reports, and only evolved into a programming language as the throwaway programs people wrote in it grew larger. It was not until Perl 5 (if then) that the language was suitable for writing serious programs, and yet it was already massively popular.

What makes a language good for throwaway programs? To start with, it must be readily available. A throwaway program is something you expect to write in an hour. So the language probably must already be installed on the computer you're using. It can't be something you have to install before you use it. It has to be there. C was there because it came with the operating system. Perl was there because it was originally a tool for system administrators, and yours had already installed it.

Being available means more than being installed, though. An interactive language, with a command-line interface, is more available than one that you have to compile and run separately. A popular programming language should be interactive, and start up fast.

Another thing you want in a throwaway program is succinctness. This is always attractive to hackers, and never more so than in a program they expect to turn out in an hour.

Libraries

Of course the ultimate in succinctness is to have the program already written for you, and merely to call it. And this brings us to what I think will be an increasingly important feature of programming languages: libraries. Perl wins because it has large libraries for manipulating strings. This class of library function is especially important for throwaway programs, which are often originally written for converting or extracting data. Many Perl programs probably begin as just a couple library calls stuck together.

I think a lot of the advances that happen in programming languages in the next fifty years will have to do with library functions. I think future programming languages will have libraries that are as carefully designed as the core language. Programming language design will not be about whether to make your language statically or dynamically typed, or object-oriented, or functional, or whatever, so much as about how to design great libraries. The kind of language designers who like to think about how to design type systems may shudder at this. It's almost like writing applications! Well, too bad. Languages are for programmers, and libraries are what programmers need.

It's hard to design good libraries. It's not simply a matter of writing a lot of code. Once the libraries get too big, it can sometimes take longer to find the function you need than to write it yourself. Libraries need to be designed using a small set of orthogonal operators, just like the core language. It ought to be possible for the programmer to *guess* what library call will do what he needs.

Efficiency

A good language, as everyone knows, should generate fast code. But in practice I don't think fast code comes primarily from things you do in the design of the language. As Knuth pointed out long ago, speed only matters in certain critical bottlenecks. And as many programmers have observed since, one is often mistaken about where these bottlenecks are.

So, in practice, the way to get fast code is to have a good profiler, rather than by, say, making the language statically typed. You don't need to know the type of every argument in every call in the program. You do need to be able to declare the types of arguments in the bottlenecks. And even more, you need to be able to find out where the bottlenecks are.

One complaint people have had with very high level languages like Lisp is that it's hard to tell what's expensive. This might be true. It might also be inevitable, if you want to have a very abstract language. And in any case I think good profiling would go a long way toward fixing the problem: you'd soon learn what was expensive.

Part of the problem here is social. Language designers like to write fast compilers. That's how they measure their skill. They think of the profiler as an add-on, at best. But in practice a good profiler may do more to improve the speed of actual programs written in the language than a compiler that generates fast code. Here, again, language designers are somewhat out of touch with their users. They do a really good job of solving slightly the wrong problem.

It might be a good idea to have an active profiler—to push performance data to the programmer instead of waiting for him to ask for it. For example, the editor could display bottlenecks in red when the programmer edits the source code. Another approach would be to somehow represent what's happening in running programs. This would be an especially big win in server-based applications, where you have lots of running programs to look at. An active profiler could show graphically what's happening in memory as a program's running, or even make sounds that tell what's happening.

Sound is a good cue to problems. At Viaweb we had a big board of dials showing what was happening to our web servers. The hands were moved by little servomotors that made a slight noise when they turned. I couldn't see the board from my desk, but I found that I could tell immediately, by the sound, when there was a problem with a server.

It might even be possible to write a profiler that would automatically detect inefficient algorithms. I would not be surprised if certain patterns of memory access turned out to be sure signs of bad algorithms. If there were a little guy running around inside the computer executing our programs, he would probably have as long and plaintive a tale to tell about his job as a federal government employee. I often have a feeling that I'm sending the processor on a lot of wild goose chases, but I've never had a good way to look at what it's doing.

A number of languages now compile into byte code, which is then executed by an interpreter. This is usually done to make the implementation easier to port, but it could be a useful language feature. It might be a good idea to make the byte code an official part of the language, and to allow programmers to use inline byte code in bottlenecks. Then such optimizations would be portable too.

The nature of speed, as perceived by the end user, may be changing. With the rise of server-based applications, more and more programs may turn out to be I/O-bound. It will be worth making I/O fast. The language can help with straightforward measures like simple, fast, formatted output functions, and also with deep structural changes like caching and persistent objects.

Users are interested in response time. But another kind of efficiency will be increasingly important: the number of simultaneous users you can support per processor. Many of the interesting applications written in the future will be server-based, and the number of users per server is the critical question for anyone hosting such applications. In the capital cost of a business offering a server-based application, this is the divisor.

For years, efficiency hasn't mattered much in most end-user applications. Developers have been able to assume that users would have increasingly fast processors sitting on their desks. And Parkinson's Law has proven as powerful as Moore's. Software has bloated to consume the resources available. That will change with server-based applications, because hardware and software will be supplied together. For companies that offer server-based applications, it will make a big difference to the bottom line how many users they can support per server.

In some applications, the processor will be the limiting factor, and execution speed will be the most important thing to optimize. But often memory will be the limit; the number of simultaneous users will be determined by the amount of memory you need for each user's data. The language can help here too. Good support for threads will enable all the users to share a single heap. It may also help to have persistent objects and/or language-level support for lazy loading.

Time

The last ingredient a popular language needs is time. No one wants to write programs in a language that might go away, as so many programming languages do. So most hackers will tend to wait until a language has been around for a couple years before even considering it.

Inventors of wonderful new things are often surprised to discover this, but you need time to get any message through to people. A friend of mine rarely does anything the first time someone asks him. He knows that people sometimes ask for things they turn out not to want. To avoid wasting his time, he waits till the third or fourth time he's asked to do something. By then whoever's asking him may be fairly annoyed, but at least they probably really do want whatever they're asking for.

Most people have learned to do a similar sort of filtering on new things they hear about. They don't even start paying attention until they've heard about something ten times. They're perfectly justified: the majority of hot new whatevers do turn out to be a waste of time, and eventually go away. By delaying learning VRML, I avoided having to learn it at all.

So anyone who invents something new has to expect to keep repeating their message for years before people will start to get it. It took us years to get it through to people that Viaweb's software didn't have to be downloaded. The good news is, simple repetition solves the problem. All you have to do is keep telling your story, and eventually people will start to hear. It's not when people notice you're there that they pay attention; it's when they notice you're still there.

It's just as well that it usually takes a while to gain momentum. Most technologies evolve a good deal even after they're first launched—programming languages especially. Nothing could be better for a new technology than a few years of being used only by a small number of early adopters. Early adopters are sophisticated and demanding, and quickly flush out whatever flaws remain in your technology. When you only have a few users you can be in close contact with all of them. And early adopters are forgiving when you improve your system, even if this causes some breakage.

There are two ways new technology gets introduced: the organic growth method, and the big bang method. The organic growth method is exemplified by the classic seat-of-the-pants underfunded garage startup. A couple guys, working in obscurity, develop some new technology. They launch it with no marketing and initially have only a few (fanatically devoted) users. They continue to improve the technology, and meanwhile their user base grows by word of mouth. Before they know it, they're big.

The other approach, the big bang method, is exemplified by the VC-backed, heavily marketed startup. They rush to develop a product, launch it with great publicity, and immediately (they hope) have a large user base.

Generally, the garage guys envy the big bang guys. The big bang guys are smooth and confident and respected by the VCs. They can afford the best of everything, and the PR campaign surrounding the launch has the side effect of making them celebrities. The organic growth guys, sitting in their garage, feel poor and unloved. And yet I think they are often mistaken to feel sorry for themselves. Organic growth seems to yield better technology and richer founders than the big bang method. If you look at the dominant technologies today, you'll find that most of them grew organically.

This pattern doesn't only apply to companies. You see it in research too. Multics and Ada were big-bang projects, and Unix and C were organic growth projects.

Redesign

"The best writing is rewriting," wrote E. B. White. Every good writer knows this, and it's true for software too. The most important part of design is redesign. Programming languages, especially, don't get redesigned enough.

To write good software you must simultaneously keep two opposing ideas in your head. You need the young hacker's naive faith in his abilities, and at the same time the veteran's skepticism. You have to be able to think *how hard can it be?* with one half of your brain while thinking *it will never work* with the other.

The trick is to realize that there's no real contradiction here. You want to be optimistic and skeptical about two different things. You have to be optimistic about the possibility of solving the problem, but skeptical about the value of whatever solution you've got so far.

People who do good work often think that whatever they're working on is no good. Others see what they've done and think it's wonderful, but the creator sees nothing but flaws. This pattern is no coincidence: worry made the work good.

If you can keep hope and worry balanced, they will drive a project forward the same way your two legs drive a bicycle forward. In the first phase of the two-cycle innovation engine, you work furiously on some problem, inspired by your confidence that you'll be able to solve it. In the second phase, you look at what you've done in the cold light of morning, and see all its flaws very clearly. But as long as your critical spirit doesn't outweigh your hope, you'll be able to look at your admittedly incomplete system and think, how hard can it be to get the rest of the way?

It's tricky to keep the two forces balanced. In young hackers, optimism predominates. They produce something, are convinced it's great, and never improve it. In old hackers, skepticism predominates, and they won't even dare to take on ambitious projects.

Anything you can do to keep the redesign cycle going is good. Prose can be rewritten over and over until you're happy with it. But software, as a rule, doesn't get redesigned enough. Prose has readers, but software has users. If a writer rewrites an essay, people who read the new version are unlikely to complain that their thoughts have been broken by some newly introduced incompatibility.

Users are a double-edged sword. They can help you improve your language, but they can also deter you from improving it. So choose your users carefully, and be slow to grow their number. Having users is like optimization: the wise course is to delay it.

Also, as a general rule, you can at any given time get away with changing more than you think. Introducing change is like pulling off a bandage: the pain is a memory almost as soon as you feel it.

Everyone knows it's not a good idea to have a language designed by a committee. Committees yield bad design. But I think the worst danger of committees is that they interfere with *redesign*. It's so much work to introduce changes that no one wants to bother. Whatever a committee decides tends to stay that way, even if most of the members don't like it.

Even a committee of two gets in the way of redesign. This happens particularly in the interfaces between pieces of software written by two different people. To change the interface both have to agree to change it at once. And so interfaces tend not to change at all, which is a problem because they tend to be one of the most ad hoc parts of any system.

One solution here might be to design systems so that interfaces are horizontal instead of vertical—so that modules are always vertically stacked strata of abstraction. Then the interface will tend to be owned by one of them. The lower of two levels will either be a language in which the upper is written, in which case the lower level will own the interface, or it will be a slave, in which case the interface can be dictated by the upper level.

The Dream Language

By way of summary, let's try describing the hacker's dream language. The dream language is clean and terse. It has an interactive toplevel that starts up fast.[3] You can write programs to solve common problems with very little code. Nearly all the code in any program you write is code that's specific to your application. Everything else has been done for you.

The syntax of the language is brief to a fault. You never have to type an unnecessary character, or even use the Shift key much.

Using big abstractions you can write the first version of a program very quickly. Later, when you want to optimize, there's a really good profiler that tells you where to focus your attention.

You can make inner loops blindingly fast, even writing inline byte code if you need to.

There are lots of good examples to learn from, and the language is intuitive enough that you can learn how to use it from examples in a couple minutes. You don't need to look in the manual much. The manual is thin, and has few warnings and qualifications.

The language has a small core, and powerful, highly orthogonal libraries that are as carefully designed as the core language. The libraries all work well together; everything in the language fits together like the parts in a fine camera. Nothing is deprecated or retained for compatibility. The source code of all the libraries is readily available. It's easy to talk to the operating system and to applications written in other languages.

The language is built in layers. The higher-level abstractions are built in a transparent way out of lower-level abstractions, which you can get hold of if you want.

Nothing is hidden from you that doesn't absolutely have to be. The language offers abstractions only as a way of saving you work, rather than as a way of telling you what to do. In fact, the language encourages you to be an equal participant in its design. You can change everything about it, including even its syntax, and anything you write has, as much as possible, the same status as what comes predefined. The dream language is not only open source, but open design.

Chapter 15

Design and Research

Visitors to this country are often surprised to find that Americans like to begin a conversation by asking "what do you do?" I've never liked this question. I've rarely had a neat answer to it. But I think I have finally solved the problem. Now, when someone asks me what I do, I look them straight in the eye and say, "I'm designing a new dialect of Lisp." I recommend this answer to anyone who doesn't like being asked what they do. The conversation will turn immediately to other topics.

I don't consider myself to be doing research on programming languages. I'm just designing one, in the same way that someone might design a building or a chair or a new typeface. I'm not trying to discover anything new. I just want to make a language that will be good to program in.

The difference between design and research seems to be a question of new versus good. Design doesn't have to be new, but it has to be good. Research doesn't have to be good, but it has to be new. I think these two paths converge at the top: the best design surpasses its predecessors by using new ideas, and the best research solves problems that are not only new, but worth solving. So ultimately design and research are aiming for the same destination, just approaching it from different directions.

What do you do differently when you treat programming languages as a design problem instead of a research topic?

The biggest difference is that you focus more on the user. Design begins by asking, who is this for and what do they need from it? A good architect, for example, does not begin by creating a design that he then imposes on the users, but by studying the intended users and figuring out what they need.

Notice I said "what they need," not "what they want." I don't mean to give the impression that working as a designer means working as a sort of short-order cook, making whatever the client tells you to. This varies from field to field in the arts, but I don't think there is any field in which the best work is done by the people who just make exactly what the customers tell them to.

The customer *is* always right in the sense that the measure of good design is how well it works for the user. If you make a novel that bores everyone, or a chair that's horribly uncomfortable to sit in, then you've done a bad job, period. It's no defense to say that the novel or chair is designed according to the most advanced theoretical principles.

And yet, making what works for the user doesn't mean simply making what the user tells you to. Users don't know what all the choices are, and are often mistaken about what they really want. It's like being a doctor. You can't just treat a patient's symptoms. When a patient tells you his symptoms, you have to figure out what's actually wrong with him, and treat that.

This focus on the user is a kind of axiom from which most of the practice of good design can be derived, and around which most design issues center.

When I say that design must be for users, I don't mean to imply that good design aims at some kind of lowest common denominator. You can pick any group of users you want. If you're designing a tool, for example, you can design it for anyone from beginners to experts, and what's good design for one group might be bad for another. The point is, you have to pick *some* group of users. I don't think you can even talk about good or bad design except with reference to some intended user.

You're most likely to get good design if the intended users include the designer himself. When you design something for a group that doesn't include you, it tends to be for people you consider less sophisticated than you, not more sophisticated. And looking down on the user, however benevolently, always seems to corrupt the designer. I suspect few housing projects in the US were designed by architects who expected to live in them. You see the same thing in programming languages. C, Lisp, and Smalltalk were created for their own designers to use. Cobol, Ada, and Java were created for other people to use.

If you think you're designing something for idiots, odds are you're not designing something good, even for idiots.

Even if you're designing something for the most sophisticated users, though, you're still designing for humans. It's different in research. In math you don't choose abstractions because they're easy for humans to understand; you choose whichever make the proof shorter. I think this is true for the sciences generally. Scientific ideas are not meant to be ergonomic.

Over in the arts, things are different. Design is all about people. The human body is a strange thing, but when you're designing a chair, that's what you're designing for, and there's no way around it. All the arts have to pander to the interests and limitations of humans. In painting, for example, all other things being equal a painting with people in it will be more interesting than one without. It is not merely an accident of history that the great paintings of the Renaissance are all full of people. If they hadn't been, painting as a medium wouldn't have the prestige it does.

Like it or not, programming languages are also for people, and I suspect the human brain is just as lumpy and idiosyncratic as the human body. Some ideas are easy for people to grasp and some aren't. For example, we seem to have a very limited capacity for dealing with detail. It's this fact that makes programming languages a good idea in the first place; if we could handle the detail, we could just program in machine language.

Remember, too, that languages are not primarily a form for finished programs, but something that programs have to be developed in. Anyone in the arts could tell you that you might want different mediums for the two situations. Marble, for example, is a nice, durable medium for finished ideas, but a hopelessly inflexible one for developing new ideas.

A program, like a proof, is a pruned version of a tree that in the past has had false starts branching off all over it. So the test of a language is not simply how clean the finished program looks in it, but how clean the path to the finished program was. A design choice that gives you elegant finished programs may not give you an elegant design process. For example, I've written a few macro-defining macros that look now like little gems, but writing them took hours of the ugliest trial and error, and frankly, I'm still not entirely sure they're correct.

We often act as if the test of a language were how good finished programs look in it. It seems so convincing when you see the same program written in two languages, and one version is much shorter. When you approach the problem from the direction of the arts, you're less likely to depend on this sort of test. You don't want to end up with a programming language like marble.

For example, it is a huge win in developing software to have an interactive toplevel, what in Lisp is called a read-eval-print loop. And when you have one, this has real effects on the design of the language. It would not work well for a language where you have to declare variables before using them. When you're just typing expressions into the toplevel, you want to be able to set x to some value and then start doing things to x. You don't want to have to declare the type of x first. You may dispute either of the premises, but if a language has to have a toplevel to be convenient, and mandatory type declarations are incompatible with a toplevel, then no language that makes type declarations mandatory could be convenient to program in.

To get good design you have to get close, and stay close, to your users. You have to calibrate your ideas on actual users constantly. One of the reasons Jane Austen's novels are so good is that she read them out loud to her family. That's why she never sinks into self-indulgently arty descriptions of landscapes, or pretentious philosophizing. (The philosophy's there, but it's woven into the story instead of being pasted onto it like a label.) If you open an average "literary" novel and imagine reading it out loud to your friends as something you'd written, you'll feel all too keenly what an imposition that kind of thing is upon the reader.

In the software world, this idea is known as Worse is Better. Actually, there are several ideas mixed together in the concept of Worse is Better, which is why people are still arguing about whether worse is actually better or not. But one of the main ideas in that mix is that if you're building something new, you should get a prototype in front of users as soon as possible.

The alternative approach might be called the Hail Mary strategy. Instead of getting a prototype out quickly and gradually refining it, you try to create the complete, finished product in one long touchdown pass. Countless startups destroyed themselves this way during the Internet Bubble. I've never heard of a case where it worked.

What people outside the software world may not realize is that Worse is Better is found throughout the arts. In drawing, for example, the idea was discovered during the Renaissance. Now almost every drawing teacher will tell you that the right way to get an accurate drawing is not to work your way slowly around the contour of an object, because errors will accumulate and you'll find at the end that the lines don't meet. Instead you should draw a few quick lines in roughly the right place, and then gradually refine this initial sketch.

In most fields, prototypes have traditionally been made out of different materials. Typefaces to be cut in metal were initially designed with a brush on paper. Statues to be cast in bronze were modelled in wax. Patterns to be embroidered on tapestries were drawn on paper with ink wash. Buildings to be constructed from stone were tested on a smaller scale in wood.

What made oil paint so exciting, when it first became popular in the fifteenth century, was that you could make the finished work *from* the prototype. You could make a preliminary drawing if you wanted to, but you weren't held to it; you could work out all the details, and even make major changes, as you finished the painting.

You can do this in software too. A prototype doesn't have to be just a model; you can refine it into the finished product. I think you should always do this when you can. It lets you take advantage of new insights you have along the way. But perhaps even more important, it's good for morale.

Morale is key in design. I'm surprised people don't talk more about it. One of my first drawing teachers told me: if you're bored when you're drawing something, the drawing will look boring. For example, suppose you have to draw a building, and you decide to draw each brick individually. You can do this if you want, but if you get bored halfway through and start making the bricks mechanically instead of observing each one, the drawing will look worse than if you had merely suggested the bricks.

Building something by gradually refining a prototype is good for morale because it keeps you engaged. In software, my rule is: always have working code. If you're writing something you'll be able to test in an hour, you have the prospect of an immediate reward to motivate you. The same is true in the arts, and particularly in oil painting. Most painters start with a blurry sketch and gradually refine it. If you work this way, then in principle you never have to end the day with something that looks unfinished. Indeed, there is even a saying among painters: "A painting is never finished. You just stop working on it." This idea will be familiar to anyone who has worked on software.

Morale is another reason that it's hard to design something for an unsophisticated user. It's hard to stay interested in something you don't like yourself. To make something good, you have to be thinking, "wow, this is really great," not "what a piece of shit; those fools will love it."

Design means making things for humans. But it's not just the user who's human. The designer is human too.

Notes

CHAPTER 1, 1–17

1 Alberti, Leon Battista, *The Use and Abuse of Books*, translated by Renée Watkins, Waveland Press, 1999.

2 So how do you fix schools? The key to the answer may be college. When you go to (a good) college, most of the problems I describe get fixed. So the solution may come from asking, how do you make life for teenage nerds more like college life?

Home-schooling offers an immediate solution, but it probably isn't the optimal one. Why don't parents home-school their kids all the way through college? Because college offers opportunities home-schooling can't duplicate? So could high school if it were done right.

CHAPTER 2, 18–33

1 Johnson wrote in the preface to his Shakespeare:

"He has long outlived his century, the term commonly fixed as the test of literary merit. Whatever advantages he might once derive from personal allusions, local customs, or temporary opinions, have for many years been lost; and every topick of merriment or motive of sorrow, which the modes of artificial life afforded him, now only obscure the scenes which they once illuminated. The effects of favour and competition are at an end; the tradition of his friendships and his enmities has perished; his works support no opinion with arguments, nor supply any faction with invectives; they can neither indulge vanity nor gratify malignity, but are read without any other reason than the desire of pleasure, and are therefore praised only as pleasure is obtained...."

2 The worst thing photography did to painting may have been to kill the best day job. Most of the great painters in history supported themselves by painting portraits. Soon after the invention of photography they were undercut by hacks who worked from photographs. (This method is also easier on the sitter.) The class of technically skilled painters then more or less disappeared, and the role of skill in the price of painting was superseded by brand (which also depends greatly on photography, or, more precisely, on photographs reproduced in books and magazines).

3 Microsoft discourages employees from contributing to open source projects, even in their spare time. But so many of the best hackers work on open source projects now that the main effect of this policy may be to make it hard for them to hire first-rate programmers.

4 What you learn about programming in college is like what you learn about books or clothes: what bad taste you had in high school.

5 Here's an example of applied empathy. At Viaweb, if we couldn't decide between two alternatives, we'd ask, what would our competitors hate most? At one point a competitor added a feature to their software that was basically useless, but since it was one of few they had that we didn't, they made much of it in the trade press. We could have tried to explain that the feature was useless, but we decided it would annoy our competitor more if we just implemented it ourselves, so we hacked together our own version that afternoon.

6 Except text editors and compilers. Hackers don't need empathy to design these, because they are themselves typical users.

7 Well, almost. They overshot the available RAM somewhat, causing much disk swapping, but this could be fixed by buying an additional disk drive.

8 Abelson, Harold, and Gerald Sussman, *Structure and Interpretation of Computer Programs*, MIT Press, 1985.

9 The way to make programs easy to read is not to stuff them with comments. I would take Abelson and Sussman's rule a step further. Programming languages should be designed to express algorithms, and only incidentally to tell computers how to execute them. A good programming language ought to be better for explaining software than English. You should only need comments when there is some kind of kludge you need to warn readers about, just as on a road there are only arrows on parts with unexpectedly sharp curves.

CHAPTER 3, 34–49

1 The Inquisition probably never intended to carry out their threat of torture. But that was because Galileo made it clear he would do whatever they asked. If he had refused, they would not simply have backed down. Not long before they had burnt the philosopher Giordano Bruno when he proved intransigent.

2 Many organizations obligingly publish lists of what you can't say within them. Unfortunately these lists are usually both incomplete, because there are things so shocking they don't even anticipate anyone saying them, and at the same time so general that they couldn't possibly be enforced literally. It's a rare university speech code that would not, taken literally, forbid Shakespeare.

3 Kundel, H. L., C. F. Nodine, and E. A. Krupinski, "Searching for lung nodules: Visual dwell indicates locations of false-positive and false-negative decisions," *Investigative Radiology*, 24 (1989), 472-478.

4 The verb "diff" is computer jargon, but it's the only word with exactly the sense I want. See Glossary.

5 It may seem from this that I am some kind of moral relativist. Far from it. I think that "judgmental" is one of the labels used in our time to suppress discussion, and that our attempts to be "non-judgmental" will seem to future eras one of the most comical things about us.

6 This makes the world confusing to kids, since what they see disagrees with what they're told. I could never understand why, for example, Portuguese "ex-

plorers" had started to work their way along the coast of Africa. In fact, they were after slaves.

De Azurara, Gomes Eannes, *Chronicle of the Discovery of Guinea*, in Almeida (ed.), *Conquests and Discoveries of Henry the Navigator*, George Allen & Unwin, 1936.

7 The kids soon learn these words from their friends, but they know they're not supposed to use them. So for a while you have a state of affairs like something from a musical comedy, where the parents use these words among their peers, but never in front of the children, and the children use the words among their peers, but never in front of their parents.

8 Viaweb's logo was a solid red circle with a white V in the middle. After we'd been using it for a while, I remember thinking, you know, this is a really powerful symbol, a red circle. Red is arguably the most basic color, and the circle the most basic shape. Together they had such visual punch. Why didn't more American companies have a red circle as their logo? Ahh, yes....

9 The fear is far the stronger of the two forces. Sometimes when I hear someone use the word "gyp" I tell them, with a serious expression, that one can't use that word anymore because it's considered disparaging to Romani (aka Gypsies). In fact dictionaries disagree about its etymology. But the reaction to this joke is nearly always one of slightly terrified compliance. There is something about fashion, in clothing or ideas, that takes away people's confidence: when they learn something new, they feel it was something they should have known already.

10 This is the one overt example in this essay of something you can't say. It violates the principal taboo of university life. Within universities it's an unspoken axiom that all areas of study are intellectually equal. No doubt this axiom helps things run more smoothly. But when you consider what an astonishing coincidence it would require for it to be true, and how convenient it would be for everyone to treat it as true even if it weren't, how can you not question it?

Particularly when you consider some of the corollaries it forces you to accept. For example, it would mean that there could not be ups and downs within an individual field. Unless all fields were oscillating in sync. (You really have to stretch to save this one.)

And then, what do you do about universities that have departments like Culinary Arts or Sports Management? If you accept this axiom, how far does it extend? Do you really want to find yourself defending the position that differential geometry is no harder than cooking?

11 Presumably, within the industry, such thoughts would be considered "negative." Another label, much like "defeatist." Never mind that, one should ask, are they true or not? Indeed, the measure of a healthy organization is probably the degree to which negative thoughts are allowed. In places where great work is being done, the attitude usually seems to be critical and sarcastic rather than "positive" and "supportive." The people I know who do great work think that they suck, but that everyone else sucks more.

12 Behar, Richard, "The Thriving Cult of Greed and Power," *Time*, 6 May 1991.

13 Healy, Patrick, "Summers hits 'anti-Semitic' actions," *Boston Globe*, 20 September 2002.

14 "Tinkerers' champion," *The Economist*, 20 June 2002.

15 By this I mean you'd have to become a professional controversialist, not that Noam Chomsky's opinions = what you can't say. If you actually said the things you can't say, you'd shock conservatives and liberals about equally—just as, if you went back to Victorian England in a time machine, your ideas would shock Whigs and Tories about equally.

16 Traub, James, "Harvard Radical," *New York Times Magazine*, 24 August 2003.

17 Miller, Arthur, *The Crucible in History and Other Essays*, Methuen, 2000.

18 Some tribes avoid "wrong" as judgmental, and instead use more neutral-sounding euphemisms like "negative" or "destructive."

CHAPTER 4, 50–55

1 I planned to learn how to pick locks too. But not just out of intellectual curiosity. When I was about halfway through grad school, the clever but truculent corps of undergrad hackers who used to administer all the computers were replaced by a professional system administrator who used to go home at 5 o'clock and leave the machine room door locked. If a computer got wedged, one was expected to wait till morning to reboot it. A completely impractical plan, since at that time we often didn't even start working till 5 PM. Fortunately, in Aiken Lab (since demolished) there was a gap between the floors, and a trapdoor right over the system administrator's office. When we needed the machine room key, we'd drop in through the ceiling and get it out of his desk drawer.

One night at about 3 AM as I was climbing down onto the sysadmin's desk, ear-splitting alarms went off all through the building. "Fuck," I thought (sorry for the profanity, but I clearly remember thinking that), "they've wired the place." I was out of that building in about thirty seconds. I scurried home (through a drenching rainstorm), trying to look nonchalant, but to my guilty conscience every car looked like a Crown Victoria. When I showed up at the Lab the next day I was already rehearsing my defense, but there was no ominous email waiting for me. It turned out the alarms had been set off by lightning during the storm.

2 It's not just the content of products that's increasingly software. As manufacturing becomes more automated, designs become software too.

3 I would gladly volunteer my name for this curve. Calling it something will make the idea stick better.

CHAPTER 5, 56–86

1 Realizing that much of the money is in the services, companies building lightweight clients have usually tried to combine the hardware with an online service. This approach has not worked well, partly because you need two different kinds of companies to build consumer electronics and to run an online service, and partly because users hate the idea. Giving away the handle and making

money on the blades may work for Gillette, but a razor is a smaller commitment than a web terminal.

Cell phone handset makers are satisfied to sell hardware without trying to capture the service revenue as well. That should probably be the model for Internet clients too. If someone just sold a nice-looking little box with a web browser that you could use to connect through any ISP, every technophobe in the country would buy one.

2 Security always depends more on not screwing up than any design decision, but the nature of server-based software will make developers pay more attention to not screwing up. Compromising a server could cause such damage that ASPs (who want to stay in business) are likely to be careful about security.

3 In 1995, when we started Viaweb, Java applets were supposed to be the technology everyone was going to use to develop server-based applications. Applets seemed to us an old-fashioned idea. Download programs to run on the client? Simpler just to go all the way and run the programs on the server. We wasted little time on applets, but countless other startups must have been lured into this tar pit. Few seem to have escaped alive.

4 This point is due to Trevor Blackwell, who adds, "The cost of writing software goes up more than linearly with its size. Perhaps this is mainly due to fixing old bugs, and the cost can be more linear if all bugs are found quickly."

5 The hardest kind of bug to find may be a variant of compound bug where one bug happens to compensate for another. When you fix one bug, the other becomes visible. But it will seem as if the fix is at fault, since that was the last thing you changed.

6 Within Viaweb we once had a contest to describe the worst thing about our software. Two customer support people tied for first prize with entries I still shiver to recall. We fixed both problems immediately.

7 Robert Morris wrote the ordering system, which shoppers used to place orders. Trevor Blackwell wrote the image generator and the manager, which merchants used to retrieve orders, view statistics, configure domain names, etc. I wrote the editor, which merchants used to build their sites. The ordering system and image generator were written in C and C++, the manager mostly in Perl, and the editor in Common Lisp.

8 I'm using "exponentially" in the colloquial sense here. Properly it should be "polynomially."

9 Price discrimination is so pervasive that I was surprised to find it was outlawed in the US by the Robinson-Patman Act of 1936. This law does not appear to be vigorously enforced.

10 In *No Logo*, Naomi Klein says that clothing brands favored by "urban youth" do not try too hard to prevent shoplifting because in their target market the shoplifters are also the fashion leaders.

11 Companies often wonder what to outsource and what not to. One possible answer: outsource any job that's not directly exposed to competitive pressure, because outsourcing it will thereby expose it to competitive pressure. (I mean

"outsource" in the sense of hiring another company to do it, not the more specific sense of hiring an overseas company.)

12 The two guys were Dan Bricklin and Bob Frankston. Dan wrote a prototype in Basic in a couple days, then over the course of the next year they worked together (mostly at night) to make a more powerful version written in 6502 machine language. Dan was at Harvard Business School at the time and Bob nominally had a day job writing software. "There was no great risk in doing a business," Bob told me. "If it failed it failed. No big deal."

13 It's not quite as easy as I make it sound. It took a long time for word of mouth to get going, and we didn't get a lot of press coverage until we hired Schwartz Communications, probably the best high-tech PR firm in the business, for $16,000/month (plus some warrants). However, it was true that the only significant channel was our own web site.

14 If the Mac was so great, why did it lose? Cost, again. Microsoft concentrated on the software business and unleashed a swarm of cheap component suppliers on Apple hardware. It did not help, either, that suits took over during a critical period. (And it hasn't lost yet. If Apple were to grow the iPod into a cell phone with a web browser, Microsoft would be in big trouble.)

15 One thing that would help web-based applications, and help keep the next generation of software from being overshadowed by Microsoft, would be a good open source browser. A small, fast browser would be a great thing in itself, and would encourage companies to build little web appliances.

Best of all, a good open source browser could cause HTTP and HTML to continue to evolve (as e.g. Perl has). Remember when every release of Netscape added new features to HTML? Why did that have to stop?

It would help web-based applications greatly to be able to distinguish between selecting a link and following it; all you'd need to do this would be a trivial enhancement of HTTP, to allow multiple URLs in a request. Cascading menus would also be good.

If you want to change the world, write a new Mosaic. Think it's too late? In 1998 a lot of people thought it was too late to launch a new search engine, but Google proved them wrong. There is always room for something new if it is significantly better.

16 Trevor Blackwell, who probably knows more about this from personal experience than anyone, writes:

"I would go farther in saying that because server-based software is so hard on the programmers, it causes a fundamental economic shift away from large companies. It requires the kind of intensity and dedication from programmers that they will only be willing to provide when it's their own company. Software companies can hire skilled people to work in a not-too-demanding environment, and can hire unskilled people to endure hardships, but they can't hire highly skilled people to bust their asses. Since capital is no longer needed, big companies have little to bring to the table."

17 I would not even use Javascript, if I were you; Viaweb didn't. Most of the Javascript I see on the Web isn't necessary, and much of it breaks. And when

you start to be able to browse actual web pages on your cell phone or PDA (or toaster), who knows if they'll even support it?

CHAPTER 6, 87–108

1 One valuable thing you tend to get only in startups is *uninterruptability*. Different kinds of work have different time quanta. Someone proofreading a manuscript could probably be interrupted every fifteen minutes with little loss of productivity. But the time quantum for hacking is very long: it might take an hour just to load a problem into your head. So the cost of having someone from personnel call you about a form you forgot to fill out can be huge.

This is why hackers give you such a baleful stare as they turn from their screen to answer your question. Inside their heads a giant house of cards is tottering.

The mere possibility of being interrupted deters hackers from starting hard projects. This is why they tend to work late at night, and why it's next to impossible to write great software in a cubicle (except late at night).

One great advantage of startups is that they don't yet have any of the people who interrupt you. There is no personnel department, and thus no form nor anyone to call you about it.

2 Faced with the idea that people working for startups might be 20 or 30 times as productive as those working for large companies, executives at large companies will naturally wonder, how could I get the people working for me to do that? The answer is simple: pay them to.

Internally most companies are run like Communist states. If you believe in free markets, why not turn your company into one?

Hypothesis: A company will be maximally profitable when each employee is paid in proportion to the wealth they generate.

3 Until recently even governments sometimes didn't grasp the distinction between money and wealth. Adam Smith (*Wealth of Nations*, v:i) mentions several that tried to preserve their "wealth" by forbidding the export of gold or silver. But having more of the medium of exchange would not make a country richer; if you have more money chasing the same amount of material wealth, the only result is higher prices.

4 There are many senses of the word "wealth," not all of them material. I'm not trying to make a deep philosophical point here about which is the true kind. I'm writing about one specific, rather technical sense of the word "wealth." What people will give you money for. This is an interesting sort of wealth to study, because it is the kind that prevents you from starving. And what people will give you money for depends on them, not you.

When you're starting a business, it's easy to slide into thinking that customers want what you do. During the Internet Bubble I talked to a woman who, because she liked the outdoors, was starting an "outdoor portal." You know what kind of business you should start if you like the outdoors? One to recover data from crashed hard disks.

What's the connection? None at all. Which is precisely my point. If you want to create wealth (in the narrow technical sense of not starving) then you should be especially skeptical about any plan that centers on things you like doing.

That is where your idea of what's valuable is least likely to coincide with other people's.

5 In the average car restoration you probably do make everyone else microscopically poorer, by doing a small amount of damage to the environment. While environmental costs should be taken into account, they don't make wealth a zero-sum game. For example, if you repair a machine that's broken because a part has come unscrewed, you create wealth with no environmental cost.

6 Many people feel confused and depressed in their early twenties. Life seemed so much more fun in college. Well, of course it was. Don't be fooled by the surface similarities. You've gone from guest to servant. It's possible to have fun in this new world. Among other things, you now get to go behind the doors that say "authorized personnel only." But the change is a shock at first, and all the worse if you're not consciously aware of it.

7 When VCs asked us how long it would take another startup to duplicate our software, we used to reply that they probably wouldn't be able to at all. I think this made us seem naive, or liars.

8 Few technologies have one clear inventor. So as a rule, if you know the "inventor" of something (the telephone, the assembly line, the airplane, the light bulb, the transistor) it is because their company made money from it, and the company's PR people worked hard to spread the story. If you don't know who invented something (the automobile, the television, the computer, the jet engine, the laser), it's because other companies made all the money.

9 This is a good plan for life in general. If you have two choices, choose the harder. If you're trying to decide whether to go out running or sit home and watch TV, go running. Probably the reason this trick works so well is that when you have two choices and one is harder, the only reason you're even considering the other is laziness. You know in the back of your mind what's the right thing to do, and this trick merely forces you to acknowledge it.

10 It is probably no accident that the middle class first appeared in northern Italy and the low countries, where there were no strong central governments. These two regions were the richest of their time and became the twin centers from which Renaissance civilization radiated. If they no longer play that role, it is because other places, like the United States, have been truer to the principles they discovered.

11 It may indeed be a sufficient condition. But if so, why didn't the Industrial Revolution happen earlier? Two possible (and not incompatible) answers: (a) It did. The Industrial Revolution was one in a series. (b) Because in medieval towns, monopolies and guild regulations initially slowed the development of new means of production.

CHAPTER 7, 109–120

1 Part of the reason this subject is so contentious is that some of those most vocal on the subject of wealth—university students, heirs, professors, politicians, and journalists—have the least experience creating it. (This phenomenon will be familiar to anyone who has overheard conversations about sports in a bar.)

Students are mostly still on the parental dole, and have not stopped to think about where that money comes from. Heirs will be on the parental dole for life. Professors and politicians live within socialist eddies of the economy, at one remove from the creation of wealth, and are paid a flat rate regardless of how hard they work. And journalists as part of their professional code segregate themselves from the revenue-collecting half of the businesses they work for (the ad sales department). Many of these people never come face to face with the fact that the money they receive represents wealth—wealth that, except in the case of journalists, someone else created earlier. They live in a world in which income *is* doled out by a central authority according to some abstract notion of fairness (or randomly, in the case of heirs), rather than given by other people in return for something they wanted, so it may seem to them unfair that things don't work the same in the rest of the economy.

(Some professors do create a great deal of wealth for society. But the money they're paid isn't a *quid pro quo*. It's more in the nature of an investment.)

2 When one reads about the origins of the Fabian Society, it sounds like something cooked up by the high-minded Edwardian child-heroes of Edith Nesbit's *The Wouldbegoods*.

3 According to a study by the Corporate Library, the median total compensation, including salary, bonus, stock grants, and the exercise of stock options, of S&P 500 CEOs in 2002 was $3.65 million. According to *Sports Illustrated*, the average NBA player's salary during the 2002-03 season was $4.54 million, and the average major league baseball player's salary at the start of the 2003 season was $2.56 million. According to the Bureau of Labor Statistics, the mean annual wage in the US in 2002 was $35,560.

4 In the early empire the price of an ordinary adult slave seems to have been about 2,000 sestertii (e.g. Horace, *Sat.* ii.7.43). A servant girl cost 600 (Martial vi.66), while Columella (iii.3.8) says that a skilled vine-dresser was worth 8,000. A doctor, P. Decimus Eros Merula, paid 50,000 sestertii for his freedom (Dessau, *Inscriptiones* 7812). Seneca (*Ep.* xxvii.7) reports that one Calvisius Sabinus paid 100,000 sestertii apiece for slaves learned in the Greek classics. Pliny (*Hist. Nat.* vii.39) says that the highest price paid for a slave up to his time was 700,000 sestertii, for the linguist (and presumably teacher) Daphnis, but that this had since been exceeded by actors buying their own freedom.

Classical Athens saw a similar variation in prices. An ordinary laborer was worth about 125 to 150 drachmae. Xenophon (*Mem.* ii.5) mentions prices ranging from 50 to 6,000 drachmae (for the manager of a silver mine).

For more on the economics of ancient slavery see:

Jones, A. H. M., "Slavery in the Ancient World," *Economic History Review*, 2:9 (1956), 185-199, reprinted in Finley, M. I. (ed.), *Slavery in Classical Antiquity*, Heffer, 1964.

5 Eratosthenes (276–195 BC) used shadow lengths in different cities to estimate the Earth's circumference. He was off by only about 2%.

6 No, and Windows, respectively.

7 One of the biggest divergences between the Daddy Model and reality is the valuation of hard work. In the Daddy Model, hard work is in itself deserving. In reality, wealth is measured by what one delivers, not how much effort it costs. If I paint someone's house, the owner shouldn't pay me extra for doing it with a toothbrush.

It will seem to someone still implicitly operating on the Daddy Model that it is unfair when someone works hard and doesn't get paid much. To help clarify the matter, get rid of everyone else and put our worker on a desert island, hunting and gathering fruit. If he's bad at it he'll work very hard and not end up with much food. Is this unfair? Who is being unfair to him?

8 Part of the reason for the tenacity of the Daddy Model may be the dual meaning of "distribution." When economists talk about "distribution of income," they mean statistical distribution. But when you use the phrase frequently, you can't help associating it with the other sense of the word (as in e.g. "distribution of alms"), and thereby subconsciously seeing wealth as something that flows from some central tap. The word "regressive" as applied to tax rates has a similar effect, at least on me; how can anything *regressive* be good?

9 "From the beginning of the reign Thomas Lord Roos was an assiduous courtier of the young Henry VIII and was soon to reap the rewards. In 1525 he was made a Knight of the Garter and given the Earldom of Rutland. In the thirties his support of the breach with Rome, his zeal in crushing the Pilgrimage of Grace, and his readiness to vote the death-penalty in the succession of spectacular treason trials that punctuated Henry's erratic matrimonial progress made him an obvious candidate for grants of monastic property."

Stone, Lawrence, *Family and Fortune: Studies in Aristocratic Finance in the Sixteenth and Seventeenth Centuries*, Oxford University Press, 1973, p. 166.

10 There is archaeological evidence for large settlements earlier, but it's hard to say what was happening in them.

Hodges, Richard and David Whitehouse, *Mohammed, Charlemagne and the Origins of Europe*, Cornell University Press, 1983.

11 William Cecil and his son Robert were each in turn the most powerful minister of the crown, and both used their position to amass fortunes among the largest of their times. Robert in particular took bribery to the point of treason. "As Secretary of State and the leading advisor to King James on foreign policy, [he] was a special recipient of favour, being offered large bribes by the Dutch not to make peace with Spain, and large bribes by Spain to make peace." (Stone, *op. cit.*, p. 17.)

12 Though Balzac made a lot of money from writing, he was notoriously improvident and was troubled by debts all his life.

13 A Timex will gain or lose about .5 seconds per day. The most accurate mechanical watch, the Patek Philippe 10 Day Tourbillon, is rated at -1.5 to +2 seconds. Its retail price is about $220,000.

14 If asked to choose which was more expensive, a well-preserved 1989 Lincoln Town Car ten-passenger limousine ($5,000) or a 2004 Mercedes S600 sedan ($122,000), the average Edwardian might well guess wrong.

15 To say anything meaningful about income trends, you have to talk about real income, or income as measured in what it can buy. But the usual way of calculating real income ignores much of the growth in wealth over time, because it depends on a consumer price index created by bolting end to end a series of numbers that are only locally accurate, and that don't include the prices of new inventions until they become so common that their prices stabilize.

So while we might think it was very much better to live in a world with antibiotics or air travel or an electric power grid than without, real income statistics calculated in the usual way will prove to us that we are only slightly richer for having these things.

Another approach would be to ask, if you were going back to the year x in a time machine, how much would you have to spend on trade goods to make your fortune? For example, if you were going back to 1970 it would certainly be less than $500, because the processing power you can get for $500 today would have been worth at least $150 million in 1970. The function goes asymptotic fairly quickly, because for times over a hundred years or so you could get all you needed in present-day trash. In 1800 an empty plastic drink bottle with a screw top would have seemed a miracle of workmanship.

16 Some will say this amounts to the same thing, because the rich have better opportunities for education. That's a valid point. It is still possible, to a degree, to buy your kids' way into top colleges by sending them to private schools that in effect hack the college admissions process.

According to a 2002 report by the National Center for Education Statistics, about 1.7% of American kids attend private, non-sectarian schools. At Princeton, 36% of the class of 2007 came from such schools. (Interestingly, the number at Harvard is significantly lower, about 28%.) Obviously this is a huge loophole. It does at least seem to be closing, not widening.

Perhaps the designers of admissions processes should take a lesson from the example of computer security, and instead of just assuming that their system can't be hacked, measure the degree to which it is.

CHAPTER 8, 121–129

1 Some of the essays in this book have been rewritten, but except for translating the probability calculations from Lisp code into mathematical notation, I left this one alone. So a few things in it are no longer true. Few spams contain the word "click" now. But the algorithm still works. A slightly improved version catches about 99.6% of current spam. For more on filtering see paulgraham.com.

2 In 2002 the lowest rate seemed to be about $200 to send a million spams. That's very cheap, 1/50th of a cent per spam. But filtering out 95% of spam, for example, would increase the spammers' cost to reach a given audience by a factor of 20. Few can have margins big enough to absorb that.

CHAPTER 9, 130–145

1 Sullivan actually said "form ever follows function," but I think the usual misquotation is closer to what modernist architects meant.

2 The engine of the Wright Flyer weighed 152 lbs. and generated 12 hp. The F414-GE-400 jet engine used in the F-18 weighs 2,445 lbs. and generates 22,000 lbs. of thrust. Assuming 1 lb. thrust = 1 hp., it delivers about 114 times as much power per weight.

Current Intel processors, meanwhile, deliver about 1700 times the processing power of those available 30 years ago.

3 Brush, Stephen G., "Why was Relativity Accepted?" *Physics in Perspective*, 1 (1999), 184-214.

CHAPTER 10, 146–154

1 The most common way of breaking into computers takes advantage of some idiosyncrasies of C. In C, when you set aside a chunk of memory (a *buffer*) for some input you're expecting, it gets allocated next to the memory containing the *return address* of the currently running code. The return address is the location in memory of the code that's going to be executed when the current code is done. It is, in effect, the next thing on the computer's to-do list.

So if someone wants to break into your computer, and they guess you're using a 256-byte buffer to store some kind of input, then by sending just over 256 bytes they can overwrite the return address. When the current code is done, control will pass to whatever location in memory they've specified. And the location they'll usually specify will be the beginning of the buffer, which they've just filled up with the machine language program of their choice. Bingo: their program is now running on your computer.

In higher-level languages this would be impossible, but in C, whenever you take input from outside and don't check the length, you've created a security hole. An attack that exploits such a hole is called a *buffer overflow attack*. There are other ways to get control of a computer in a buffer overflow attack, but overwriting the return address is the classic method.

Curiously, airline hijackings are also buffer overflow attacks. In an ordinary airliner, passengers and cockpit are adjacent, just as data and code are adjacent in a C program. By overflowing into the cockpit, hijackers in effect promote themselves from data to code.

2 Note to hackers: this is merely a metaphor. Do not attempt to drive a Yugo with a jet engine bolted to the roof.

Arguably, the Yugojet phenomenon is not new. Fortran also owes its popularity largely to its libraries.

3 Cipolla, Carlo, *Guns, Sails, and Empires: Technological Innovation and the Early Phases of European Expansion 1400-1700*, Pantheon, 1965.

CHAPTER 11, 155–168

1 I believe Lisp Machine Lisp was the first language to embody the principle that declarations (except those of dynamic variables) were merely optimization advice, and would not change the meaning of a correct program. Common Lisp seems to have been the first to state this explicitly.

1 Viaweb at first had two parts: the editor, written in Common Lisp, which people used to build their sites, and the ordering system, written in C, which handled orders. The first version was mostly Lisp, because the ordering system was small.

In January 2003, Yahoo released a new version of the editor written in C++ and Perl. But to translate this program into C++ they literally had to write a Lisp interpreter: the source files of all the page-generating templates are still, as far as I know, Lisp code. (See Greenspun's Tenth Rule, p. 198.)

2 Robert says I didn't need to be secretive, because even if our competitors had known we were using Lisp, they wouldn't have understood why: "If they were that smart they'd already be programming in Lisp."

3 All languages are equally powerful in the sense of being Turing-equivalent, but that's not the sense of the word programmers care about. (No one wants to program a Turing machine.) The kind of power programmers care about may not be formally definable, but one way to explain it would be to say that it refers to features you could only get in the less powerful language by writing an interpreter for the more powerful language in it. If language A has an operator for removing spaces from strings and language B doesn't, that probably doesn't make A more powerful, because you can probably write a subroutine to do it in B. But if A supports, say, recursion, and B doesn't, that's not likely to be something you can fix by writing library functions.

4 Or possibly a lattice, narrowing toward the top. It's not the shape that matters here but the idea that there is at least a partial order.

5 It is a bit misleading to treat macros as a separate feature. In practice their usefulness is greatly enhanced by other Lisp features like lexical closures and rest parameters.

6 As a result, comparisons of programming languages either take the form of religious wars or undergraduate textbooks so determinedly neutral that they're really works of anthropology. People who value their peace, or want tenure, avoid the topic. But the question is only half a religious one; there is something there worth studying, especially if you want to design new languages.

1 After putting this essay online I got an apparently genuine email beginning:

Pointy haired? Aren't all hairs pointed? If this is the best insulting term for a boss that you can come up with it's easy to see how deservedly you guys have earned the nickname "nerd".

2 The IBM 704 CPU was about the size of a refrigerator, but a lot heavier. The CPU weighed 3150 pounds, and the 4K of RAM was in a separate box weighing another 4000 pounds. The Sub-Zero 690, one of the largest household refrigerators, weighs 656 pounds.

3 Steve Russell also wrote the first (digital) computer game, Spacewar, in 1962.

4 A number of Lisp features, including programs expressed as lists and a form of recursion, were implemented in IPL-V. But it was more of an assembly language; a program consisted of a sequence of opcode/address pairs.

Newell, Allen (ed.), *Information Processing Language-V Manual*, Prentice-Hall, 1961.

5 If you want to trick a pointy-haired boss into letting you write software in Lisp, you could try telling him it's XML.

6 Muehlbauer, Jen, "Orbitz Reaches New Heights," *New Architect*, April 2002.

7 Here is the accumulator generator in other Lisp dialects:

```
Scheme:  (define (foo n)
            (lambda (i) (set! n (+ n i)) n))
Goo:     (df foo (n) (op incf n _)))
Arc:     (def foo (n) [++ n _])
```

8 Peter Norvig found that 16 of the 23 patterns in *Design Patterns* were "invisible or simpler" in Lisp (www.norvig.com/design-patterns).

CHAPTER 14, 200–215

1 A hello-world program is a program that does nothing but print the words "Hello, world!" In Java you'd write:

```
public class Hello {
    public static void main(String[] args) {
        System.out.println("Hello, world!");
    }
}
```

Someone who has never written a program probably looks at this and wonders, why do you need to say so much to get the the computer to print a message? Curiously, the reaction of experienced programmers is identical.

2 In *When the Air Hits Your Brain*, neurosurgeon Frank Vertosick recounts a conversation in which his chief resident, Gary, talks about the difference between surgeons and internists ("fleas"):

> Gary and I ordered a large pizza and found an open booth. The chief lit a cigarette. "Look at those goddamn fleas, jabbering about some disease they'll see once in their lifetimes. That's the trouble with fleas, they only like the bizarre stuff. They hate their bread and butter cases. That's the difference between us and the fucking fleas. See, we love big juicy lumbar disc herniations, but they hate hypertension. . . . "

It's hard to think of a lumbar disc herniation as juicy (except literally). But I think I know what they mean. I've often had a juicy bug to track down. Someone who's not a programmer would find it hard to imagine that there could be pleasure in a bug. Surely it's better if everything just works. And yet there is undeniably a grim satisfaction in hunting down certain sorts of bugs.

Acknowledgments

First on the list of people I have to thank is Sarah Harlin. After writing an essay I usually showed it to her first. And she usually crossed out half of it and told me to rewrite the rest. She has a perfect ear for prose rhythm, and barks at superfluous words like a dog after a squirrel.

If these essays are any good it's because most grew out of conversations with her or with Robert Morris, Trevor Blackwell, or Jackie McDonough. I'm lucky to know them.

The book benefits from the ideas of several other friends with whom I've talked about these questions over the past several years: Ken Anderson, Chip Coldwell, Matthias Felleisen, Dan Friedman, Daniel Giffin, Shiro Kawai, Lisa Randall, Eric Raymond, Olin Shivers, Bob van der Zwaan, and David Weinberger. Eric Raymond I owe special thanks not just for his ideas but for his example in writing about hacking.

I owe thanks to many others for help and ideas, including Jülide Aker, Chris Anderson, Jonathan Bachrach, Ingrid Bassett, Jeff Bates, Alan Bawden, Andrew Cohen, Cindy Cohn, Kate Courteau, Maria Daniels, Rich Draves, Jon Erickson, John Foderaro, Bob Frankston, Erann Gat, Phil Greenspun, Ann Gregg, Amy Harmon, Andy Hertzfeld, Jeremy Hylton, Brad Karp, Shriram Krishnamurthi, Fritz Kunze, Joel Lehrer, Henry Leitner, Larry Lessig, Simon London, John McCarthy, Doug McIlroy, Rob Malda, Julie Mallozzi, Matz, Larry Mihalko, Mark Nitzberg, North Shore United, Peter Norvig, the Parmets, Sesha Pratap, Joel Rainey, Jonathan Rees, Guido van Rossum, Barry Shein, the Sloos, Mike Smith, Ryan Stanley, Guy Steele, Sam Steingold, Anton van Straaten, Greg Sullivan, Brad Templeton, Dave Touretzky, Mike Vanier, the Weickers, JonL White, Stephen Wolfram, and Bill Yerazunis.

This book looks good because the design was really done by typography god Gino Lee, not me. I know enough about book design to do whatever Gino says. Chip Coldwell spent hours beating on fonts and Amy Hendrickson days writing LaTex macros to achieve the appearance of ease you see here. The cover, curiously, was in a sense designed by Robert Morris, who fired up the Gimp and did some surgery on the previous version. Thanks to Gilberte Houbart for her ingenuity and persistence in extracting images from sources all over the world.

The guys at O'Reilly did an excellent job: Allen Noren, whose genuine interest in making good books is enough to restore one's faith in the book business; Betsy Waliszewski, whose vision for a more popular book stealthily became mine; Matt Hutchinson, Robert Romano, and Claire Cloutier, who made production run smoothly; and Tim O'Reilly, who shows what publishing can be when a publisher is a person rather than a conglomerate.

Extra special thanks to Jessica Livingston. Her advice improved every part of this book, from the front cover to the index. Her unfailing encouragement made the book better too: by telling me constantly that lots of people would want to read it, she frightened me into trying hard to make it something lots of people would want to read.

I learned about hacking from many people, but I learned about painting mostly from one: Idelle Weber, a great teacher all the better for teaching by example. I'm deeply indebted to her and her husband Julian for years of kindness.

Thanks finally to my father, for teaching me skepticism, and to my mother, for teaching me imagination. Having her for a mom has been like seeing the world in color.

Image Credits

Glossary

abstract Hiding details. When a language is more abstract, you can write programs using a smaller number of (individually more powerful) operations.

Ada An *object-oriented* language designed by a committee for the DoD in the late 1970s. Turned out about like you would expect.

AI, artificial intelligence A general term for several kinds of work that attempt to make machines think. The more mathematical have had some success (e.g. in computer vision).

Algol A programming language initially designed in 1958 by a committee (bad) of very smart (good) people. Rarely used to write programs, but had a great influence on succeeding languages.

algorithm A method for doing something. Recipes are examples of algorithms.

alphanumeric characters Letters and digits.

API Application Program Interface. The list of commands an *operating system* or *library* will accept from *applications*.

APL An extremely succinct language designed in the early 1960s by Ken Iverson. Used especially in numerical applications. Its modern descendant is J.

application A program that is not infrastructure. E.g. a word processor, but not an *operating system*. Not a precise term.

Arc A *vaporware Lisp* dialect.

array What in school you called a matrix: an n-dimensional collection of numbered pigeonholes for storing data.

ASP Application Service Provider. A company that lets you use software on their computers via a network, as opposed to installing and running the software on your own computer.

assembly language A more programmer-friendly form of *machine language*. The commands are the same but you can use more convenient names.

B&D language Bondage & discipline language. A language that makes the programmer follow strict rules.

bandwidth The rate at which a connection can transmit data.

Bayesian Using Bayes's Rule, which says how to combine statistical evidence.

binary When used with an article (e.g. "a binary"), *object code*. When used without an article, a way of representing numbers in base 2 instead of the more familiar base 10. Successive digits (starting from the right) represent powers of two instead of powers of ten. So 101, in binary, represents the number we write as 5 in decimal. Most computers represent data in binary, because it's easier to design circuits with two states (on or off) than ten.

bit manipulation Performing simple transformations to large areas of a computer's memory. For example, moving a window on the screen.

bloatcode A programmer who makes programs longer than they should be.

block-structured Describes a language in which programs have subsidiary parts instead of simply being a list of commands.

Blub Paradox The inability to understand the power of programming languages more powerful than the ones you're used to thinking in.

bottom-up programming A style of programming that works from the other direction than the earlier top-down style. Instead of subdividing a task down into smaller units, you build a "language" of ideas up toward your task. The two techniques can be combined.

bound Constrained by a particular resource. E.g. I/O-bound, memory-bound, CPU-bound.

branch A *machine language goto* command.

Brooks's Hypothesis That the number of lines of code programmers can produce per day is constant, regardless of the of the language they're using.

bug A mistake in a program. Predates computers; in the early twentieth century it was common to speak of "ironing out the bugs" in a Broadway play.

buffer A segment of memory used to hold a sequence of data the program expects as input, or is accumulating for output.

buffer overflow attack See p. 234.

byte code Any language like *machine language*, but not of any specific computer. Because byte code is like machine language, it is easy to write a byte code *interpreter*, which reads byte code programs and executes the corresponding machine language commands.

C A beautifully simple language developed by Dennis Ritchie in the early 1970s. Widely used in infrastructure like *operating systems* and routers.

C++ An attempt to add *object-oriented* capabilities to *C*, designed by Bjarne Stroustrup in 1983. Popular because its *syntax* is like C's, and it can be intermixed with C programs.

CGI script Common Gateway Interface script. A program that a *web server* runs when it needs to compute something (e.g. search results) rather than just sending you a pre-existing web page. The key limitation of CGI scripts is that they generate only one page before terminating, rather than remaining in memory and having an ongoing conversation with the user, like desktop software.

checksum A way of summing up all the information in a *file* to get one number that can be used to identify it. One (not very good) way to calculate a checksum, for example, would be to use the number of characters.

circular definition See *infinite loop.*

class In *object-oriented* programming, a *data type*.

click trail The series of *HTTP* requests sent to a *web server* by one specific user. Usually equates to the series of web pages they visited.

client A computer or device that submits requests to a *server*.

Cobol A primitive language designed in the early 1960s for use in business applications. Only recently succeeded by *Java* as the most popular language.

code When unqualified, *source code*.

collocated Located, especially at an ISP.

comment Part of a program that is ignored by the computer. Usually inserted as an annotation for human readers.

Common Lisp A popular dialect of *Lisp* designed by a committee in the 1980s.

compiler A program that translates programs written in a more powerful, succinct language (a *high-level language*) into the simpler commands (*machine language*) that the computer hardware understands. See also: *interpreter*.

complexity The time complexity of an *algorithm* is how fast the time required to complete it grows as the size of the input grows. For example, if you have to search a room for a specific person by looking at each in turn, the time required to find him will be proportionate to the number of people. Such an algorithm is called $O(n)$, meaning it takes time proportionate to n, the size of the data. Whereas if you wanted to find the two people in the room who looked most like siblings, you'd probably take time proportionate to the square of the number of people, because you might have to compare every pair, and the number of pairs is the square of the number of people. Such an algorithm is $O(n^2)$.

conditional A *high-level* language *expression* (or *statement*) in which different code is executed depending on whether or not some condition is true. For example: if it is sunny, then go for a walk, otherwise stay inside and read.

content-based filtering Filtering email based on what it says, rather than, for example, where on the Internet it came from.

CPU Central Processing Unit. The part of a computer, usually now a single chip, where computations are carried out. The concept is growing blurred, because there are now processors within e.g. graphics cards and hard disks.

crash When a *bug* causes an *operating system* or *application* to stop working. Or, when applied to hard disks, a hardware malfunction.

cruft Debris.

cycle The minimum time required to execute a *machine instruction*. A computer with a clock speed of 1 GHz has a billion cycles per second, meaning it can execute up to a billion machine instructions per second.

DARPA Defense Advanced Research Projects Agency. Has funded much of the computer research in the United States.

data structure A format for data with multiple parts. For example, you could use one consisting of a pair of numbers to represent points on a graph.

data type A category of data that a language can deal with. Typical data types include integers (1), floating-point numbers, which in school you called decimals (1.234), and character *strings* ("monster").

dynamic typing The opposite of *static typing.*

debugging Finding and fixing mistakes in a program.

declaration An element of a program that is more of a description than a command. The most common are *type* declarations, where you say what type of values a variable may have.

deprecated Said of practices supported by a standard whose authors now wish they had not allowed them.

design war A competition where the best design wins, rather than e.g. marketing or control of sales outlets.

device driver Component of an *operating system* that knows how to talk to a specific device, like a printer.

diff An unselective and microscopically thorough comparison between two versions of something. From the *Unix* diff utility, which compares *files.*

embedded language A language defined within another language, usually for a specific kind of problem. For example, if you define a series of commands for manipulating images, you can start to think of them as a language for manipulating images. See *bottom-up programming.*

end user Euphemism for unsophisticated user.

environment Software to help in writing programs, e.g. editors and *profilers.*

expression A quantum of code that when executed yields a value. E.g. the expression 2 + 3 will yield 5.

field One of the parts of a *data structure.*

file A sequence of characters or *binary* digits, usually stored on disk.

Fortran A programming language widely used for numerical applications. Originally designed by a group at IBM in 1956, it has evolved greatly since.

FreeBSD An *open source* dialect of *Unix.*

freeware Software distributed for free.

function A *subroutine* that, when called, yields a value, which becomes the value of the call. In some languages, functions are a *data type.*

garbage collection Recovering memory that is no longer needed by a program automatically, instead of requiring the programmer to explicitly (and often mistakenly) declare when he is finished using it.

glue program A program to sequence or move data between *applications.*

goto A command that transfers control to another part of a program. Because there is no mechanism for returning to a goto, as there is to a *subroutine* call, programs that use gotos tend to become *spaghetti.* Rare now.

Greenspun's Tenth Rule "Any sufficiently complicated *C* or *Fortran* program contains an ad hoc informally-specified *bug*-ridden slow implementation of half of *Common Lisp.*"

hack A solution that somehow breaks the rules. Can be either good or bad.

hacker (1) A good programmer. (2) Someone who breaks into computers.

hash table A *data structure* like a database in which you can store chunks of data under individual keys and later retrieve the data stored under a given key.

headers The part at the top of an email containing information about it. The average user sees only the From, To, Date, Subject, and Cc lines, but there are others describing e.g. the path the email took.

heuristic Rule of thumb.

high-level Substantially more *abstract* than *machine language.*

HTML HyperText Markup Language. The notation used to express web pages.

HTTP HyperText Transfer Protocol. The protocol that web browsers and *servers* use to communicate with one another.

indented Like an outline, *source code* is indented to show its structure. When code says to do a list of things *n* times, for example, the list of things is usually indented to show that it's within a loop. In most languages indentation is something you add to make programs easier to read, but in some (e.g. Python) it is significant, meaning it affects the behavior of the program.

infinite loop See *circular definition.*

interpreter Like a *compiler*, an interpreter accepts programs written in a *high-level language*, but instead of translating the whole program into *machine language* and then running that, the interpreter examines the program one piece at a time and executes the corresponding machine language commands.

inner loop Part of a program that gets executed particularly often.

instrument To modify a program to keep track of everything it does, so that if it's slow or uses too much memory, you can find out why.

Intel box A computer with an Intel processor.

I/O Input and output. Usually, printing and reading characters or *binary* data.

IT Information Technology. Computer infrastructure, or the people in charge of maintaining it. Term used mainly in big or nontechnical companies.

Java An attempt at a better *C++* by James Gosling. Originally called Oak, it was renamed Java by Sun when they adopted it in the hope of inserting a Sun-controlled layer between *operating systems* and *applications.* That didn't work, but Java is popular anyway, partly due to Sun's huge marketing effort, and partly because there is demand for a better C++.

Javascript A *scripting language* for web browsers designed by Brendan Eich. It has no intrinsic connection to *Java*, which is in most ways inferior. Unduly maligned because it is used mainly to do cheesy things on web sites.

kludge A bad *hack.* (Rhymes with stooge.)

larval startup A startup in the earliest phase, when the potential founders are not sure they want to start a company.

legacy software Software an organization still needs, which is not written the way they wish it were, and which they can't afford to or don't dare to rewrite.

lexical closure A *function* that refers to a variable defined not within it, but in the surrounding code. The accumulator generators on page 195 yield closures.

LFSP Language for Smart People. A language that puts power over safety.

library A collection of existing code for performing a specific task.

Linux An *open source* dialect of *Unix*. Called GNU Linux by the fastidious, because while the kernel (the innermost part) was written by Linus Torvalds, more of the code comes from Richard Stallman's GNU Project.

Lisp A family of languages deriving from one John McCarthy discovered in the late 1950s. The two best known dialects are *Common Lisp* and *Scheme*. Recent *open source* languages contain increasing amounts of Lisp DNA.

list A series of pieces of data, often of varying *types*, which can be joined together like trains to make bigger lists.

literal representation A way of referring directly to data in a *high-level language*. In most languages, the literal representation of five is 5. (The *expression* 2 + 3 has the same value, but is not a literal representation.)

low-level Less *abstract*; allowing only simple commands, like *machine language*.

machine instruction One machine language command.

machine language The list of commands a processor knows how to obey. Also, a sequence of such commands.

macro A program that generates programs. The means for doing this vary between languages, so a "macro" in one language may mean something much more powerful than in another.

mainframe A big computer based on designs from the 1960s and 70s.

math envy The worry that one is not as smart as mathematicians, especially when manifested in work with a gratuitously mathematical flavor.

metacircular When the *interpreter* of a language is written in that language. More a technique for describing languages than implementing them.

method In *object-oriented* programming, a *subroutine* considered as a property of some *class* of things. For example, the area method of the circle class might be a subroutine for calculating the areas of circles.

module A group of subroutines and variables considered as a unit. Generally only specifically noted ones are accessible to code outside the module.

Moore's Law The official version of Moore's Law is that the number of transistors on a chip doubles every two years. But most people use the term to mean that processors get twice as fast every 18 months. Arguably more business plan than law, because Gordon Moore was a founder of Intel.

number crunching Performing straightforward operations on large amounts of numerical data.

object A term with many meanings. In the most general sense, an instance of a *data type*. E.g. a particular *string*, or a particular integer.

object code *Machine language*, as the output of a *compiler*.

OO, object-oriented A way of organizing programs so that the code for performing a certain task on different *classes* of data is broken up into separate pieces (*methods*) for each. See p. 152.

Occam's Razor That one should prefer the simpler of two theories.

open source Software whose *source code* is freely distributed and can be modified by anyone, usually on the condition that the modifications also be made freely available. *Linux* and *FreeBSD* are well-known open source *operating systems*.

orthogonal Independent of one another and therefore combinable in many ways. Classic Lego is more orthogonal than a plastic model kit.

OS, operating system The program that controls the running of other programs. *Unix*, *FreeBSD*, *Linux*, *OSX*, and the Windows family are operating systems.

optimization Changing a program to make it more efficient.

parallel computer A computer whose hardware can perform multiple computations simultaneously. Not a sharply delineated category, because all modern processors use some amount of parallelism to increase speed.

Parkinson's Law That the resources required to complete a task will expand to consume the resources available.

parser A program that reads input and produces a *parse tree*.

parse tree The *data structure* into which a *compiler* translates the characters that make up your program, as the first stage of translating it into *machine language*.

Pascal Algol derivative designed in the early 1970s by Niklaus Wirth.

patch A piece of code released to fix a flaw in an earlier program.

PDA Personal Digital Assistant. A small computer you carry with you. Usually has an easier but more limited interface than a regular computer.

Perl An *open source* language developed by Larry Wall. Initially intended for manipulating *strings* of characters, it became popular because this is a large part of what programmers do. Famous for its complex (but concise) *syntax*, and its rapid and promiscuous evolution.

pipe A way of joining *operating system* commands so that the output of one becomes the input of another.

pointer A piece of data whose value is the location in memory of another.

pointer arithmetic Finding things in memory by adding certain amounts to already known locations. A *low-level* technique.

pointy-haired boss Character in the cartoon strip *Dilbert* by Scott Adams. Generically, an inept and overbearing middle manager.

polynomial When applied to growth, means that y grows as a power of x, e.g. as the square or cube of x. The resulting curve gets steeper over time.

portable Able to be moved to new hardware. Programs written in *high-level languages* are (more) portable than *machine language* programs, because they assume (almost) nothing about the hardware.

portal Web site.

premature design Deciding too early what a program should do.

premature optimization Tuning a program for performance before you're finished writing it. The software equivalent of marrying young.

process In an *operating system* that can control multiple programs at once (as all modern OSes can), one of those programs.

programming language A high-level language is what the compiler uses as input to generate object code. (Just kidding; see Chapter 10.)

profiler A program that watches your program while it's running and tells you which parts consume most resources. See *inner loop*.

pseudocode A language for expressing *algorithms* "on paper" rather than to computers. Arguably, this whole concept is an artifact of using languages that are too *low-level*.

Python An *open source* language developed by Guido van Rossum. Strongly *object-oriented* in flavor, it is seen by fans as a cleaner alternative to *Perl*.

QA Quality Assurance. In software, people who detect and catalog *bugs*.

recursive An *algorithm* that refers to itself. A policeman's algorithm for interrogating people is recursive: ask the person if they know about the crime, or if they know anyone who does, and if they do, interrogate them too.

RAID Redundant Array of Independent Disks. A piece of hardware that uses multiple hard disks to simulate one hard disk that (in theory) never *crashes*.

read-eval-print loop A *toplevel*.

regular expression A pattern used like a sieve to retrieve elements of *strings*.

RISC Reduced Instruction Set Computer. A computer whose *machine language* commands do little, but run fast. The aim is to make a better target for *compilers*, in the same way fine granularity film yields sharper images.

Ruby A newer *open source* competitor for *Perl* and *Python* developed by Yukihiro "matz" Matsumoto.

scan To look at a series of characters and divide it up into *tokens*.

Scheme An elegant but prim dialect of *Lisp* designed by Guy Steele and Gerry Sussman in 1975.

scripting language A language used to customize a program. Sometimes *open source* languages like *Perl* and *Python* are called scripting languages, but this usage is meaningless.

server A computer on a network that responds to requests from other computers.

SETI@home Search for Extra-Terrestrial Intelligence etc. A project to search the electromagnetic background for signals from other life forms, using the spare *cycles* of desktop computers connected to the Internet.

s-expression A *token*, or zero or more s-expressions enclosed in parentheses.

Smalltalk The canonical *object-oriented* language, designed by Alan Kay in 1972.

socket In *Unix*, a channel through which *processes* can communicate across a network.

software engineer A formal term for programmer.

spaghetti Code whose structure has so many twists and turns that no one can understand it, including the author.

spam Unsolicited mass email, usually advertising. From a Monty Python skit in which Vikings drown out conversation with choruses of "Spam, Spam, Spam."

spec Specification. An informal description of what a program should do.

SSH Secure SHell. A program for connecting securely to a remote computer.

SSL Secure Sockets Layer. A protocol for transmitting data securely over the Web.

state machine A theoretical machine that can be in some set of possible states, with connections between states when certain conditions are true.

statement A quantum of code that does not yield a value. To be any use it must thus have some effect, e.g. print something. Arguably, this whole concept is a mistake; in some languages there are only *expressions*.

static typing A language is statically typed if the type of value that every variable can have has to be known at the time the program is written.

string A sequence of characters, usually denoted `"like this"`.

subroutine A distinct chunk of code. When at some point in a program you want to run this code, you *call* it, and when the subroutine is finished, control returns to the point where the call occurred. In a cookbook, a recipe for making icing might be a subroutine of a cake recipe, and the call might be "make icing using the recipe on page x."

subset A concept included in another. Baking is a subset of cooking.

suits Nontechnical people, especially managers. Derives from the clothes they wore before they started dressing like hackers during the 1990s.

symbol A *data type* whose instances are *tokens*. Like *strings* except (a) a symbol is a single unit, not a sequence of characters, and (b) there is generally only one symbol with a given name, whereas there might be several strings containing the same characters.

syntax The form used to express the ideas in a program. To give x the value 10, different languages might say x = 10, x <- 10, or (= x 10).

system administrator Someone who installs computer hardware and software and keeps networks running properly.

system administrator disease The implicit belief by system administrators that the infrastructure they oversee is an end in itself, rather than a tool there for users. More generally, the attitude that customers are a nuisance, rather than the reason your job exists. Endemic in jobs not exposed to competition.

throwaway program A program written to satisfy some temporary need.

token A sequence of characters as one unit. A more general term for "word."

toplevel An interface to a programming language in which you have an ongoing conversation with the language, as you do with *Unix*, rather than simply *compiling* programs and then running them.

tree A *data structure* each instance of which can refer to two or more other instances. For example, a family tree.

Turing-complete A language is Turing-complete if any program written in it can be translated into a *Turing machine* program and vice versa. All programming languages are Turing-complete, meaning they are all (in a theoretical sense) equivalent in power. Aka Turing-equivalent.

Turing machine A simple imaginary computer whose properties are used to prove theorems about computation. It is currently believed that you can't get anything more powerful, in the sense that you can't define a computer whose programs couldn't be translated into Turing machine programs. But no one can say for sure, because "computer" isn't formally defined.

type *Data type.*

UDP A protocol for broadcasting information on networks.

UI User Interface.

Unix The *operating system* from which most current ones derive. The term is used both generically and is a trademark of a company that ended up with the rights to an early variant. Originally developed at Bell Labs by Ken Thompson and Dennis Ritchie in the early 1970s.

vector A one dimensional *array*; a sequence.

uptime Percentage of time a computer, particularly a *server*, is doing what it is supposed to. Also, the time since a computer last *crashed*.

URL Uniform Resource Locator. The address of a web page. More precisely, a request to a *web server*, usually for a web page, but possibly to run a program (e.g. a web search).

vaporware Software that is talked about but not yet available.

VC, venture capitalist One who supplies money to start or refinance a company in return for some of the stock.

version 1.0 The very first version of something, with the implication that it will be incomplete or broken.

VT100 A popular computer terminal in the 1980s.

web server A *server* that responds to *HTTP* requests.

wedged In an unresponsive state. Said especially of *servers*.

wysiwyg "What you see is what you get." (Pronounced whizzy wig.) E.g. a word processor where what you see on the screen looks like the page that will come out of your printer.

XML A format for organizing data.

Index

The cover of this book was designed and produced in Adobe Photoshop 5.5 and QuarkXpress 4.1 with Sabon and Interstate fonts. Cover image of Pieter Bruegel's *Tower of Babel* is copyright © Corbis.

The interior was designed using LATEX, written by Leslie Lamport atop Donald Knuth's TEX, with additional macros by Amy Hendrickson, and set in MVB Verdigris, Computer Modern, and Computer Modern Typewriter. The book was previewed using gv, by Johannes Plass and Tim Theisen, which is built on Ghostscript, by L. Peter Deutsch.

Matt Hutchinson was the production editor and copyeditor for *Hackers & Painters*. Reg Aubry, David Futato, and Claire Cloutier provided quality control. Paul Graham made the index.

CPSIA information can be obtained at www.ICGtesting.com
Printed in the USA
BVOW04s0414080714

358445BV00023B/320/P

9 781449 389550